Kevin Lygo is an expert in Islamic and Byzantine art who
has travelled across Europe and the Middle East extensively.
He has previously edited the publications *Portraits of the Masters:
Bronze Sculptures of the Tibetan Buddhist Lineages* (2003) and
Pages of the Qur'an. A study of Islamic Calligraphy (2011). He is
Director of Television at ITV and was formerly Director of
Television at Channel 4. **Bettany Hughes** is an award-winning
historian, author and broadcaster. **Robert Peston** is a journalist,
writer and the Political Editor of ITV News.

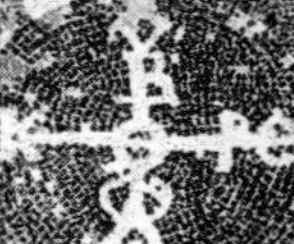
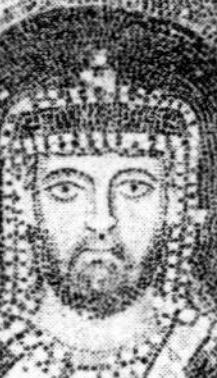
ΑΛΕ
ΞΑΝ
ΔΡΟΣ
ΠΙCΤΟΣ
ΕΝ

THE EMPERORS OF BYZANTIUM

KEVIN LYGO

Foreword by
ROBERT PESTON

Introduction by
BETTANY HUGHES

With 30 illustrations

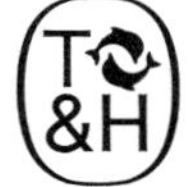

COVER: Constantine IX, detail of mosaic, Hagia Sophia ('Church of Holy Wisdom'), Istanbul, *c.* 1028–34 and 1042–55, ozdereisa/123RF.com.

FRONTISPIECE: Full-length portrait of Alexander, *c.* 913. Uncovered in 1958 beneath layers of Turkish plaster in Hagia Sophia.

First published in the United Kingdom in 2022 by
Thames & Hudson Ltd, 6–24 Britannia Street, London WC1X 9JD

First published in the United States of America in 2022 by
Thames & Hudson Inc., 500 Fifth Avenue, New York, New York 10110

This compact paperback edition published in 2024

The Emperors of Byzantium © 2022 and 2024 Thames & Hudson Ltd, London

Text © 2022 Kevin Lygo
Foreword © 2022 Robert Peston
Introduction © 2022 Bettany Hughes

Designed by P D Burgess
Cover designed by Steve O Connell

EU Authorized Representative: Interart S.A.R.L.
19 rue Charles Auray, 93500 Pantin, Paris, France
productsafety@thameshudson.co.uk
interart.fr

A CIP catalogue record for this book is available from the British Library

ISBN 978-0-500-29799-5
02

Printed and bound in the United Kingdom by CPI (UK) Ltd

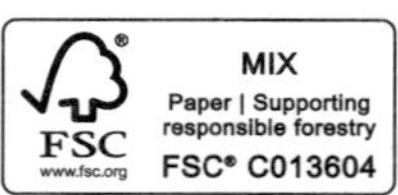

Be the first to know about our new releases,
exclusive content and author events by visiting
thamesandhudson.com
thamesandhudsonusa.com
thamesandhudson.com.au

CONTENTS

FOREWORD

I studied history in a state school in the 1970s, when the subject had not degraded into current affairs. But even before the teaching of history became just another battleground for culture wars between Right and Left, neocons and born-again socialists, teenagers were expected neither to notice nor care that the curriculum went from the Romans straight to the Ottomans, with about a thousand years more or less ignored. If you'd asked me what had happened during this intervening period, I would have muttered something about the Dark Ages, transposing to Eurasia the cultural degradation of Western Europe.

I assume that the enduring Eastern part of Rome's hegemony was ignored in North London and beyond because the flamboyant Christianity it fostered was an affront to the dull and sober established Church of England. I was well into my twenties before I had a grasp of the origins and importance of the Orthodox church, which came about mainly because I was lucky enough to have Greek Cypriot friends, whose gifts to me were the music of Cat Stevens and a couple of invitations to boisterous, enormous nuptials. Later, in 1989, when I visited Kiev to report on the collapse of the Soviet Union, I concluded that Communism might be crumbling, but Orthodoxy was probably set fair for another millennium. The ebullient primate I met there was explicit that dictators might come and go, but he and his fellow clerics would not be budged.

My idea of Byzantium was derived almost wholly from English Literature set texts, in particular W. B. Yeats's poem of that name and his 'Sailing to Byzantium'. Both summon up a dreamlike, mythical place of emperors, gold-leafed 'handiwork', soldiery and ghosts. It turns out, according to Kevin Lygo, that Yeats wasn't so far from the truth. As Yeats wrote, 'Byzantium was the centre of European civilisation and the source of its spiritual philosophy.'

High civilization is not the same as compassion or squeamishness. Kevin Lygo's epic narrative of imperial succession tells of every kind of familial betrayal, exile and homicide, including some that make *Game of Thrones* seem restrained (which is presumably because, as George R. R. Martin has said, his influences were largely French and English medieval history). This is why 'Byzantine' is in the lexicon as a synonym for 'complex' and 'impenetrable', used especially as an epithet for plotting and scheming.

But along with the blood, gore and deviousness, there was great art, architecture, philosophy and jurisprudence. Justinian's magnificent 6th-century Orthodox cathedral, Hagia Sophia – the glory of Byzantine architecture – has defined the great city on the Bosphorus for 1,500 years. The widely criticized decision of Turkey's president, Recep Tayyip Erdoğan, to turn Sophia into a working mosque is proof of its enduring symbolic power. Another living monument to Byzantine culture is the Cyrillic script, which honours in its name a Byzantine saint, Cyril, who together with St Methodius helped spread the alphabet throughout the Slavic territories, as a medium for propagating the Orthodox faith and reinforcing the power of Constantinople rather than Rome.

The other paradox of my school education – as, I assume, for most of my generation – is that we were taught that the Fall of Constantinople in 1453 to the Muslim Ottomans was a defining moment, marking – in the cliché – the end of the medieval age. But we were never told about the way that the Byzantine Empire stopped the great Muslim expansion of the 7th and 8th centuries, by repelling first the Umayyads and then the Abbasids. Whether you think of 'Europe' as a Christian or a secular and liberal concept, it would not exist today had Byzantium not been its iron girdle for a thousand years. Irrespective of the volatile nature of international politics, we are defined by European history and European values. And for all that we need to thank the Byzantine emperors.

Robert Peston

INTRODUCTION

History is measured by absence and presence. What we choose to leave out can be as articulate as that which is left in – and there is one perplexing, critical gap that is crying out to be filled: the story of the empire of Byzantium and of her rulers.

This was a time and a place too important not to know. Byzantium was an ambitious, world-class power, holding sway in the hotspots of human history for over a thousand years. It was a radical, pioneering force: the vigorous medieval continuation of the Roman Empire (Rome never really fell – it just moved 800 miles towards the rising sun), a child of Eastern influences and a prime interface with early Islam. Byzantium was also a place where women had more power and advantage than anywhere else in Europe or North Africa; where the court elite developed a rubric for lawmaking that still forms the basis of European law today; and whose national and political boundaries still demarcate millions of lives. Christianity as a territory-based religion was pioneered here; so too the cult of the Virgin Mary. Sitting atop this pyramid of people and power and ideas was the emperor. Originally a Latin title, *imperator*, meaning a successful Roman general, by the time of the establishment of Byzantium in 330 CE the word signified a body and an ideal invested with quasi-divine authority.

So a comprehensive and vivid timeline of the rulers of this epoch-shaping, game-changing force is long overdue. Byzantium might be the empire that time forgot, but we neglect it today at our peril. Ninety-two emperors add up to a huge total-sum of historical experience and cogent influence. Their domain forged many incidental details of our own lives; the use of the fork, anointing crowned heads of state with chrism, the word 'soldier' (from the favoured currency of Byzantium, the *solidus*), Russian 'tzars' (from the name *Caesar*), even drum majorettes (tossing batons was a move popularized by the successors of the Byzantines, the Ottomans, and their marching military bands of Christian Janissary slaves). The story of Byzantium's leaders is a framework around which we can start to stretch and decorate the rich, wonderful, sometimes mysterious world of the Byzantines, applying embellishments like those on the famous automata – roaring lions and singing birds – many Byzantine emperor-kings so loved to employ in their palaces.

So why is there a history-hole that needs to be filled? There are two explanations, one physical and one psychological. In 1204 Byzantium witnessed one of the most shaming chapters in world history. Christian Crusaders, having first targeted Jerusalem, then turned their ire and swords on Constantinople, masking raw land-grab and power play in a thin excuse of doctrinal differences. They destroyed the body of Byzantium. But they also destroyed its identity and spirit. And once Byzantine humiliation had been charted in clerical and courtly annals and in the collective memory, it became acceptable to downgrade what the Byzantines had achieved. It was easy to brand Byzantium as a failed experiment, a degenerate husk, because the enemies of the Byzantines had consumed or burnt or sold or censored or damned much of what they had thought, produced and broadcast for close on a millennium.

Rather than a world power, Byzantium and her rulers were memorialized as oddities. They were perceived as louche, lush, corrupted and corrupting parasites who practised the wrong kind of Christianity. With its courts dominated by the influence of eunuchs (some scholars have estimated there would have been over 1 thousand in Byzantium in its heyday), and a proclivity for the gaudy theatricals and complex, ancient governmental traditions that had become a hallmark of courtly life, it was easy to demonize what lay east of the Alps. And so the word 'Byzantine', in both English and French, came to mean obscure, labyrinthine, obfuscating.

But it was not so. Byzantine emperors (and a scattering of empresses) were the summation of an idea of blistering originality and ambition. For the Byzantine emperors, they were at the centre of a new world, with a new, ethical project: to Christianize the planet. Their religious and political headquarters, Constantinople, provided social care to thousands each day and a sanctuary for refugees; from 562 CE one *quaestor* in the city performed special duties as a refugee and immigrant official. Justinian, the great reforming emperor whose code is still referenced by modern European law, and his wife, Theodora, sponsored radical legal initiatives – safe houses for sex workers and single mothers, the death penalty for rape, the prohibition of pimping and infanticide.

These men and women ruled territories that stretched across a million square miles, and their influence and reputation reached even farther. In the 6th century fake emperor portraits adorned imitation Byzantine coins found in the graves of Chinese noblemen in Xingjiang; and imperial palaces, in what the Chinese called the 'Fortunate City', were by the 10th century described as boasting doors of ivory, columns of lapis lazuli and floors of gold. It is little surprise that many of the emperor's scholars and clerics set down to write new world histories from the hyper-connected Byzantine capital.

Theirs was a heady world. The descriptions of the city of Constantinople in its prime are rich and wonderful. The main street that led from the Golden Gate (terminus of the Egnatian Way, the ancient Roman road that still runs from Rome to Istanbul across south-eastern Italy, Albania and Greece), along which the emperors processed, was flanked with lavender. The court itself was colour-coded: the highest ranks were allowed to wear red boots or white cloaks, and future emperors were literally 'born in the purple', in a room built with porphyry – the purple stone from Egypt particularly valued by Byzantine's rulers – and draped in purple-dyed silks.

Although Istanbul/Constantinople is famously described as the powerhouse where East meets West, it is far, far more than that: it is also, critically, where North meets South. Take Emperor

Theophilos, whose envoys brought a sorry group of Viking refugees to the court of Charlemagne's son, Louis the Pious, in 839 CE. The emperor's personal guard, the Varangians, took their name from the Norse *var*, a pledge of loyalty. And the influence of these northern people, who were known as Rus' and who called Constantinople *Miklagard*, or 'Big City', can be traced in the Byzantine double-headed eagles that fly on the Russian flag today.

Sometimes portrayed as mere figureheads, many emperors in fact were driving forces of geopolitical change. That same Theophilos, although he was often at war with Baghdad, also drew inspiration from the city's caliph, Harun al-Rashid, importing Islamic designs into Byzantine architecture, whence they made their way into the Western world. Others were less fortunate: Jovian never even set foot in the capital, and Basiliskos was starved to death in a dry cistern in Cappadocia. So from the first Byzantine emperor (Constantine I, proclaimed emperor in York in 306 CE) to the last (Constantine XI Palaiologos, who was crowned in southern Greece in the satellite kingdom of Mystras, and whose undiscovered body gave rise to the hope that he would one day return to defend his imperial city against the Ottoman forces of Mehmed II, soon to be Mehmed the Conqueror), the emperors and empresses were more than entitled women and men. In their own eyes, the Eastern Roman Caesars were the one true God's favoured representatives on earth and the channel for a cosmic mission. This was to promulgate an ecumenical understanding of the world – ecumenical in the ancient Greek sense of a single, common ideal that had the potential to reach, and change, the inhabited world.

The story of the emperors of Byzantium is a history that matters. More than ever now we need to be the age that opens rather than closes minds, that has a vision for the potential of global unity, and that stops writing humans and experiences out of history, and instead writes them back in. Enjoy this compendium – it counts.

Bettany Hughes

CONSTANTINIAN DYNASTY

(306–363)

The Constantinian dynasty was founded by Constantine the Great's father, Constantius Chlorus, and continued the line of the Roman Empire's *augusti*, who had ruled from Rome since the time of Augustus. It was also referred to as the 'Neo-Flavian' dynasty, since all Constantine's family included the name Flavius, which recalled the 1st century dynasty of the same name. Constantine the Great and his descendants ruled over the 'Late Roman Empire', also known as the 'Eastern Roman Empire'. It was, however, the formal adoption of Christianity as the state religion and the move to the newly built city of Constantinople ('the city of Constantine'), also known as the 'New Rome', that marked the beginning of what would become the Byzantine Empire, which ruled for over 1,100 years.

Constantine I the Great

September 324 – May 337

Wearing his late father's royal cloak, Constantine appeared from his father's quarters and demonstrated to everyone that, indeed, his father still reigned through him.

EUSEBIUS, *c.* 338

In matters of state, his own family was expendable.

MICHAEL PSELLOS, *c.* 1060

Constantine the Great, who sits chronologically between Jesus Christ and the Prophet Muhammad, was one of the few individuals who we can legitimately claim to have changed the shape of the world and redefined it in their own image.

Three momentous decisions were at the heart of this transformation. Constantine was the first emperor of the Romans to embrace Christianity, and he made it the chosen religion of the state. He also moved the centre of the empire away from Rome to Byzantion (the name of the original Greek settlement) on the Thracian mainland, where he built a magnificent city in his own honour: Constantinople, 'the city of Constantine'. Third, he reformed the monetary system, introducing the *solidus* as the basis of a new currency that became the gold standard and lasted for 700 years.

Yet very little is known about the personality of this extraordinary man. Historians of Constantine's time and for the next few hundred years were utterly partisan in their descriptions. In an attempt to mythologize and almost deify him, all trace of his character was deliberately removed from the records, and we are left with the rather clinical portrait of a demigod who could do no wrong. Certainly, his achievements as the emperor of the Romans are numerous, astounding and unrivalled, and it was he who set a course for the empire of Byzantium for the next 1,100 years.

Constantine was born in Naissus (Nis in Serbia today). His father was Constantius, *caesar* of the western part of the empire; Constantine therefore spent little time with him, as Constantius would have been away on campaigns for most of his life. Constantine was sent to the court of Diocletian, *augustus* of the East, to receive a first-rate education and also act as a sort of hostage, a guarantee of Constantius's loyalty to Diocletian. Constantine's mother, Helena, was a more influential force on him, particularly when it came to her devotion to Christianity. She was a Greek woman of lowly birth – some reports describe her as a slave whom Constantius picked up on campaign – and Constantine was their only child. She was divorced and discarded by Constantius when he married the more politically appropriate daughter of the Roman emperor Maximian, Theodora, around 289. When Constantine was sent to Nicomedia on campaign, Helena travelled with him.

For many years Constantine fought on behalf of Diocletian against the Sassanians in Syria and the barbarians on the Danube. In 303 he returned to the eastern capital, Nicomedia, as a seasoned and successful general still in his twenties. It is here that he would have witnessed first-hand the implementation of Diocletian's policy of the 'Great Persecution'. Christians throughout the empire were ruthlessly persecuted, their lands confiscated, their churches and scriptures destroyed, and their priests imprisoned. Constantine's role in this policy is unclear: he claimed to have had little to do with it, although later admitted that he did not actively try to stop it being pursued.

The retirement and eventual death of Diocletian forced Constantine to return to Gaul and the court of his father, where the two of them crossed the Channel into Britain and proceeded to campaign against the Picts north of Hadrian's Wall. Constantius became severely ill and died in 306, and Constantine was instantly proclaimed *augustus* in York, making him responsible for Britain and Gaul.

For the next four years Constantine steadily strengthened his position among his fellow rulers. In 310 Maximian was defeated in battle by Constantine's forces and was 'encouraged' to commit suicide. Licinius, *augustus* of the eastern provinces, was offered Constantia, the half-sister of Constantine, as a wife to cement his alliance with Constantine, and accepted.

The remaining ruler opposed to Constantine, the emperor Maxentius, declared war on him but was beaten back by Constantine's army on several occasions before they met in the final battle at the Milvian Bridge, outside Rome. The defeat of Maxentius is significant not only because it reduced to just two the number of people who ruled, giving Constantine command over half the empire, but also because it was alleged that this was the moment Constantine first embraced Christianity.

According to some sources, the day before Constantine had a vision of a cross of light in the sky over the sun, bearing a Greek

　　　　CONSTANTINIAN DYNASTY

inscription that translates as 'With this sign, you shall win.' That night he had a dream in which Christ appeared with the same sign and told him to make an army standard in the form of the *labarum* (a military banner). On it he should inscribe the first two letters of the Greek word *Christos*, a *chi* and a *rho*. This Constantine duly did, placing the chi-rho symbol (which resembles an X with a P running directly through it) on the shields of all his men. He was victorious. Constantine then met with Licinius to attend the marriage of Constantia, and together the two formulated the Edict of Milan, which ended the persecution of Christians and returned their property and churches to them. An uneasy alliance was forged between Licinius and Constantine, until 18 September 324 when the two sides met in battle at Chrysopolis, the pagan Licinius against the Christian Constantine. Constantine's forces prevailed. Both Licinius and his accomplice Martinian were initially spared death and banished to Thessalonica and Cappadocia, respectively. The next day, 19 September, Constantine was crowned sole emperor of the Romans.

A newly united empire needed a new city to do it justice, and almost immediately on becoming emperor Constantine selected the Greek town of Byzantion. The significance of the location cannot be overestimated. It was situated at the meeting point of two continents, protected by the Bosphorus to the east, the Golden Horn to the north and the Sea of Marmara to the south, and therefore accessible by land on only one front. Constantine himself – guided by an angel, according to legend – walked the new perimeter of the city, drawing a line in the earth with his sword to mark where the walls should be built. The new city was founded in 324 and dedicated on 11 May 330. It was the first Christian city built by any Roman, and Constantine's subsequent ambitious building projects were evidence of his grand designs for this 'New Rome': Constantinople.

As the city took shape, it became obvious that the major difference from the old capital, Rome, on which all the general planning was based, was that it was first and foremost a Christian city. Churches were built in abundance. The church of the Holy Apostles was constructed on the site of an old temple to Aphrodite. Like Rome, it was to have a forum and seven hills, and its inhabitants were to be exempt from taxes, benefiting from the emperor's generous provisions of free food and lavish entertainment in purpose-built arenas. Constantine laid the foundations of cisterns, vast baths and, of course, his Great Palace, and instigated the building of the cathedral of Hagia Sophia. He was to have brought to his capital the holiest of relics, including fragments of the True Cross, the Rod of Moses and many more.

In these early days of Christianity, there was no model for what a large church or cathedral should look like. Constantine, or his builders, decided that it should take the form of a basilica: a vast, open space, rectangular in shape, where congregations could gather to worship and attend religious services. Aisles would be placed on either side of a central nave separated by colonnades, and a wooden roof would be higher above the nave than the aisles, allowing light to enter the building through a series of windows at clerestory level. The interior decoration was to take on the most beautiful and varied designs: marble columns, revetments of granite, porphyry and coloured marble, mosaic work and paintings – all were to play their part in adorning the religious building and expressing wonder to God Almighty. Constantine had built similar structures without a Christian purpose in both Trier and Rome, and this new form of architecture was to dominate the physical manifestation of the Christian world until the present day.

Alongside the new architecture was the issue of the role of art in Christianity. Should it exist at all? Could God be portrayed? What did an angel look like? All these questions and many more had to be addressed by the first Byzantine artists. What age is Christ? Does he have a beard or is he clean-shaven? What should he be wearing? What colour were his eyes? There are no contemporary descriptions of Jesus, let alone a contemporary portrait, so some

   CONSTANTINIAN DYNASTY

300 years after his death it was the Byzantines who decided, to a large extent, how he is perceived today.

Constantine wished to make Constantinople the greatest city in the world, and to this end he scoured the empire for works of art to adorn his capital. Many of them can be seen even today, and some are still in situ in modern Istanbul, such as the Column of Constantine.

In matters of religion Constantine remains an enigma. His own faith has been the subject of much debate, ranging from the view that it was just a cynical, politically motivated ploy to curry favour with a large sect, to the idea that he had a genuine belief that grew throughout his reign, culminating in a baptism on his deathbed. There can be no doubt that many around him, including the early Christian scholar Hosius of Cordoba, would have attributed his victory at the Milvian Bridge to a direct intervention through the power of Christ and would have believed that the cross in the sky was a sign from God. Constantine was not an intellectual, nor was he a scholar, and the intricate contradictions of theology were probably of little interest to him, yet as the first Christian emperor all his actions were subject to intense scrutiny. The first controversy with which he came into contact – one of many that would inform Christianity for the whole of the Byzantine era – was Donatism. Essentially, this was an African issue, concerning those who had been persecuted under Diocletian, had renounced their Christian beliefs in order to save themselves from torture and death and who now, with the ban on all matters Christian lifted, wished to be readmitted to the church. The African church was split between those who wanted the persecuted *traditores* to return, the Orthodox, and those who followed Bishop Donatus, who did not. Despite Constantine's best efforts to settle this dispute, he, as ultimate head of the church, was forced to decide. He chose the Orthodox party and, when the Donatists refused to obey, Constantine had the army force them into submission. Many were martyred, such that by 316 Constantine had unwittingly carried out the first official persecution in favour of Christianity.

In Alexandria, the intellectual centre of the empire at this point, a priest named Arius led a group that was vehemently opposed to the Orthodox view on the nature of Christ. Constantine called a council of all the church leaders, an ecumenical council, in Nicaea in 325, specifically to identify these areas of difference and reach agreement. What emerged was the Nicene Creed, which set out the doctrine that Christ was begotten, not made, of the same substance as the Father. This meant that the Father and the Son were equally God and that both had existed for all eternity. But, to Constantine's dismay, the Arians refused to accept the creed and the split remained. Another question then arose: if one of these views was heretical, why did God not punish the wrongdoers? This issue was to haunt the Byzantine Empire for centuries, and never really reached a satisfactory conclusion. Constantine learnt that religion was never going to be the unifying force for the empire that he hoped it would be.

The personality of Constantine is still puzzling. The man who ruled the largest territory in the world, who never lost a battle, who brought Christianity into the mainstream and who built magnificent monuments throughout the world was also a ruthless murderer. The list of his family members who suffered under his orders is extraordinary. He forced his father-in-law Maximian to commit suicide, killed his brother-in-law Maxentius in battle, executed his other brother-in-law Licinius after promising to spare his life, executed his 10-year-old nephew Valerius, executed his son Crispus, and allegedly murdered his wife, Fausta, in a hot bath after suspecting her of having an affair with Crispus, her stepson. It is not hard to see why pagans believed his conversion to Christianity and deathbed baptism were a last-ditch attempt to absolve himself of these crimes.

Constantine's mother, Helena, was spared any family violence, and seems to have been the person with whom he had the longest, most constant relationship throughout his life. She was undoubtedly an important and influential figure in Constantine's dealings with religion, being a devout Christian herself. Her journey to the

Holy Land in her old age established the act of pilgrimage as a worthwhile Christian activity, and wherever she went, with the help of Constantine's vast treasury, she built churches. She supported the building of the church of the Holy Nativity in Bethlehem and the church of the Eleona on the Mount of Olives, Jerusalem, and the so-called Chapel of St Helen, founded on the traditional site of the Burning Bush (now part of St Catherine's Monastery, Sinai). In the place where she found three pieces of wood supposedly from the True Cross, Constantine ordered the construction of the great church of the Holy Sepulchre. She also uncovered three nails from the True Cross and had them brought back to Constantinople for all to see. She is a saint of the Eastern Orthodox church, and her tomb, a magnificent structure in porphyry, is in the Vatican Museum. Her strength of character and ambition are something that she surely passed on to her son.

Frustrating though it is to try to find clues to the personality of Constantine, there can be no doubt that he deserves his epithet of 'the Great'. He built the foundations of the Eastern Roman Empire, and had a lasting and dominating influence on the future ninety-one emperors of Byzantium.

Constantius II

September 337 – November 361

Of Constantius II:
Swarthy, with watchful, bulging eyes, he had soft hair and close-shaven cheeks that were clean and smooth; he was peculiarly long of body but very short in the leg, enabling him to excel at running and jumping.
AMMIANUS MARCELLINUS, MID-390S

Of Constans I:
Because of this victory, Constans became more arrogant, and at the same stage he was wilful and insufficiently cautious on account of

*his age. Furthermore, he was detestable because of the depravity
of his subordinates and passionate in his greed and in his contempt
for the soldiers.*

Sextus Aurelius Victor, c. 360

All three sons of Constantine the Great assumed joint *augusti* status on their father's death. Constantine II was *augustus* in Gaul, Constantius II was *augustus* in the East, and Constans I was *augustus* in Italy. They had two half-brothers, born to Theodora, Constantine I's second wife: Julius Constantius and Delmatius, who were both killed on the orders of Constantius II, as were Delmatius's two young sons and Julius Constantius's elder son. Constantius's two brothers-in-law, Flavius Optatus and Popilius Nepotianus (both married to his half-sisters), were also murdered. It was a bloody beginning.

In 337 the three brothers came together to carve up the empire between them. Constantine II as the eldest, though only 20 years old, kept Gaul, Spain and Britain. Constantius II ruled over the East, which included Asia Minor and Egypt. Constans I, who was only 14 years old, ruled over Africa, Italy, Thrace, the Danube and Macedonia. Constantine II always felt himself superior to the other two, and when his youngest brother, Constans, would not do as he was asked, Constantine II decided to move against him. In 340 Constantine II invaded Constans's territory of Italy, but Constans was waiting for him, ambushed his elder brother and killed him. His body was tossed into the river Alsa and forgotten.

Now there were just two brothers left to rule the empire, and Constans was still only about 17 years old. His youth and his obvious predilection for cavorting with male Germanic prisoners led him to neglect both his soldiers and the Danubian frontier, which became increasingly undefended. While he was out hunting with his friends one day, a soldier in Constans's army from Britain named Magnentius decided to pronounce himself emperor and had the young and feckless Constans I hunted down and murdered.

                          CONSTANTINIAN DYNASTY

On hearing the news, the sole remaining heir of Constantine the Great, Constantius II, marched with his army to stifle this rebellion. He married off his recently widowed sister Constantina to a young cousin, Gallus, and made him *caesar* of the East. The pursuit of Magnentius took almost two years, but he was eventually found, and his army defeated in 351 in Croatia. Two years later, tired of running and hiding, Magnentius took his own life.

Constantius II, now sole *augustus*, began to believe that Gallus was plotting against him. This was entirely in keeping with the way all three brothers had thought and behaved; indeed, they had learnt this all at the knee of their father. If there was any doubt as to a person's loyalty, it was better to have them killed before you found out the truth – an approach that could almost have served as the family motto. Gallus was duly despatched, leaving poor Constantina, Constantius's sister, widowed for a second time.

Constantius II, now undisputed ruler of the empire, was clever enough to realize that he could not be everywhere in his vast lands at the same time. He needed to appoint someone who could look after the administration of the capital while Constantius was either dealing with the Germanic tribes attacking him from across the Danube or attempting to contain the ever-constant threat of the mighty Persian Empire in the East. The only person he could think to trust was his nephew Flavius Claudius Julianus, or Julian – a young scholar and intellectual with no military or political experience. He had stayed loyal to Constantius II, or at least neutral, throughout the internecine fighting of the previous years and had shown no real interest in the affairs of state. Julian's own father, Julius Constantius, and his elder brother had been murdered on the orders of his uncle when he was just a small boy, and it is hard to imagine that these events did not shape the opinion he must have formed of his emperor. These caveats notwithstanding, Constantius made him *caesar* of Gaul, and Julian was quickly sent to his new province in 355.

Constantius II was having a difficult time in the East. The great Sassanian Empire of Persia and the mighty forces of the Roman

Empire were engaged in seemingly endless hostilities. Upon hearing that his appointed *caesar* in the West was enjoying some military success and organizing the empire efficiently, Constantius is likely to have been surprised and, given the track record of family rivalry, more than a little concerned. In 359 he was served with an ultimatum by the Sassanian king Shapur, to the effect that Constantius II should concede much of the territory currently occupied by Roman troops, including vast areas between the Tigris and the Euphrates, as well as all the lands of Christian Armenia. If Constantius did not agree to these terms, the whole might of the Sassanian forces would fall upon him. Constantius knew that he could not defeat the Persians in a pitched battle and so sent word to his nephew Julian that he should immediately send half of the Western army to help defend the eastern borders of the empire. On hearing this, Julian's men demanded en masse that he become emperor in his own right, leaving Constantius to his own fate. Needless to say, Julian accepted. Constantius was understandably furious and demanded that Julian step down. But by now Julian was an experienced politician and soldier. He had been highly successful in defending and even extending the Western Empire. He had the loyalty of his troops, and his memory of the murders only recently inflicted on his family by Constantius came to the fore. He prepared for civil war with his cousin and emperor. It was all or nothing for him now.

Constantius II marched over 1,100 km (700 miles) westwards and prepared to do battle; it could never be denied that a member of this family was always prepared to fight. Julian marched with his army from Gaul towards Constantinople. However, when Constantius reached Tarsus, in Cilicia, he became seriously ill with a fever and, at a small village called Mopsucrenae, in November 361 he died. The world now belonged to Julian.

Constantius II had been a ruthless but effective leader. He had fought every enemy that the world outside Rome had thrown at him – Gauls, Franks, Alemanni and Sassanians – and of course his own brothers. On the great religious questions of the day, Constantius

   CONSTANTINIAN DYNASTY

was undoubtedly a devout Christian, and one who openly favoured the Arian sect. He believed that Jesus Christ was of similar substance to, but not the same as, God the Father. Despite the fact that this view had been declared heresy by the Council of Nicaea, he was confident in his beliefs and was not averse to persecuting Orthodox Athanasian Christians and pagan worshippers alike. He had married three times: his first wife had died young, and his second was his great love, the beautiful Macedonian Eusebia, but neither had given him any children; his last wife, Faustina of Antioch, outlived him but had borne him no sons. Ultimately, Constantius's achievements amounted to little more than the maintenance of the vast empire he had inherited. At his funeral, in the church of the Holy Apostles, he was afforded all the honours due to an emperor by the very man he had underestimated and put in power, now known to history as Julian 'the Apostate'.

Julian the Apostate
November 361 – June 363

Godless but pragmatic.
PRUDENTIUS, *c.* 400

As his portraits fade, his writings will live on for ever.
LIBANIUS OF ANTIOCH, *c.* 370

Most famous for being the last pagan emperor of the Roman Empire, Julian was a complex character whose copious writings reveal much more than simply a portrait of a man who wished to deny the Christian faith. He ruled for less than two years, and yet he has been remembered through history with more interest and granted more significance than many of his greater fellow emperors.

Julian was the first emperor to be born in the new capital, Constantinople. In some ways his life was set on its course by the brutal murder of his father and elder brother on the orders of Constantius II. Julian was about 6 years old at the time; and whether or not he actually witnessed the murder of his family, he would certainly have been aware of the man responsible for it. His mother had also died, and he was banished to the remote fortress of Marcellum, in Cappadocia. He shared his exile with his half-brother Gallus, whose youth initially saved him from slaughter but who would later meet the same fate as the rest of their family: death at the hands of their emperor cousin.

During his teenage years, Julian was a capable and keen scholar. Receiving the best education from a variety of famous intellectuals, he was familiar with Christian teachings but soon began to fall under the spell of classical literature and the works of Greek antiquity. When he was studying in Athens, it is said that he joined the cult of Helios-Mithra, and this belief in the old pagan gods would never leave him. In the world of Constantine the Great and Constantius II, it was dangerous to turn one's back on Christian customs: it was not until after he had become emperor that Julian stopped pretending and revealed his pagan ways.

It was while Julian was in Athens that he received a summons from Constantius to join him in Milan. When they finally met, he must have been relieved to have escaped punishment from the ever-vindictive emperor, and instead he was made *caesar* of Gaul. To everyone's surprise, Julian quickly demonstrated that he was no puppet of his uncle, nor was he idle in fulfilling his duties, and he quickly established himself as a very capable military leader and civil administrator. He won the support and admiration of his men, since he was both fair and considerate in all his dealings with them. When Constantius II demanded that he send more than half his army from Gaul to the eastern provinces to help fight the Persians, Julian was genuinely torn. He had promised his men and their families a life in Gaul, but while he prevaricated they made the decision for him by declaring him as the new emperor. This would have troubled Julian, as he had tried to be honest and loyal to the empire all his life and had not deliberately agitated for this position, but

  CONSTANTINIAN DYNASTY

after successfully ruling a large province for several years he had undoubtedly developed a taste for power. He accepted the challenge and led a coup against Constantius. The two men marched at the head of their respective armies to join battle, but fortuitously for Julian the emperor contracted a fever and died quite suddenly. Julian was now sole ruler of the entire Roman Empire.

He travelled straight to Constantinople, where he oversaw the funeral of his predecessor in the church of the Holy Apostles. Once the ceremony was over, Julian instantly dropped his Christian ways, openly flaunted his pagan beliefs and never set foot in a church again.

Julian wanted to restore the 'old religion' to the empire. He did not persecute the Christians or close down the churches, since he sincerely believed that, once it had been shown the error of its ways, the population would see that the old gods were better than the one new Christian god and would soon renounce its faith. He was, as we can now see, completely misguided. The people were too entrenched in the Christian way of thinking. They enjoyed the simplicity of the church's message, and they enjoyed the rituals and ceremonies. Julian travelled the country making blood sacrifices at old pagan temples, but this just alienated him more from his people, who gave him the nickname 'butcher' because he slaughtered so many animals. Gradually they grew tired of his endless speechmaking, his obsession with largely impenetrable philosophies, and even his austere way of living. They wanted their emperor to be superior to them, to represent splendour and pomp. What they had in Julian was a man who discharged thousands of his staff, wanted no personal wealth or luxury, and, since the death of his wife, Helena, many years before, had assumed a vow of celibacy. This man was simply no fun at all. His stamping out of corruption, his reforms of the tax system and refining of the rule of law to help the common man – these benefits were lost on his subjects. Towards the end of his life, Julian came to see that his earnest belief in the power of the old religion to triumph over

Christianity was not enough. He started to strip some churches of their wealth, forbade the teaching of Christianity in schools and generally became more zealous, but the people simply refused to agree with his beliefs.

Always taking his imperial duties seriously, Julian decided to try to defeat the Sassanians once and for all. He took his army into Persia and at first was successful, winning battles and surrounding the ancient city of Ctesiphon. However, he was indecisive at a crucial moment and retreated from the field, intending to restock and replenish his troops. It was as he was retreating that a spear hurled into the fray pierced his body. According to Libanius of Antioch, it was a Roman spear from the hand of his own troops; whatever the truth, the 31-year-old emperor was dead, the last non-Christian to lead the empire.

A curious figure, Julian is one of the most documented of the emperors partly because he wrote so copiously about himself and his beliefs; these works, mostly written in Greek, have survived in various forms to this day. Sincere, intelligent and loyal, even to his murdering predecessor, he was simply out of step with the times. He had failed as an emperor and left no lasting legacy. His obsession with his outmoded religion had led him down a path that his subjects would not follow. There was no going back for the people of the Roman world. They were Christians now, and Julian the Apostate was gone.

NON-DYNASTIC RULER

Jovian

June 363 – February 364

His stride was stately and his manner always positive. His eyes were grey ... He was a glutton in his eating, and revelled in the company of wine and women.

AMMIANUS MARCELLINUS, MID-390S

The brief reign of Flavius Jovian was significant for two reasons. First, he accelerated the end of the last vestiges of Roman paganism (although it continued, sporadically, in various forms) and re-established Christianity as the official religion of the empire, as it would remain until the end of the empire itself, over a thousand years later. Second, he ceded to the Sassanians much of the territory that had been held by the empire for many years.

After the death of Julian during the campaign against the Sassanians, the soldiers selected Jovian from among their ranks and continued their retreat with him at the head, Shapur II and the Sassanians chasing and attacking them in small groups, delaying the defeated and straggling horde from reaching safety deep within their own territory. Eventually Jovian was forced to reach a humiliating settlement with Shapur. The treaty did allow for thirty years of peace, but terms included the surrender of five frontier provinces and eighteen important fortresses. What was equally damaging was an agreement to refuse aid to the Christian kingdom of Armenia, whose king, Arsaces, was now totally at the mercy of the Sassanians.

Jovian and his army trudged back towards Constantinople. He seemed less concerned about giving up hard-won territory than getting back to his palace and asserting his authority in the capital. For many weeks the army marched westwards until they reached the town of Nisibis, one of the cities he had agreed to surrender to Shapur. Rather than endure further humiliation by seeking refuge in a place he had only just given up, he refused to enter the town, even though his men were presumably exhausted and their supplies pitifully low. The army was now turning against the leader who just a few months previously they had so quickly chosen as the right man to take over from Julian. Many, including the soldier-historian Ammianus Marcellinus, had found his surrender to Shapur both cowardly and unnecessary. Jovian had previously been seen as a fun-loving, committed Christian, a relief after the lecturing pagan that was Julian, but the mood had changed and Jovian was no longer in favour with his men. Jovian ordered the entire population of Nisibis to evacuate the town rather than welcome the victorious Sassanians. This mass migration of people was carried out reluctantly, many dying on the long journey away from their homes. Marching on to Antioch, Jovian passed a decree that restored full rights and privileges to all Christians throughout the empire.

Eight months after their humiliating retreat from Shapur II, the weary forces had just passed Ankara, in Anatolia, and were nearing the historically significant city of Nicaea when they stopped to camp at a small village named Dadastana. After a particularly lavish banquet, Jovian retired to his bed, fell asleep and never woke up. Some suspected foul play, others that he had overindulged in wine and mushrooms or perhaps suffocated from the charcoal fires in his bedchamber.

Whatever the cause of his demise, Jovian was no more. He was an emperor who had never set foot in his capital. He had been an unlikely candidate for the crown from the beginning, and all he had achieved was to sign an unpopular and disastrous peace treaty

　　　　　　　　　　　　　　　　NON-DYNASTIC RULER

with the old enemy of the empire, the Sassanians. He had restored Christianity as the state religion, but this could perhaps have been accomplished by almost any other ruler. Jovian was buried alongside previous emperors in the church of the Holy Apostles, in the capital from which he never ruled.

VALENTINIAN DYNASTY

(364–379)

The house of Valentinian – connected to the Constantine's family through the marriage of one of Constantine's granddaughters, Flavia Maxima Constantia, to the emperor Gratian – ruled for five generations. Valentinian I split the empire into East and West, and thus laid the foundations for the eventual rise of the eastern provinces, as Rome became besieged by northern Goths, Visigoths and Vandals. The Valentinians continued to rule in the West after the Theodosian dynasty had replaced them in the East, so that the two dynasties ruled concurrently until 455.

Valentinian I
February 364 – March 375 (*Whole Empire*)

Valens
March 364 – August 378 (*Eastern Empire*)

Of Valens:
He was greedy for money, intolerant of hard work, feigned frugality and was inclined to cruelty; he had an unsophisticated mind.
AMMIANUS MARCELLINUS, MID-390S

In the 360s it was still the army that held power within the empire. It chose the new emperors, a practice that would continue with the selection of another one of their own: a young and distinguished general from Pannonia (today in the west of Hungary) called Flavius Valentianus. Valentinian chose Milan and Trier as his imperial headquarters, and his time was spent dealing with the northern borders of the Rhineland, fighting the Alemanni and the Franks. He also had to contend with the Picts and the Scots in Britain, and the provinces in North Africa that were constantly being harried by the Moors. This was a full-time occupation that left little time for managing Constantinople and the Eastern Empire – to the extent that history's perception of Valentinian as emperor would be undermined. Presumably he realized that he could not control the vast, sprawling empire on his own, and to the surprise of many he chose his younger brother Valens to sit alongside him as co-emperor, giving him complete responsibility for the eastern lands.

Valens was in many ways the opposite of his charismatic elder brother. The contemporary historian Ammianus Marcellinus paints an unflattering picture of the 36-year-old Valens, describing him as 'knock-kneed and somewhat pot-bellied'. As an Arian Christian, Valens was never popular with the majority of his subjects, who were largely Orthodox, but even the pagan soldier-historian Ammianus conceded that, as an administrator, Valens was effective. During his reign the nobles suffered the loss of some of their power, but the plight of the common man was undoubtedly improved. Unlike his brother, who seemed uninterested in the religious squabbles of the Nicene and Arian factions, Valens turned to persecuting Orthodox Christians. Although he favoured Antioch as his main residence, certainly spending more time there than in Constantinople, he did recognize that the capital needed building works in order to maintain its position as the greatest city on earth. He famously built the Aqueduct of Valens, which still stands, some 1,700 years later.

One incident was to define Valens's reign above all others. In about 376 a new force, the Huns, arrived north of the Danube and began to drive out the Goths, the existing inhabitants of what is now Romania. They were a fierce group, and the Goths decided that they would move en masse south of the Danube and seek a deal with the Roman forces. Valens approved, and allowed the Goths to come and settle within the empire's lands, on the condition that they became members of the imperial army and helped defend the frontier. Valens hoped that the Goths would thus have stability and a homeland away from the invading Huns, and the Romans would have an ally between the Huns and themselves. Unfortunately, the provision of food and safety for the immigrant Goths was found wanting. Indeed, the local governors exploited the new arrivals by selling them food at exorbitant prices, and even selling some of them as slaves to other parts of the empire. This led to riots and then a full-scale revolt in 377. Valens marched with his army from the eastern provinces to Thrace, where the Goths were looting and plundering the local towns and villages. After a long march, and greatly under-estimating the strength of the Goths' army, Valens launched into battle on the baking hot plains outside Adrianople. Woefully mishandling the tactics, Valens and his men were heavily defeated, and the emperor was obliged to flee into the countryside and hide. The victorious Goths decided to burn every house and farm they could find, and hiding in one of these was Valens himself. Presumed to have been either burned to death or found and killed, Valens was the first emperor to lose his life in battle for over a hundred years. Valentinian I had died three years earlier, in 375 – apparently from a burst blood vessel in his brain brought on by shouting at the Quadi (a Germanic people living in today's Moravia) over some disagreement – having put his young son Gratian in charge at the tender age of 16 years old.

The death of Valens was a low point in the history of the new empire. He mishandled a needless battle and left a young and inexperienced man in charge. As Valens's body was never recovered, he was denied a burial place among his fellow emperors in Constantinople.

Gratian

August 367 – August 383
August 378 – January 379 (*sole emperor*)

Gratian, the son of Valentinian I, spent his life serving in the army. He fought many campaigns along the Rhine and the Danube, combatting the increasingly powerful Hunic tribes. He had very little contact with Byzantium, and it is not certain he ever visited the city. However, for a brief period of five months following the death of his uncle Valens, he was the sole ruler of the whole empire.

THEODOSIAN DYNASTY

(379–457)

The Theodosian dynasty produced five emperors including the first woman emperor, Pulcheria, who briefly reigned alone before marrying Marcian. Ruling alongside the Valentinians, they were prolific builders, and many of their constructions remain today, notably in Ravenna and Istanbul. The dynasty's rule was effective and largely harmonious. It ended because Pulcheria and Marcian had no children; Leo was selected in an orderly manner to succeed them.

Theodosios I

19 January 379 – 17 January 395

He was handsome in face and body, fair skinned, with blond hair and a thin, curved nose.
LEO GRAMMATICUS, SCRIBE OF SYMEON THE LOGOTHETE, *c.* 970

A large silver ceremonial dish in the Real Academia de la Historia, Madrid, shows Theodosios I with his two co-emperors seated either side of him: his young son Arcadius and the Western emperor Valentinian II. Such iconography was common in Roman art and would soon develop into the 'Christ in Majesty' image that became commonplace for the representation of Christ in Byzantine art. This *missorium* dish, of exquisite quality, was made for the 10th anniversary of Theodosios's reign. Discovered in his native Spain at the turn of the 19th century, it was still intact but broken by its finders so that each could take his share of the sale price. Certainly, it was a clumsy act of vandalism but also strangely symbolic, given that Theodosios I was the last to rule the empire as a whole before he split East and West apart for ever.

In January 379 it was the emperor of the West, Gratian, who selected Theodosios to be emperor of the East. It seemed a curious appointment, as Theodosios was living in northern Spain, retired at the age of just 32, looking after his estates in the manner of a Roman nobleman. Gratian would have known that the young Theodosios had served on campaigns with his father, a highly regarded general, and was respected as a military commander in his own right.

According to the 5th-century historian Sozomen, as a child Theodosios suffered from a life-threatening sickness and came close to death. Following his parents' decision to have him baptized, he made a miraculous recovery – an event that perhaps sowed the seeds of his ardent religious beliefs. Theodosios was fervently Orthodox, and a defining characteristic of his time as emperor was the comprehensive establishment of Orthodox Christianity as the official state religion, along with the active persecution of non-believers. Until now, the emperors, starting with Constantine the Great, had allowed other religions to continue more or less unhindered, but Theodosios passed legislation that made Orthodox Christianity compulsory, crushing any other religion, whether it was pagan or, indeed, any other form of Christianity.

The Nicene doctrine of Christianity affirmed that Jesus the Son was equal to God the Father and of 'one substance' with the Father. The Greek word *homoousios* ('of one substance') was central to this argument, since those who disagreed believed instead that Jesus was merely 'like' God the Father, using the word *homoios* instead. Both Constantius II and Valens had followed the *homoios* line, but Theodosios was determined to stamp it out. The Council of Nicaea, in 325, had condemned the teaching of Arius, who believed Christ to be subordinate to God the Father. Despite the official position, many – labelled 'Arians' – had taken to supporting the doctrine. In particular, the eastern territories of Syria and Anatolia had an affinity to the Arian version of Christianity, but Theodosios made

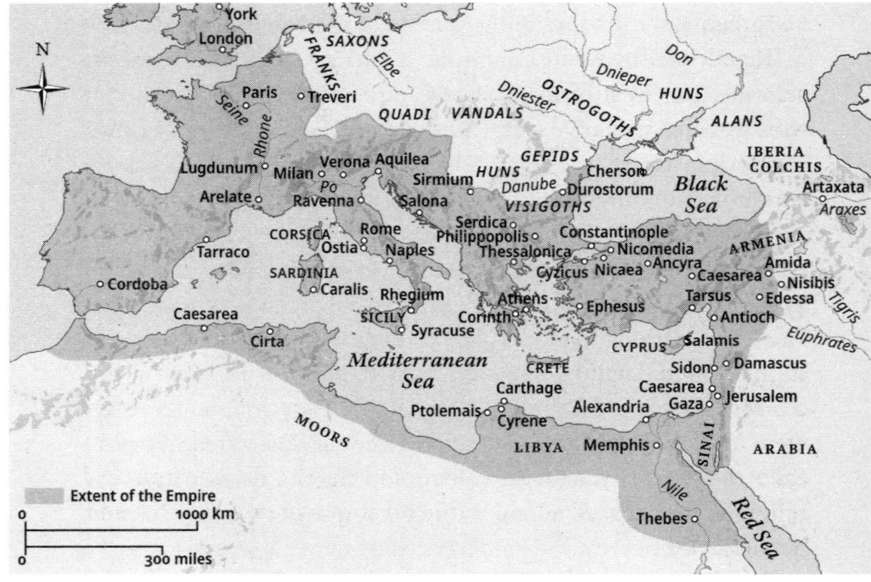

it illegal and drove it underground. The old Roman religions were also banned, and temples were either destroyed or requisitioned for other uses. Old religious practices, be they Manichaean or pagan, were strictly forbidden, and their adherents persecuted.

Theodosios's first acts of military significance were conducted against the Goths. These warriors of Germanic origin were allied with other Northern European tribes to fight the Roman Empire in its northern areas of Pannonia and Dacia. Theodosios was largely successful in these campaigns, but it took several years before he gained full control of the area, during which time he often suffered from the same physical weakness that had plagued him since childhood and was unable to command his troops in person. The Goths were absorbed into the ranks of the Roman Empire, and their

  THEODOSIAN DYNASTY

leader, Athanaric, was invited to Constantinople. He was apparently so overwhelmed by the sumptuous sights of the capital that he agreed to serve the emperor and make peace with him.

Theodosios had continued the tradition established by Constantine the Great of decorating the imperial capital with great works of art, primarily sculptures taken from all over the empire. Today the Obelisk of Theodosios, whose base shows reliefs of the emperor and his family, still stands in the Hippodrome. Moving such a massive stone structure across the empire was a formidable task: this obelisk originally came from Karnak in Egypt, was transported to Alexandria, and then was taken by ship to Constantinople. There was nothing to rival these buildings and statues: the wealth, sophisticated engineering and demonstration of power were clear for all to see. It was a political tactic that Byzantine emperors were to deploy for many centuries to come. The seductive powers of the great city, with the splendour of its rituals, pageants and religious services, all added to the mystique of the emperor and his subjects.

Ruthlessness was also a favoured tactic. When in 390 the people of Thessalonica rioted against the presence of the local garrison installed by Theodosios, mainly because they were Goths and not Romans, Theodosios retaliated in the most brutal manner. The people were summoned to the circus, set upon by troops loyal to the emperor and massacred in their thousands. Needless to say, the remaining inhabitants did not riot again.

In 395, while in Milan, Theodosios, ever sickly, died of a fever. His two sons from his first marriage, Honorius and Arcadius, assumed the roles of emperors of the West and East respectively. They were both young and needed experienced guardians to help them. Theodosios's other surviving child was his daughter, Galla Placidia, from his second wife, Galla, the daughter of Valentinian I. Galla Placidia would become an empress in Rome and was highly influential in Roman politics throughout her life. The Roman Empire would never again be ruled by a single emperor.

Arcadius

January 395 – May 408

Arcadius was small, almost deformed, and very dark in his complexion.

George Kedrenos, 1050s

Arcadius was about 17 years old when he inherited the Eastern Empire from his father, Theodosios; his younger brother, Honorius, was made emperor of the West at only 11 years of age. Neither appeared to possess their father's leadership skills, and both were easily manipulated and subsequently rather ineffective as emperors. They were separated from each other at their father's death, so that there was never much brotherly love between them and they spent some years openly hostile to one another. Neither showed much interest in governing in his own right, and there is little record of them trying to break free from their respective political guardians.

For the first few years of his reign, Arcadius was subservient to his guardian Flavius Rufinus, who was *magister officiorum* and eventual praetorian prefect of the East, in all matters of government. Rufinus had been a trusted ally of Theodosios, and there seems to have been no objection to his appointment as guardian to the young emperor. Rufinus's ambition was all-consuming, and he immediately came into conflict with his equivalent minister in the West, Honorius's guardian, Stilicho. The two hated each other, bound by their mutual desire for power, and this hostility resulted in military disaster. Rufinus appeared to refuse to help the Western army defeat the Visigoth chief Alaric, which allowed Alaric to escape and eventually sack Rome in 410, contributing to the eventual transformation of the Roman Western Empire. Rufinus had arranged for the young Arcadius to marry his daughter, but as the marriage day arrived it appeared that a group of court eunuchs under the influence of the high-ranking official Eutropius were fearful of Rufinus's growing power and persuaded the young man to marry another.

This public humiliation enraged Rufinus, and now he had to face the new empress, Aelia Eudoxia. Here he had met his match as far as ambition was concerned, and he was soon exiled.

Eudoxia, the new empress of the East, and the eunuch Eutropius now dominated the life of the court. Corruption became commonplace, with Eutropius openly selling off high positions in government to the highest bidders. Eudoxia was at the centre of court life and interfered in matters of state whenever she pleased. Her lewd behaviour, extravagant clothes and propensity to throw lavish parties were criticized by the patriarch of Constantinople, John Chrysostom, a towering figure in the church. He had been a clergyman in Antioch for much of his life, and as a great preacher and orator had established a devoted following. His clashes with Eudoxia resulted in his being banished from the capital for a short period, before he returned to continue his tirades against her from the pulpit. On the day of his banishment there was an earthquake in the capital, which the ever-superstitious people believed was a sign of God's anger at his exile, and Eudoxia pleaded for his return. But when Eudoxia had a silver statue of herself made and placed near the church of the Holy Apostles, it was too much for the puritanical patriarch to bear. In his *Historia ecclesiastica* (church history), Socrates of Constantinople quotes Chrysostom as saying: 'Again, Herodias raves; again, she is troubled; she dances again; and again, desires to receive John's head in a charger,' comparing himself to John the Baptist and Eudoxia to Salome. Eventually, in 404, Eudoxia and Arcadius, her weak-willed husband, sent Chrysostom into permanent exile in Armenia, where he died three years later. His influence lasted long after he had departed, however, and Constantinople was recognized as the most important episcopacy in the east, eclipsing Alexandria.

At the turn of the 4th century the Goths had played an increasingly dominant part in the military affairs of the empire. These Germanic peoples were subject to a Roman prejudice that bordered on xenophobia. When a Gothic general, Gainas, was made head of

the Byzantine army, the population of Constantinople reacted violently, causing a riot in which many Goths were killed. Just as in
Rome over the previous centuries, the mob in Constantinople could
quickly become dangerous and quite capable of large-scale massa-
cres. Gainas, a trusted general of Theodosios and Arcadius, had to
flee for his life and, despite trying to rally his troops once he reached
the Thracian border, was tracked down by Arcadius and defeated.
A column was erected in the capital celebrating the defeat of the
Goths, and Arcadius and his empress, Eudoxia, won back the support of the people.

Eudoxia had four daughters and one son, named Theodosios
after his grandfather, who at the tender age of just 9 months
was crowned as co-emperor with his father. There is a poignant
account by Porphyrios of Gaza of Arcadius being overwhelmed
with emotion at the baptism of his son: 'His face was more cheerful
and radiant than the purple robe he was wearing.'

In 404, as Eudoxia was giving birth to a seventh child, complica-
tions arose, and both she and the child died. Four years later, at the
age of 31, Arcadius contracted an illness and he, too, died, leaving
his son, Theodosios, as the child emperor. Arcadius's reign was of
little consequence, and he had a minimal effect on what was happening in the empire as a whole. He left his infant son an orphan,
with an entire empire to manage.

Theodosios II
May 408 – July 450

*Despite being born in the purple, Theodosios the Younger was no
more than an average man, and yet, strangely, people he encountered
found him almost wise.*
JOHN OF ANTIOCH, 610–26

Proclaimed co-*augustus* before the age of 1, the infant Theodosios
became sole emperor of the East when he was just 7. A sickly child,

  THEODOSIAN DYNASTY

he grew up to be bookish (hence his nickname 'the Calligrapher'), introverted and generally uninterested in the empire's military affairs. His entire reign of forty-two years was spent under the dominating influence of others.

At first, it was the government official and praetorian prefect to Theodosios's father, Anthemius, who really ran the empire. Then, in 414, his elder sister Pulcheria was officially proclaimed *augusta* and acted as regent. She was only 15 years old herself at the time, but would go on to dominate Byzantine politics in both the East and the West for the next fifty years.

Throughout his childhood and teenage years, Theodosios had little to do with the affairs of state and concentrated on his study and education. At the age of 19, he married a beautiful and intelligent woman called Athenais (later renamed Eudokia), the daughter of an Athenian professor. According to the rather unreliable chronicler John Malalas, the impressionable young emperor had seen this dazzling woman argue a legal case in the capital and had fallen in love with her at first sight. The highly intellectual couple founded the first university of Constantinople and fostered a culture of learning throughout their court and in the city at large.

The emperor's wife began to clash with his sister (they were both powerful and ambitious women) over matters of state and their relationship to Theodosios, who was uncomfortably caught between them. In 438, Eudokia decided she would go on a pilgrimage to Jerusalem and search for holy relics to bring back to the capital. On her return, relations between the emperor and his wife were strained, and the mild-mannered Theodosios looked for an excuse to banish her. The opportunity presented itself. John Malalas claims that the emperor's life-long friend Paulinus was seen eating an apple that Theodosios had given to his wife, and when questioned about it Eudokia lied and claimed that she had eaten it. This untruth made Theodosios believe that they were having an affair: he had Eudokia banished from the capital and the poor Paulinus executed. The imperial couple had seemed so well suited, and their split was both sudden and unexpected. They had only one child who survived infancy, a daughter named Licinia who was to marry the Western emperor Valentinian III.

Throughout this time the empire was under almost constant attack from the Huns, who were led by two chiefs, Attila and Bleda. They were particularly successful in the West, where they defeated the Western army on several occasions and ran riot through vast territories that had once been a stronghold of the Romans. Theodosios relied on the good military sense of two Alanic generals, Ardabur and then his son Aspar, who played a significant role throughout the Theodosian period and beyond.

In the East, it was more the policy to bribe the enemy to stay away from imperial lands – an approach that drained the treasury of 700 pounds of gold. This desire to avoid war was to become a defining feature of the Byzantine state and, although bribery was not always possible, it allowed many emperors to remain in power, buying them time to regroup if necessary and enabling them to survive for many hundreds of years when a direct confrontation with the enemy may well have resulted in annihilation.

Closer to the emperor's heart were the great theological debates of the time. Theodosios had come into the orbit of a monk from Syria named Nestorios, a famous orator and preacher whom he appointed archbishop of Constantinople in 428. Nestorios, with the full support of the emperor, tried to reconcile the two factions in the debate about the nature of Christ, but he was accused of espousing the view that Christ's human and divine natures were separate. At the Council of Ephesus in 431 the Orthodox establishment denounced him. His brand of heresy would be known as Nestorianism.

Perhaps Theodosios's greatest achievement was the creation of the Codex Theodosianus, a collation of all the laws and edicts made since the time of Constantine. This would form the basis of the rule of law in the empire and became the cornerstone of the far more extensive codex prepared by Justinian a hundred years later.

The final years of Theodosios's reign saw a power struggle between Pulcheria and an influential eunuch named Chrysaphius, who had risen to high rank within the government but was generally believed to be corrupt and untrustworthy. It was only after the death of Theodosios that Pulcheria could have Chrysaphius removed from power and executed.

Theodosios had spent a lifetime in gentle courtly activity and intellectual pursuits. Aside from the end of his marriage, he had lived a charmed life and been considered a kind and honest ruler. His death was similarly understated, in that it was as arbitrary as falling off his horse. Today the remnants of the great Theodosian walls in Constantinople are still standing; started by the emperor's guardian, Anthemius, these building works would serve the capital and the empire well in the centuries to come.

Pulcheria & Marcian
July 450 – January 457

For the first time in the history of the empire, a woman was in power. Theodosios's sister Pulcheria reigned for four months before the Roman senate demanded she marry, as they refused to recognize a woman ruling alone (the eastern part of the empire seemed less concerned by this state of affairs). Ever the politician and pragmatist, Pulcheria believed the general Flavius Marcian to be the best choice and married him in 450. He had been a soldier serving under the influential head of the army, Aspar, and came with an unblemished reputation for honesty and loyal service, at one point having been captured by the Vandals in Northern Africa.

Aged 51 when she married, Pulcheria maintained a vow of celibacy that she had taken when just 14 years old; Marcian, to his credit, respected this wish for the duration of their married life. She and Marcian were both fervent Christians, and in 451 they together arranged for the convening of the Fourth Ecumenical

Council of Chalcedon. Here, it was finally agreed by an assembly of several hundred bishops, as well as the two reigning emperors, that Jesus had both a divine and a human nature, united in one person (*hypostasis*), with neither division nor confusion. These conclusions were followed up with laws and actions that prevented the Nestorians and the Eutychianists, another heretical group, from expressing dissent – a decision that forced these different sects, already on the fringes of the empire in Syria, to flee from persecution and set up their own religious organizations in neighbouring lands and beyond. To this day, there are still Nestorian Christian communities in China, India and Iran. The Orthodox church was thus stabilized for a long period, which endeared both Pulcheria and Marcian to the religious orthodoxy in perpetuity. Pulcheria died in 453 and, adored by the population of Constantinople, was made a saint.

Marcian ruled the empire with great efficiency. He refused to pay Attila and his Huns the annual tribute that Theodosios had given, and thereby risked an all-out attack. However, he forced the Germanic armies to turn westwards, leaving the eastern lands relatively unscathed. Diplomatically skilful, Marcian managed to sow dissent among the confederation of Hunic tribes, allowing some to become protected vassals of the empire in exchange for their service in the army when required. He built up the reserves of the treasury by cutting expenditure rather than increasing taxes and, of course, by refusing to pay vast sums of gold to the Huns. On his death, he left the empire with 7 million *solidi* in the treasury. Following the legacy left by Pulcheria, he built several important monuments, most now gone, although a column dedicated to Marcian still stands in Constantinople.

Marcian died in 457 after contracting gangrene and was buried in the church of the Holy Apostles next to Pulcheria. Their reign was considered one of the most successful by those who followed. It was relatively peaceful and prosperous, and there was no evidence of the large-scale persecution that was so common in these times. There can be little doubt that they were fortunate as well: the traditional enemies of Byzantium, the Huns and the Sassanians, were preoccupied with others, and there were no natural disasters to wreak havoc in the wider population. There is some evidence to suggest that a colossal statue in Barletta, Italy, is a portrait of Marcian: it wears both military and regal attire, a fitting reminder of the dual roles of the Byzantine emperor. He had no children to succeed him and it was up to the long-serving and faithful Aspar once again to select an emperor that could do justice to the office.

LEONID DYNASTY

(457–518)

Leo's selection as emperor by the loyal general Aspar the Alan ushered in a period of consolidation for the Eastern Empire. Leo I's daughter Ariadne became empress in her own right, and was the wife of two further emperors and mother to another. There was some dissent towards the end of their reign but, with the death of Zeno and the marriage of his widow, Ariadne, to Anastasios Dikoros, order was restored, and a stable, financially successful empire was established. This would make it possible for Justinian I the Great to fulfil his ambitions of restoring the empire to its former 'Roman' borders.

Leo I

February 457 – January 474

Leo was very thin, wore no beard and had piercing eyes.
LEO GRAMMATICUS, SCRIBE OF SYMEON THE LOGOTHETE, *c.* 970

The emperor should dispense pity to those on whom he looks, just as the sun dispenses warmth to those on whom it shines.
LEO I, *c.* 470 (ATTRIBUTED)

Aspar the Alan, *magister militum* (master of the army) under two successive emperors and Marcian's king-maker, now selected his next protégé to sit on the throne. Flavius Valerius Leo was a Thracian army officer of humble origins (it was rumoured that he and his wife Verina once worked in a butcher shop; the claim is unsubstantiated but makes the point), but he had proved himself a capable commander and rose to the rank of *comes*, a chief of staff to Aspar. At a relatively mature age – he was in his mid-50s – he was installed as emperor of the Eastern Empire and held the distinction of being the first emperor to be crowned by the patriarch of Constantinople. This was a practice that was to become commonplace, symbolically linking the emperor ever more closely with the church and establishing a religious significance in the act of coronation itself.

Relations between Aspar and Leo started to deteriorate as soon as the emperor was installed. If Aspar had thought that his old subordinate was going to be a puppet ruler, he was sorely disappointed. The army, under Aspar, had become dominated by Germanic soldiers over the previous century, and the empire was increasingly dependent on these Romanized 'foreign' troops to defend their lands and their way of life. To exacerbate matters, the enemies of the empire were often Germanic peoples themselves, specifically the Huns and the Vandals. To counterbalance their influence Leo began to appoint more Isaurians than Germans to prominent military positions, and the balance of power soon shifted away from Aspar's coterie to this large tribe of famous fighters from southern Anatolia. In order to ally himself fully with the Isaurians, Leo married his eldest daughter, Ariadne, to the Isaurian chieftain Tarasikodissa Zeno. This infuriated Aspar and, when his son Ardabur was accused of devising a plot to kill Leo and was subsequently put to death, relations between the emperor and his general were ruined forever.

Leo's wife, Aelia Verina, was to play an important role in these years of the empire's history. Empress consort to Leo, mother to Leo II, sister of the usurper emperor Basiliskos, and mother-in-law to Zeno, she was at the heart of Eastern Roman politics for almost forty years. A second significant figure is Theodoric, a young Ostrogoth prince Leo had taken as hostage to ensure that the Ostrogoths fulfilled their side of a treaty with the empire. This extraordinarily charismatic and clever young man learnt a great deal about the Byzantines and their way of life while living among them, and always remained on good terms with Leo, who had given him the best possible education.

In 467 Leo initiated an enormous military expedition in conjunction with the Western Roman Empire. He helped install the new Western emperor Anthemius, and together they sent the largest force ever to leave Constantinople to attack the Vandals in North Africa, as punishment for the sacking of Rome twelve years earlier. Over 1,000 ships carrying up to 100,000 men were dispatched under the command of Basiliskos, the brother-in-law of Leo I. It was a complete disaster. The fleet was destroyed, and thousands of men killed. After this defeat, the victorious Vandals began raiding the empire, and Leo was forced to sue for a very expensive peace with the Vandal chief Gaiseric.

Despite the North African catastrophe, Leo's reign was defined largely by the functional stability of the government that he had left behind, which continued for many years beyond his death. While the Western Roman Empire succumbed to the pressure of its enemies, the Eastern half survived and settled itself for the times ahead. Leo's family, through his wife, Verina, and daughter Ariadne, was to dominate Eastern Roman court life and politics for almost forty years.

Leo had ruled steadily for seventeen years and died of dysentery in 474 aged about 73, a grand age in the 5th century.

Leo II
January 474 – November 474

Leo II was only 7 years old when his grandfather, Leo I, died, having made him co-emperor. His father, Zeno, was understandably unhappy with this arrangement, and could not understand why his father-in-law had bypassed him and Ariadne, Leo I's own daughter. He immediately complained to the senate, who allowed him to become co-emperor after four weeks of sole rule by Leo II. Zeno was an Isaurian and, although this was better than being a Hun in the eyes of the ever xenophobic and critical populace of Constantinople, it was still considered an unsuitable background for becoming emperor. Leo I had most certainly grasped this fact, and had decided that the line of succession would skip a generation, meaning that his grandson, of more noble birth than his son-in-law, would inherit the throne. The problem was short-lived, however, as the young Leo II died only a few months after becoming emperor. His father, Zeno, now ruled alone. Naturally, since this was a Roman dynastic affair, there are unfounded rumours of wrongdoing in Leo II's untimely death. Had Ariadne or the unpopular Isaurian Zeno assassinated their own child to achieve the highest office? The behaviour of Verina towards her son-in-law certainly suggests there was no love lost between them.

Zeno

February 474 – January 475 (*first reign as co-emperor*)

Zeno was like the Greeks' description of Pan: hairy-legged, goat-like, with wild hair. Black of skin and ridiculous in physique.
LEO GRAMMATICUS, SCRIBE OF SYMEON THE LOGOTHETE, *c.* 970

Zeno holds the dubious distinction of being the only Byzantine emperor ever to succeed his own son. Deeply unpopular with the people, he ruled during a period plagued by constant rebellions and insurrections, most notably from his own family.

Born in 425 in Rousomblada, Isauria (southern Anatolia), as Tarasikodissa, Zeno gratefully changed his name upon marrying Ariadne, the daughter of Leo I. Owing to his Isaurian heritage and his Monophysite beliefs, Zeno was never considered fit to be emperor by many of the people of Constantinople, including his father-in-law, and his infant son was made emperor ahead of him.

After Leo II's early death, Zeno became sole emperor and managed to hold on for just a year before he was usurped by Basiliskos, the brother of the widowed empress Verina. Rumours suggest that this redoubtable woman had started an affair with Patricius, the *magister officiorum* under her husband, Leo I, and wanted to marry him and have him installed as the new emperor. Despite Zeno being married to her daughter Ariadne, Verina arranged a coup against him, and together with her own brother Basiliskos forced Zeno and his family to flee the capital for his homeland of Isauria.

Verina must have thought she had succeeded, but she had not considered her brother Basiliskos, who had other ideas. As soon as he was able, he had Patricius arrested and murdered, and sent the two leading generals of the Isaurian troops, the brothers Illus and Trocundes, to hunt down Zeno and capture him.

Basiliskos
January 475 – August 476

After Basiliskos's successful coup against Zeno, he chased him out of the city and incited a riot throughout Constantinople during which all remaining Isaurians were brutally killed. Without any strong Isaurian military presence in the capital, Basiliskos was able to seize the throne for himself.

Basiliskos is not always perceived as one of the Byzantine emperors, since he was a usurper who could not rid himself of the rightful heir to the throne. But rule he did. He had inherited a virtually empty treasury, as Zeno had taken the entire contents with him on fleeing the capital. The tried and tested Roman practice of selling off high government positions was used to raise money quickly, together with punitive tax increases on the population. Naturally this turned the population against Basiliskos; combined with the recent memory that he had been the general in charge of the disastrous defeat at the hands of the Vandals in North Africa in 468, it meant that Basiliskos never gained the trust and respect of the people. There was a devastating fire in the capital, which burnt down churches and houses and destroyed the great library built up by the emperor Julian. Always superstitious, the people of Constantinople saw this as a bad omen. To compound matters, Basiliskos was openly a Monophysite, believing Jesus and God to be one; since the majority of Orthodox Christians in the empire were Chalcedonians, believing Christ to have both a divine and a human nature, his beliefs were always going to cause unrest.

After just over a year as emperor, Basiliskos met his nemesis once again. Zeno had raised an army in Isauria and marched on Constantinople. Almost everyone had turned against Basiliskos by this point; his two generals, Illus and Trocundes, both switched sides and stood behind Zeno. Even Verina turned on her brother in revenge, since he had so foolishly executed her lover Patricius. As Zeno approached the city and it became clear to Basiliskos that the battle was lost, he begged Zeno not to spill the blood of himself or his family. Zeno agreed, sent him to Cappadocia and had him thrown in a dry cistern and starved to death, thereby only technically keeping his promise. He was thus able to reclaim the throne.

Zeno
August 476 – April 491 (*second reign*)

Having fled Constantinople (disguised as peasants in an old farm wagon, according to some), Zeno and his empress consort Ariadne now returned victorious to Constantinople, where Basiliskos capitulated without a fight. Zeno was once again emperor of the East, with a renewed ambition to restore the empire to the way it had been before his departure.

Zeno's second reign lasted nearly fifteen years, but was plagued by revolts, insurrections and attempted coups. In 479 Marcian, the son of the Western emperor Anthemius, led a coup from inside the walls of Constantinople, very nearly killing Zeno and his followers. In response, the capable general Illus had managed to move a unit of loyal soldiers into the city, had convinced Marcian's own soldiers to change sides and then captured Marcian himself, who was by now hiding in the church of the Holy Apostles. Just five years later, Illus decided that he wanted the empire for himself and led an army against the forces of the emperor, but he too was thwarted and beheaded. Verina, Ariadne's mother, had never been supportive of Zeno and was continually conspiring with others to usurp him. The mother–daughter relationship was a difficult one, and Zeno and Verina were continually plotting against each other. Zeno had banished Verina to a convent, but she had evidently left it to join Illus in his failed attempt to dethrone her son-in-law. She died during the siege of Papyrus, which began in 484, but her body was allowed back to the capital to be buried next to that of her daughter.

The Ostrogoths were active throughout this decade, and Zeno had been desperately trying to play one group off against another, with some success. However, following the death of Theodoric Strabo in 481, Theodoric the Great became king of all the Ostrogoths, and there were to be no more divisions between them. At first, Zeno was allied to Theodoric, making him consul in 484 – a position never before held by a barbarian under a Roman emperor. Theodoric even fought alongside Zeno in the siege of Papyrus against Illus. In 487, however, Theodoric turned on Zeno once again and tried to capture Constantinople, going as far as to cut off the water supply. Zeno promised Theodoric money and support, and pledged that, should he invade Italy, he could keep the lands he conquered with the emperor's blessing. After some years of fierce fighting, Theodoric did indeed defeat Odoacer, king of Italy, and became its effective ruler.

This constant fighting left little time for Zeno to accomplish much else during his reign. His strong Monophysite beliefs did encourage him to issue his famous *Henotikon* in 482. This document, an

'Act of Union', was designed to put a stop to disagreements between the Monophysites and the Chalcedonians concerning the nature of Christ. It was too vague to appease the Orthodox Christians, however, and not forceful enough to promote the Monophysite position, and as a result both sides reacted angrily, criticizing the emperor for his indecisiveness. The decree was openly ignored.

Zeno died on 9 April 491, after seventeen years as the emperor of the East. Now that the Western Empire had lost control, he was the last emperor of the Romans to boast a lineage going back to the time of Augustus.

Anastasios I Dikoros
April 491 – July 518

He was very tall, with short hair, a good figure and a round face, and with both hair and beard greying; one eye was grey and the other was black, yet his eyesight was perfect, and he often shaved his beard.
JOHN MALALAS, BEFORE 565

He was endowed with every virtue.
EMPRESS ARIADNE, *c.* 491 (ATTRIBUTED)

When the emperor Zeno died, the senate insisted that the widowed empress Ariadne marry a man 'suitable' to be the next emperor. The mob of Constantinople knew what they wanted – or, more exactly, what they did not want: no more Isaurians, and no more heretics. They wanted a Christian. As they gathered at the Hippodrome staring up at the widowed empress, they chanted: 'Give the empire an Orthodox emperor. Give the empire a Roman emperor.'

Ariadne chose an unlikely candidate in the shape of the *silentiarios* Anastasios. A *silentiarios* was a court official not without a degree of respect and responsibility; there were only thirty of them, and they were all distinguished men who were trusted personally by the emperor. Perhaps it was noticed by the empress that

Anastasios, even at the age of about 62, was an imposing and handsome man, with one grey eye and one black (a variation in colour,
today known as 'heterochromia', that gave rise to his epithet
Dikoros, or 'two-pupilled'). Originally from Dyrrachium (now
Durres in Albania), he was probably regarded as someone who
could rid the empire of the detested Isaurians and restore some
semblance of order until another, younger leader could be found.
However, the empire got more than it bargained for, as Anastasios
was to reign for twenty-seven years, dying peacefully at the age of
nearly 90, the oldest emperor ever to reign over Byzantium.

Numismatists, in a rather outdated way, still regard Emperor
Anastasios I's reign as the beginning of the age of Byzantium, owing
to his transformation of the entire fiscal system. This financial engineering, prompted by the emperor's parsimonious nature and
attention to bureaucratic detail, marked the start of a quiet revolution in the administration of empire that lasted for many years.
Anastasios may have been perceived as a killjoy, banning the hunting of wild animals in circuses, forbidding late-night feasts and
licentiousness, and cutting government expenditure on lavish
entertainments, but this introduction of financial rigour would
serve the empire well for the coming century. He even sold off
Zeno's imperial clothes, finding them too small for him, and put
the money in the public purse. At his death, he left the treasury
with 320,000 pounds of gold stacked up and ready to pay for the
expansionist policies of his successors.

Anastasios's policy of financial revolution was two-fold. First,
he changed the tax system, abolishing the highly unpopular tax
on receipts paid by the poor, and insisting that taxes be paid with
money rather than goods, which had become common practice.
This led to a significantly more efficient system, cutting out a lot
of corruption and favouring the free flow of commerce. He also
put an end to the policy of supplying soldiers with their uniform
and arms, instead giving them a generous allowance so they could
buy their own. This proved a highly popular move, cutting out yet

more bureaucracy and encouraging Roman citizens to join up rather than relying on mercenaries. Second, he introduced three new denominations of gold coinage. Up until this point the monetary system had been cumbersome and complex, but in 498 he brought in half and third denominations for the *solidus*, and then five coins of copper. This new currency allowed trade to flourish and remained the basis of Byzantine coinage for centuries to come.

There was one issue that would hound him to the end of his reign: the ongoing religious controversy surrounding the nature of Christ. Anastasios was a devout Christian who had given sermons in Hagia Sophia and had even been considered for the post of patriarch of Antioch. At heart he was a Monophysite, which placed him at odds with the Orthodox patriarch Euphemius of Constantinople. Although Anastasios was forced to sign a written declaration of his belief in Orthodoxy by Euphemius, he may have done so out of pragmatism or because he held that his understanding was the Orthodox way. However, many believed that he had heretical views, chief among them Longinus, the exiled brother of the former emperor Zeno, and a ragtag army was raised to challenge Anastasios's claim to the throne. The forces were defeated, but dissent continued for many years.

Over the previous years two factions had grown up within the city, the Blues and the Greens. They had started as two groups of supporters at the games at the Hippodrome but had evolved into a sort of local militia, each with its own religious and political beliefs, which could hold great sway in the running of the city. One group was aligned more closely with the Orthodox faith, and many within it were old supporters of the Isaurians. The other was more anti-Isaurian in nature and favoured the policies and beliefs of the current emperor, even if it would never see itself as heretical. Fighting often broke out between the two groups, and almost the entire city was aligned with one of them. When unrest occurred, it could therefore escalate until it encompassed the whole population, and it quickly became violent. People were killed, property was destroyed, and even the emperor at times found himself in danger. In 511 the oft-cited words 'Holy God, Holy and Mighty, Holy and Immortal,' were read out in the cathedral, followed by the phrase 'who was crucified for us'. This was too much for strict followers of the Chalcedonian doctrine, according to which it was not the man Jesus who was crucified but God himself. The uproar that ensued was particularly frenzied, and many died in the fighting. It was only the appearance of the now aged Emperor Anastasios himself and his offer of resignation that managed to quieten the masses. He assured them that, if he remained in authority, those words would never be uttered again. The mob were placated, and normal life could continue.

It is hard today to imagine how intensely emotional people felt over this apparently obscure detail of religious doctrine. That a disagreement over the nature and definition of Christ and his relationship to God could lead them to murder, and ultimately to war, seems fantastical, but such was the fervour of religion among all people in the empire.

As he reached the age of 88, a year after his wife, Ariadne, had died, the childless Anastasios began to think of his successor. According to the author of the *Anonymus Valesianus* chronicles, Anastasios – perplexed as to how to choose between his three nephews – decided to invite them to stay, having placed under one of the three beds a note that read: 'Regnum'. Whoever sat on this bed would be chosen as emperor. However, when the three came to sit, two of them sat together and nobody chose the bed with the note. Anastasios, like many of his time, was deeply superstitious, and his nephews had failed in their task. He therefore decided that the first person he saw the following morning would be declared as the emperor of Byzantium. That person was Justin, commander of the imperial guards known as *excubitores*, and – true to his word – Anastasios pronounced him his successor.

Anastasios died suddenly but peacefully on 1 July 518; several sources relate how a thunderstorm raged and lightning struck his palace, which some took as a sign of divine disapproval of his Monophystism. The belief that natural phenomena – particularly catastrophic events such as earthquakes, volcanic eruptions and tsunamis – were some sort of divine intervention, often to punish the wrongdoings of leaders, was constant throughout the whole of the Byzantine age.

What could not be denied was that Anastasios had left the empire in a very strong state. Rich, dominant, and with no particularly powerful enemies to threaten them, his successors would have much to thank him for.

JUSTINIAN DYNASTY
(518–602)

Ruling over what was often cited as the 'golden age' of the early Byzantine Empire, the Justinian dynasty was founded by a military man named Justin, who quickly employed his brilliant young nephew Justinian to advise him. Justinian the Great succeeded his uncle, and he and his wife, Theodora, ruled for forty years, expanding the borders of the empire to their widest point. Most of the territories that had been lost to invaders over the previous 200 years were reclaimed, including North Africa, Italy and southern Spain. Justinian's domestic achievements were also significant: he laid down the foundations of modern law, the Codex Justinianus, and began construction of the great Christian church of Hagia Sophia in 532. The mosaics of Ravenna remain one of the finest works of Byzantine art in the early medieval era.

Justin I
July 518 – August 527

The emperor Anastasios promoted Justin to captain of the palace guards, and because of this position he rose to the imperial throne when Anastasios died, despite having one foot in the grave and being utterly untutored. In fact he was illiterate, which was unprecedented among the Romans.

PROCOPIUS, *c.* 550

Of average height, but well built, he was handsome, with thick grey hair and a fine complexion. A veteran of battle, he was unschooled but generous.

JOHN MALALAS, BEFORE 565

Justin I was the founder of the Justinian dynasty, which was to rule for almost a hundred years. As is so often the case with the emperors of Byzantium, accounts of his rule are full of contradiction, from the manner of his selection to the highest office right up to the precise role of his brilliant nephew Justinian. What cannot be denied is that, diplomatically and financially, he kept the empire on a steady course and that the appointment of Justinian as his successor helped establish the great period named after him, the so-called 'Age of Justinian'.

Dismissed as a peasant, possibly a swineherd, the young Justin fled his home in Illyria when it was besieged by barbarians and came to Constantinople with his brothers, owning nothing, so the story goes, except some bread. From here he joined the palace guard, most probably the select band of *excubitores*, and served faithfully for nearly forty years, rising through the ranks to become their commander (*comes excubitorum*). He had a distinguished service record, notching up victorious battles against both the Persian and the Isaurians. According to Procopius, Justin was illiterate and had poor Greek, such that he could sign 'I have read' on documents only with the help of a stencil.

Yet Justin and his family by now occupied exalted positions within Byzantine society. His sister, Vigilantia, married a man named Sabbatius, with whom she had three children, one of whom, Petrus Sabbatius Justinianus, would become Justin's close confidant and, in due course, Emperor Justinian I. Justin himself married a former slave, originally named Lupicina (later Euphemia), whom he had purchased after one particular battle and who then allegedly served as his army cook. He seems to have had no other romantic attachments, and the two of them never had any children of their own. When he became emperor at the age of 60, he brought his wife and his peasant mother to live with him in the sumptuous palace of the capital.

The legend of Anastasios's arbitrary selection of Justin to be his successor is almost certainly false: it is much more likely that he employed cunning duplicity to obtain the position. According to the chronicler John Malalas, two officials who were trying to bribe people to vote for their candidate, Theocritus, entrusted Justin with the distribution of a large sum of money among the army and others to buy their support. Justin duly handed out the money but let everyone believe it was from him. As a result, it seems most likely that Justin appeared before the public at the Hippodrome and was overwhelmingly voted in as emperor.

Once in power, Justin quickly had his opponents assassinated, particularly those supporters of Anastasios who were known to have held anti-Chalcedonian sympathies. A purge of the Monophysites followed and, having deftly arranged an alliance with Pope Hormisdas in Rome, Justin managed to resolve the Acacian schism between the Western and Eastern Christian churches. The alliance with Rome and his embrace of the Orthodox Chalcedonian position on the dual nature of Christ stabilized relations with the whole of Italy. At this time Theodoric, king of the Ostrogoths, was in power there; an Arian in his beliefs, he was thus in conflict with the pope and the Orthodox Chalcedonians. In 523 Justin issued a decree denouncing Arianism, and thus Theodoric himself. The new pope, John I, was sent by Theodoric to visit Justin and try to overturn the ruling. Under the strict direction of his nephew Justinian, now appointed as *comes domesticorum*, commander of the imperial guard, Justin received the pope, and in full view of the crowds in Constantinople prostrated himself, alongside his patriarch, at the pope's feet. With the two churches seemingly united, Pope John returned to Theodoric, delivering the good news of reconciliation, and the bad news that there would be no renunciation of the edict against Arianism. The pope was promptly thrown in prison and died a few days later.

Justin continued to position himself as the religious head of the people, not just their emperor. He even changed the reverse of his coinage, transforming the old pagan symbol of Victory portrayed as a woman into the figure of Victory in the form of an angel, thus emphasizing the empire as a fundamentally Christian state.

In 526 there was a terrible earthquake in Antioch. The city was destroyed, and some 250,000 people died. Justin immediately made funds available to help and rebuild the city. With the empire's finances in such rude health, Justin began building programmes that his successor was to take to even greater heights. Justin was also an enthusiastic patron of the arts and commissioned a vast mural in the palace depicting his rise from swineherd to emperor. All that he instigated is now lost, or Justinian claimed the credit for it.

Suffering from a wound in his leg that had bothered Justin for many years and become septic, in April 527 he made his nephew, who by now was essentially running the empire, co-emperor. Four months later Justin I died in his bed, content that he had served the empire well and that he had left it in the capable hands of his formidable nephew, Justinian I.

Justinian I
August 527 – November 565

Murdering the innocent and stealing their lands was nothing to him. Thousands could die at his whim. He destroyed all the good institutions. He was incredibly stupid and no different from a senseless donkey.
PROCOPIUS, c. 550

Justinian the Great is something of an enigma. Without question he is preeminent among Byzantine's emperors, expanding the empire's territories to their furthest reach and reconquering lands that had been lost over the previous centuries. He instituted a fundamental work of jurisprudence, the *Corpus juris civilis*, that was then the most comprehensive body of legal codification ever undertaken, and built magnificent monuments to Christianity, not least Hagia Sophia. Yet one great literary work by Procopius, who knew him well and served alongside him for many years, paints

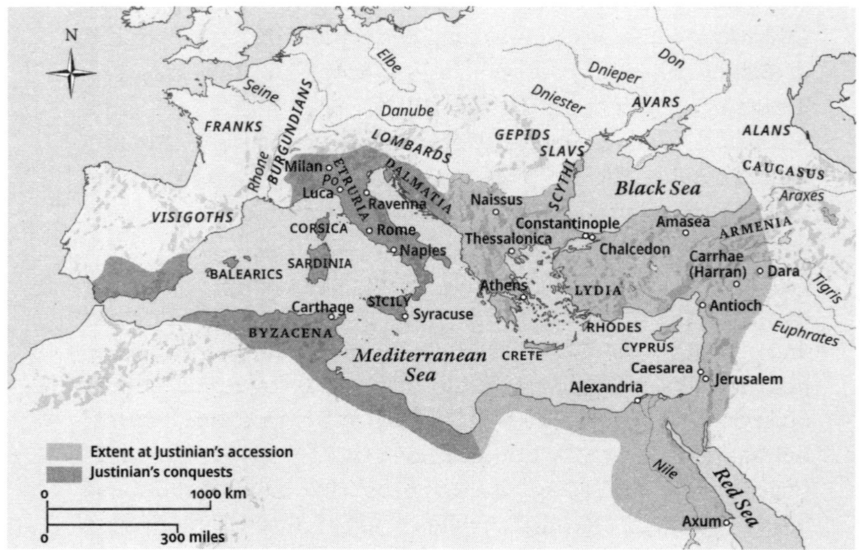

him as a petty, vindictive tyrant who was easily manipulated by his wife, Theodora. Should the *Secret History* be interpreted as a contemporary literary form that is largely satirical and plays with the truth, or an honest, private account based on Procopius's close-up exposure to those who shaped the known world? Either way, Justinian emerges as a ruler of enormous energy and capability, who formalized both the idea and the reality of Byzantium as the most powerful empire on earth.

Born Petrus Sabbatius in 482 in Tauresium, in modern-day Macedonia, Justinian is often cited as the last emperor to be a native Latin speaker. His parents were peasants, probably farmers, and it was his uncle Justin who changed the course of his life by bringing him to Constantinople, adopting him as his own and generally giving him a start that could not have been bettered. Having received a classical education, he changed his name to Justinian in honour of his uncle and was welcomed into the *excubitores*, the emperor's personal bodyguard, where he served for a number of years. From the beginning of his uncle's reign, Justinian was by his side. Made consul in 521 and then co-emperor when Justin was ill in 527, Justinian rose unopposed to become full emperor upon Justin's death later that year.

During this period Justinian met the woman who was to change his life. Theodora was the daughter of circus performers in the Hippodrome; her father was a bear-tamer and her mother a dancer. It is generally understood that she was an actress, and most probably a prostitute. Procopius goes into lewd detail as to her pornographic performances on stage as a young girl, claiming that on one occasion she used trained geese to peck at her in surprising places. Marriage to an actress was strictly forbidden, but Justinian must have been so sure of wanting to wed this woman, twenty years his junior, that he made his uncle pass a law that allowed inter-marriage between the classes. Whatever the truth of her humble and lurid beginnings, Theodora would become one of the most influential and extraordinary women of any Byzantine era, helping to shape and determine the direction of the empire alongside her authoritarian and dominating husband.

From the first days of his reign, Justinian had a very clear vision of what he wanted to achieve as he started to manoeuvre his vast resources into place. His task: to lead the empire to salvation and re-establish it as the dominant force in the world. He would indeed reconquer most of the lands lost to the barbarians over the previous centuries: North Africa from the Vandals, Italy from the Ostrogoths, and the eastern provinces from the Sassanians. The Mediterranean Sea would once again become a Roman lake. The Byzantines – who never used that word to describe themselves – saw themselves as Romans and their emperors as the continuation of a long line from Augustus. However, they were now also a Christian people, looking more East than West, and regarded their emperor as their divinely appointed leader; Justinian, for his part, saw his role as God's vice regent on earth.

The first real test for Justinian's leadership came in January 532 in the form of a historic uprising by the populace known as the Nika riots (they cheered *Nika*, or 'Victory', as they rampaged through the city). For many years there had been two factions that supported different charioteers in the races at the Hippodrome, the Blues and the Greens. They were also politicized and dangerous; emperors in the past had usually supported one or the other, ultimately balancing out the factions' power. Theodora and Justinian, however, felt sufficiently confident in their own authority to oppose both factions as they saw fit. This caused the opposing groups to unite and fight against the state rather than each other, which led to a rapid escalation in the rioting. When some of the rioters were eventually condemned to death for inciting violence, two managed to survive the hanging, and the crowd in the Hippodrome asked the emperor for them to be spared. The refusal of Justinian to show leniency to these two men led to a further riot that lasted for days. The crowd burned buildings to the ground, including the main palace gate (the Chalke), the famous baths of Zeuxippos, and the great church of Hagia Sophia itself. Justinian attempted to calm the crowd by sacking both his ministers, Tribonian and John the Cappadocian, but this did not go far enough. The aristocracy resented Justinian's imposition of punitive taxes and clampdown on corrupt practices, and, fuelled by the crowd, they now wanted to install Hypatios, the nephew of Anastasios, on the throne and rid themselves of both the emperor and his lowly empress. According to Procopius, at this point Justinian contemplated fleeing the capital on a boat he had waiting for him in the harbour, but Theodora stepped in and urged her husband to fight, saying that he could go if he wished, but she was staying since she found 'kingship to be an appropriate burial shroud'. So stay and fight Justinian did. He ordered his general Belisarios to confront the assembled rioters in the Hippodrome, which he did, using extreme violence. Some 30,000 people were said to have been slain by the emperor's troops, and the riot ended instantly. Leading aristocrats were rounded up and executed, including the hapless pretender, Hypatios. Procopius tells us that Theodora was more ruthless in these reprisals than her husband, but whatever the truth, the Nika riots were a watershed moment. Justinian had been shown to be merciless when he needed to be, and from that time on he was never again challenged so openly.

The destruction of the city afforded Justinian an opportunity to rebuild parts of it that had been burnt down or demolished. Foremost among them was the site of Hagia Sophia, the church of Holy Wisdom and Constantinople's cathedral. Work began just forty-five days after the riots had ended, which suggests that Justinian had already decided to rebuild it. He chose two theoretical mathematicians as his architects, Anthemius of Tralles and Isidore of Miletus, neither of whom had any experience in construction. It was the largest single building ever undertaken by the Romans, some 78 × 72 m (256 × 236 ft) at its base, with a dome 31 m (102 ft) in diameter and rising 62 m (203 ft) from the floor at its highest point. On either side of the central dome are two semi-domes, and the exterior walls are pierced with large windows. The effect these breathtaking proportions must have had on the population and visitors to the city in the 6th century can hardly be overestimated.

Other buildings in the capital were also constructed: the church of SS Sergius and Bakchos, reputedly instigated by Theodora herself; the church of Hagia Irene; the church of the Virgin of Pege; and many more. This extravagant building activity was not confined to the capital but was spread throughout the empire, most famously in Ravenna. Here, the church of San Vitale, with its mosaics of Justinian and his beloved Theodora, was built after the conquest of Italy by Justinian's forces. Sadly, Theodora died of cancer one year after it was completed, and neither she nor Justinian ever visited this masterpiece.

Throughout most of Justinian's long reign there were constant wars with his neighbours. Aggressive conflicts with the Sassanians in the east lasted for over twenty years and resulted in a stalemate, which kept the borders more or less intact. A peace treaty was agreed with the young king Khusro that lasted for some years but was broken sporadically. More successful was Justinian's conquest of North Africa and the expulsion of the Vandals from history, with the help of Justinian's trusted general Belisarios. Time and time again during Justinian's reign, Belisarios was called upon to help, and even brought out of retirement to solve difficult problems on every front of the empire. Belisarios's wife, Antonina, was a favourite of Theodora, and the two of them wielded enormous influence throughout the palace – an influence that, according to Procopius, was not always benign. These two intelligent, ambitious and powerful women dominated much of court life in Constantinople and beyond.

In Italy, the Armenian eunuch General Narses was ordered to take over from the now ageing Belisarios and he, too, proved successful. Although it took many years, the Ostrogoths, for so long the major force throughout Italy, were finally defeated. Not content with this epic reconquest, Justinian sent a force to southern Spain, where he was once again triumphant, defeating the Visigoths and occupying a large part of the coastline. This was the highpoint of Justinian's expansion and restored territories the Roman Empire had enjoyed in its heyday.

Of course, all these wars and lavish building programmes came at an enormous cost. Justinian was very fortunate in having inherited a stable and wealthy treasury. Anastasios I and Justin I had made Justinian's expansion possible thanks to their prudent organization and fiscal policies that had filled the government coffers with gold. But even with all the resources of the empire at his disposal, the expense of Justinian's military success was enormous. Once the land in Italy had been reconquered, there was little economic growth owing to the scale of destruction and resulting fall in population. In later times Justinian was blamed for stretching the empire's resources too thinly over a large geographical area, but it is hard to imagine that any ruler could resist a triumphant march across lands that were previously lost. Victory followed victory on the battlefield, and buildings continued to be erected at an astonishing rate on the back of this well-earned sense of confidence and invincibility.

However, there was one area Justinian could not control. The 530s–550s witnessed a series of natural disasters. The climate was dramatically affected by vast dust storms that lasted for months, blocking out the sun and causing crops to fail, with resulting famines – quite possibly caused by enormous volcanic explosions in other parts of the world, such as at Krakatoa and Rabaul in the east, Iceland in the north, and Ilopango in the west. An enormous earthquake in Beirut in 551 triggered a tsunami that reportedly killed some 30,000 people and damaged coastal towns throughout the Eastern Mediterranean. But the greatest disaster was yet to come: in 542 the bubonic plague appeared in Constantinople for the first time. Ships from Egypt transporting grain also introduced rats and fleas that would lead to devastation. It was estimated that some 30 million people died of this plague. Justinian himself contracted the disease but survived. Procopius claims that 10,000 people a day were dying in the capital; bodies lay rotting in the street as the living could not carry the dead away fast enough. In the plague's aftermath, wars became more protracted, taxes were more onerous, and the psychological damage suffered by the population greatly affected the daily activity of the empire. Many people subscribed to the Christian belief that they were witnessing the 'End of Days'. The world was created in 5500 BC, they said, and the 6th millennium was thought to herald the Day of Judgment, hence the superstition that these natural disasters were all a sign of God's displeasure.

Although the empire survived, it was rocked to its foundations and took generations to recover. Theodora died in 548 and, although she was only 40 years old, she left behind a husband now in his 60s, weary with government and destined to spend the remaining years of his life alone and childless.

This was also a difficult time for the relationship between the emperor and the church. Justinian's position was that, if the empire was to be unified, there must also be a unified position on doctrinal matters. He believed that the Orthodox, Nicaean version of Christianity should prevail. Those who differed from this view were systematically persecuted and excluded from any positions of authority within the empire. He was ruthless in this policy, the result that many sects were virtually wiped out, either by burning or drowning. Justice was undoubtedly important to Justinian, but it was his own form of justice, and nobody was going to stand in its way.

Justinian ruled over a larger and more diverse population than any who came after him. A great proportion of his building works survive, and the decoration that adorned them, primarily in mosaic, is widely seen as a high point in the first phase of Byzantine art. His codification of Roman law was unsurpassed, and his attempt to unite the peoples of Christianity through the establishment of a universal Christian creed was genuine and came as close to reconciling the Orthodox and the Monophysites as any other. Justinian died around 83 years of age, having ruled for thirty-eight years.

Justin II
November 565 – October 578

Strikingly handsome, he was well-built, and a blue-eyed blond.
SYMEON THE LOGOTHETE, *c*. 970

Do not let this attire inflame you as it did me.
JUSTIN II, 574

Justinian the Great was always going to be a hard act to follow, and his nephew Justin – about 45 years old at the time of his accession, son of the emperor's sister Vigilantia – was never really up to the task. According to the poet Corippus, even his selection, which was witnessed by only one man, was open to question, as Justinian had a second nephew called Justin who some claimed was the rightful heir. This other Justin was found murdered in his

JUSTINIAN DYNASTY

bed a year later, and many suspected Justin II's wife, Sophia, and Justin II himself to be involved.

At first, the new emperor behaved impeccably, paying off his uncle's debts, rewarding those who had helped him, administering justice in person and proclaiming universal religious tolerance. Constantly alongside him was his wife, Sophia, a niece of the redoubtable Empress Theodora and a woman who would take an increasingly active role in the affairs of state. Justin's biggest problem was the state of the treasury, as his ambitious uncle had spent most of the empire's money. Justinian had also pledged significant amounts to various foreign powers on his extensive borders, and Justin II had no real means of defending much of this newly acquired territory.

Justin's first action, although understandable, was in fact disastrous. He refused to pay the tributes that had been promised to the Avars in the north, and when they inevitably retaliated by plundering the whole of the Balkans Justin was unable to contain them. Similarly, in the east the Sassanian king Khusro rebelled against Justin for not paying the agreed and customary tribute. The ensuing war with Persia lasted for many years. Most dramatic of all was the Lombards' victory in Italy: this territory, so hard won by his uncle, was lost within a few years. Throughout most of Justin's reign, the plague was still circulating in parts of the empire, claiming many lives and making normal activity, such as travel and tax-collecting, very difficult. As if this were not enough, in the fifth year of his reign, around 570, the Prophet Muhammad was born. Within a hundred years the Muslim armies had swarmed across much of the empire and would remain a constant foe.

According to John of Ephesus, Justin suffered increasingly from mental illness, becoming violent at times, attacking those around him with biting and screaming. His wife, Sophia, had a calming effect on him; and there is a story that, in an effort to divert him, servants transported him around the palace on a little cart while music was played. When his behaviour became more unmanageable,

Sophia was made his regent and essentially ruled alone. She was instrumental in taking economic control of the empire and greatly reduced expenditure within the imperial household. She sent gifts to foreign statesmen in order to gain favour, notably the relic of the True Cross that was sent to the pope in Rome, one of the oldest relics now in the Vatican Museums. The gathering of such holy relics was a constant preoccupation of the Byzantine emperors, and in the early days of the 6th century important artefacts had been brought to the capital. Justin and Sophia repaired at least two churches to the Virgin Mary, in the district of Blachernae and in the Chalkoprateia, and feasts of the Virgin – her birth and Dormition – were officially established as public holidays. This policy helped cement the capital as the holiest place in Christendom, outstripping Rome, Antioch and even Jerusalem; it also resulted in more pilgrims coming to the city, bringing prestige and money.

Since Justin and Sophia had no children, the empress became preoccupied with the question of who was going to take over when Justin died. To this end she selected the handsome young commander of the *excubitores*, Tiberios, as her 'adopted son'. As Justin II finally succumbed to his illness, he formally appointed Tiberios as *augustus*, his successor. One of his speeches, as recorded by the historian Theophylact Simocatta, revealed a man who fully understood the burdens of leadership: 'Behold, God magnifies you; God grants you this apparel, not I; honour him, that you may also be honoured by him.'

Justin II was an emperor who had been handed an impossible task. The empire was too large and not sufficiently rich to sustain its position as the true successor to the Roman Empire. With Empress Sophia by his side, Justin did succeed in establishing financial stability where others failed, and attempted to reconcile the religious differences between the Chalcedonians and the Monophysites. As the only emperor who can truly be described as certifiably mad, his tragedy was that he knew it, and his triumph that he ceded control for the greater good of his empire.

Tiberios II Constantine
September 578 – August 582

He was handsomely built, with a broad chest, beautiful blue eyes,
a blond beard and blond hair, and fair-skinned, with a fresh and
expressive face; he was good and generous to a fault.
SYMEON THE LOGOTHETE, *c.* 970

While Justin was still alive, Tiberios and Sophia continued his parsimonious policies, but as soon as he died Tiberios changed tack. Throughout his short reign, Tiberios gave money to the poor, stamped out the selling of government posts, appeased the enemies on the borders by means of tributes and diplomacy, and relaxed the persecution of the Monophysites. There were still many battles to be fought with the Avars in the Balkans, but he eventually allowed them to settle on Byzantine lands in return for their help in defending the borders. In the east he paid tributes to the Persians to stop them advancing into Byzantine territory, although Persian Armenia remained an area of hostility. In Italy, the Lombards proved more resilient than expected; and although he reclaimed Rome, Tiberios lost most of the other territories.

Tiberios could afford this generosity because Justin II had been frugal with the treasury reserves, but also because he discovered some hitherto undiscovered stashes of gold, both within the palace grounds and in the form of treasure that the eunuch Narses had hidden in the cistern of his abode in Italy, amounting to several million *solidi*. By spreading this money liberally among the people and the army he endeared himself to both groups for the whole of his short reign. He also removed a tax on bread and wine, which greatly benefited the poor.

The widowed Empress Sophia, however, was not so pleased, and relations between them became strained. Sophia had initially hoped that she could adopt Tiberios as her son, but he refused. Then, in desperation, she insisted that he marry her, but again

Tiberios refused, as he was already married, to a woman named Ino. Sophia had banned Ino and their children from coming to the imperial palace, so Tiberios simply travelled back and forth between the palace and his wife's home as he chose. Once he was officially recognized as *augustus*, his family moved in, and in the tradition of Byzantium Ino changed her name to a more suitable one for an empress: Anastasia. This infuriated Sophia, who attempted a coup against Tiberios with the help of a high-ranking general called Justinian. The plot was discovered, and Justinian was removed from his post and replaced by a very capable general and long-time friend of Tiberios called Maurice. The dowager empress was well treated but given only a small allowance. It is typical of Tiberios that he did not take vengeance on these would-be usurpers, but merely forgave them.

After only four years Tiberios became increasingly ill. To help him run the empire he made Maurice more powerful by betrothing him to his daughter Constantina, and the day before he died he elevated Maurice to the rank of *augustus*. Tiberios died on 14 August 582, having uttered these typically kind words recorded by Paul the Deacon: 'Let my sovereignty be delivered to you with this girl [Constantina]. Be happy in the use of it, mindful always to love equity and justice.'

Maurice Tiberios

August 582 – November 602

Maurice was of average height, robust, with fair skin, a round face and reddish-gold hair, slightly balding and without any beard since he shaved every day, as is the custom of the Romans.

SYMEON THE LOGOTHETE, *c.* 970

Maurice Tiberios is sometimes regarded as the last emperor of the 'Roman Empire' as it is traditionally perceived. With his death, the age of Late Antiquity was over, and the new era of the Byzantines, of the Eastern Roman Empire, was to begin.

Although born within the heartland of the empire in Cappadocia, Maurice would not have been a native Latin speaker but Greek, and unflinchingly Chalcedonian in his Christian beliefs. His successes during his twenty-year reign were many. He had proved himself a very competent and experienced military commander under Tiberios I in both the north, against the Avars, and in the east against the Persians. Once he was crowned emperor he focused on the eastern borders and a long and hard campaign in which he helped the Persians defeat their rebellious general Bahram Chobin and re-establish Khusro II on the Sassanian throne. In return for the Byzantine army's help, the young Khusro entered into an 'eternal peace' with his neighbour and no longer demanded the tributes promised to his predecessors. These were very favourable terms: Maurice had successfully extended his territories against the Sassanians and secured a lasting truce. This enabled him to concentrate on other parts of his vast empire, where in both Africa and Italy he created exarchates – essentially self-governing areas where an appointed exarch, or viceroy, would have virtual autonomy over both military and civil matters, as long as they were subservient to the emperor in Constantinople. Maurice's first key appointment was to install Herakleios the Elder as exarch of Carthage, a post that was of great significance to the future line of emperors. The exarch system proved highly effective and helped maintain these territories for decades to come.

Maurice's ability to organize and execute his policies was impressive. As he grew older, he became harder on those who would not adhere strictly to his wishes and, keeping a tight grip on the finances, he raised taxes and paid his soldiers less money than they were used to. One episode that illustrates his meanness is his refusal in 598 to pay a ransom to free some 12,000 Byzantine soldiers who had been captured by the Avars. It was a relatively small sum, but Maurice was getting ever more frugal and remained determined not to pay.

As a result, all the soldiers were massacred. Despite an angry uprising within the army, led by an officer called Phokas, the emperor showed no remorse.

There had been a custom that soldiers on campaign would return home in the winter season to see their families, sell their booty, sort out their affairs and rest in their native towns and villages. At the end of a campaign against the Avars north of the Danube in 602, just a year or so after the massacre, Maurice decided it was too expensive to allow his troops to return home for Christmas and ordered them to remain in the Balkans. Not only would they remain in hostile territory, he ordained: they would also embark on a new offensive in the freezing Balkan winter and have to support themselves on what the land would provide. This would be his undoing.

The troops rebelled and, led by their popular commander, Phokas, they decided to mutiny. Proclaiming Phokas as the new emperor, they marched on the capital in November 602. Not only did Maurice and his family sense that soldiers were coming to the capital to depose him, but riots started to break out in the city itself and their safety was seriously threatened. The 63-year-old emperor and most of his family fled to the harbour, where a ship was to take them to safety. Phokas marched triumphantly into the capital and set up his new government. He quickly found Maurice and his family in hiding and ordered them to be killed. It is recorded by Theophylact Simocatta that Maurice was made to endure the horrific spectacle of his six sons being decapitated in front of him, one of them just 1 year old. Then he too was beheaded. His wife and three daughters were spared but sent to a monastery, where they attempted a coup against Phokas but were discovered and then executed a few years later.

Maurice had met the most terrible end after what had been many years of great success. He had quelled the Persians, established the exarchates in Italy and Africa, and overseen a period of prosperity. But his naturally parsimonious nature was his ruin, leading to the rebellion of the troops and the rioting of the Green faction in Constantinople. His policies and his decisions were often correct for the empire but not necessarily for the people.

The first Byzantine emperor ever to be killed in an uprising, Maurice had achieved so much and promised much more. Previous emperors had been unable to father heirs, but he had many healthy and capable children who could have established a dynasty for generations to come. As for Phokas, the usurper would prove to be a disaster.

NON-DYNASTIC USURPER

Phokas
November 602 – October 610

You all know only too well what a cloud of dust the devil has stirred up under the successor of Maurice of blessed memory, for he has stifled love and sown mutual hatred throughout the whole land.
JOHN, ARCHBISHOP OF THESSALONIKI, *c.* 610–20

He was deformed, with a puffed-up face, red hair, and eyebrows that knitted together. His beard was neat and short, and on his cheek he had a scar that flared up whenever he was angry.
SYMEON THE LOGOTHETE, *c.* 970

Little is known of Phokas before his soldiers raised him on a shield and declared him emperor in 602. While serving as an army centurion north of the Danube, he had led the successful rebellion against Maurice. Phokas's savage murder of both the emperor and his six children set the tone for his entire eight-year reign. He hurled their butchered bodies into the sea, where they washed up on the shores of Chalcedon – an act that portended a time of violence and terror.

Even if we take into account the desire of historians to favour Herakleios, his successor, Phokas was unprepared, and certainly unfit, to rule. He was obsessed with rooting out traitors and enemies. A probable psychopath, he took torture to new levels: eyes were pierced, tongues torn out, hands and feet were routinely amputated, and murder was rife. His drinking and carousing were legendary, and after assassinating anyone he found suspicious he installed his own relatives in all the chief positions of the army and the government. He ignored real threats to the empire on his borders and allowed the territories in the north and the east to be overrun by invaders. The Sassanians used the killing of Emperor Maurice, the man with whom they had concluded the 'eternal' peace treaty, as an excuse to invade Byzantine lands in the eastern provinces. Their great king, Khusro II, took the city of Dara, as well as the lands of Mesopotamia, Syria and most of Anatolia. In the north, the Avars and the Slavs made repeated raids against the Byzantine forces who retreated at almost every turn. The Balkans were overrun, and the great city of Constantinople was becoming increasingly surrounded.

The particularly Byzantine phenomenon of the Blues and the Greens circus factions, which had been largely quiet since Justinian's clampdown following the Nika riots, flared up again, with riots throughout the capital and beyond. Nobody was safe, and eventually it became too much for the population. A rebellion led by Herakleios the Elder, the exarch of Carthage, moved towards the capital to dethrone the hated emperor.

The one quarter from which Phokas did, mystifyingly, receive praise was the church in Italy, and in particular Pope Gregory the Great. He praised Phokas as a liberator and compared the emperor's wife, Leontia, to Pulcheria, the wife of Marcian, herself described as a new Helena. Phokas later declared Rome 'the head of all churches', and Pope Boniface III continued to hold this brutal emperor in high esteem. There is a column still standing in the Roman Forum dedicated to Phokas, which has been called 'the last monument of classical antiquity'.

According to all contemporaneous accounts, Phokas had no redeeming qualities at all, but we must remember that they were written under the auspices of Herakleios and his successors. Nevertheless, Phokas was certainly a despot, and his end came almost too late to save the empire from annihilation. The superstitious and deeply religious population believed that God appointed the emperors for a reason, and in an effort to understand his appalling behaviour they assumed that they had been given him as a punishment for sins committed in the past.

When Herakleios, the son of Herakleios the Elder, entered Constantinople, he faced no resistance from the troops or from the people. Phokas was summoned. According to John of Antioch, he met his fate swiftly: Herakleios was waiting for him, and asked the question, 'Is it thus that you have governed the empire?' Phokas replied with his last words on earth: 'Will you govern it any better?' Herakleios kicked Phokas and beheaded him on the spot. John of Antioch continues, 'They cut off his right arm, hand and genitals. They put the flesh on their spears and dragged Phokas, his brother Domentiolos, Bonosos and Leontios, his *sacellarius*, through the city. Eventually they burned them in the Forum of the Ox.'

So ended the brutal reign of one of Byzantium's most notorious emperors. The empire was in a terrible state: finances depleted, the north invaded by Slavs and Avars, the east and south overrun by the Sassanian Persians, and Italy all but lost to the Lombards. In Constantinople the people were depressed and fearful of the marauders who were almost at the city gates. It would need a leader of exceptional ability to drag them away from the cliff edge.

NON-DYNASTIC USURPER

HERAKLIAN DYNASTY

(610–695)

The near hundred-year rule of the family of Herakleios saw monumental events take place both within and without the empire's borders. After sailing from Carthage to overthrow the tyrant Phokas, Herakleios had to fight the Sassanian Persians in the east and the newly established kingdom of the Bulgars to the north. He eventually defeated the Sassanians and famously recovered relics of the True Cross from their capital, Ctesiphon, returning them to Jerusalem. However, the death of the Prophet Muhammad in 632 ushered in a new foe that would undo much of his success, and the Arab Muslim armies conquered much of the territory Herakleios had won years before. The second half of the 7th century saw the empire besieged from all sides, with Constans II even trying to move the capital from Constantinople to Syracuse. This period culminated in the banishment of Justinian II, cruel and unpopular at the age of just 23, which ushered in a period of great instability.

Herakleios

October 610 – January 641

Herakleios was one of the wisest of men and among the most determined, clever, thoughtful and opinionated of kings. He ruled the Romans with true leadership and splendour.

IBN KATHIR, *c.* 1370

Of average height, robust, with a broad chest, beautiful blue eyes, golden hair, fair complexion, and a wide, thick beard.

SYMEON THE LOGOTHETE, *c.* 970

At the point that he cut off the head of his predecessor, Herakleios faced a myriad of problems. Thirty-five years old, he married Eudokia, his sweetheart from his native Carthage, at the same time as he was crowned emperor. Eudokia and Herakleios were adored by the citizens of the capital, as liberators and as a symbol of all that was good and God-given.

The young emperor must have been relieved and excited by all that had recently occurred. He had met no opposition from the forces of Phokas, and the empire was now his. But this euphoria did not last long. Eudokia gave birth to the future emperor Constantine III, but lived for only two more years before dying of epilepsy. It is recorded in the so-called Stichometry of Nicephorus that, when her coffin passed through the streets of Constantinople, a woman launched a gob of spit from an upstairs window, which landed on the coffin. The woman was torn out of her house and executed by burning.

Herakleios began to grasp the dire position in which he found the empire. The Persians, under their dynamic leader Khusro II, had used Phokas's murder of their ally Maurice as an excuse to break their truce and attack Byzantine lands. Phokas had done nothing to stop the Sassanian armies from advancing into Armenia and the Caucasus, and they had swiftly taken control of areas close to the traditional Persian borders. During the first years of Herakleios's reign, the Sassanian armies advanced further into Byzantine territories and swept through Syria, Mesopotamia and Palestine. The Persians captured Jerusalem, slaughtered thousands of Christians and stole the most holy relic of all, the remnants of the True Cross. To the deeply religious and superstitious Byzantines, this was a crucially symbolic moment in their history, and they looked to their emperor to save them. As if this were not enough, Herakleios had similar problems in the north. The Avars and the Slavs could see how the Byzantine armies were obliged to move farther from the capital to combat the Persian advance in the south, and so they attacked the northern borders, invading the Balkans and coming within a few miles of

    HERAKLIAN DYNASTY

Constantinople itself. In one skirmish Herakleios was almost captured, and escaped death in battle only narrowly. Realizing that he could not fight enemies on two fronts, he concluded a peace treaty with the Avars, paying them a vast annual tribute to keep them quiet while he dealt with the bigger threat of the Persians' advance.

Herakleios embarked on a significant reorganization of the government. Stamping out the corruption that had flourished under Phokas, he established a hierarchy that was fair and efficient in raising tax revenues and establishing a rule of law. He reorganized the imperial army so that it was fit and ready for the battles ahead, and he tried his best to resolve the religious differences that were still causing rifts between the Monophysites and the Chalcedonians. He decreed a new doctrine called Monothelitism, which stated that Christ had two natures but only one will. Alas, neither side was placated, and religious harmony was truly restored only when the majority of non-Chalcedonians were captured and lost to the Muslim Arab forces in the eastern provinces. Herakleios was also the emperor who changed the official language of the state from Latin to Greek, taking the title *basileus* ('king' or 'emperor') – a move that marked a shift from Rome towards a Greek and Eastern Christian culture.

Herakleios then gambled everything on one audacious move. He would leave his family and his capital under the protection of his trusted and capable patriarch Sergios, and take the fight to the Persians in a surprise and sustained attack. The city's great Theodosian Walls were still impregnable and were well defended from within. Herakleios set out for Bithynia, on the coast of the Black Sea, and began preparations to lead his army personally against the Persians. He paid his troops by melting down church treasures to turn into coin, will the full support of the far-sighted Sergios. He took with him an *acheiropoieton* – a religious icon said to have come into existence miraculously, without human intervention. Usually showing Christ or the Virgin Mary, these holy pictures were sometimes held aloft on the walls of the capital or carried as standards into battle to protect the forces of Byzantium. In the case of the Sassanian Persians, they may well have worked, as Herakleios defeated them time and time again.

As the Persians suffered setbacks they began to quarrel among themselves – a situation that Herakleios exploited to great effect. He even courted a Turkic group known as the Gokturks to fight the Sassanians from the north, which culminated in the triumphant Battle of Nineveh in 627. The defeat of Khusro II and his armies after some twenty-six years of almost continuous fighting left the Persian king in an impossible position, and he was eventually captured and killed by his own son, Kavadh II. Herakleios sacked the Persian city of Dastagird and plundered everything he could, including some 300 Byzantine and Roman standards accumulated there during centuries of fighting. A peace treaty was agreed between Herakleios and Kavadh II, allowing Herakleios to reclaim vast territories that had been lost over previous decades. His greatest moment of triumph was the retaking of Jerusalem. The image of Herakleios holding up the True Cross as he rode a chariot through the city gates has been recreated throughout Christian art, from the great medals of the Duc du Berry, to 15th-century paintings in Spain and Piero della Francesca's frescoes in Arezzo. Whether or not this event actually took place, and whether the True Cross was indeed that on which Christ had been crucified some 600 years before, is secondary only to the revivifying effect this historic moment had on the Christian world.

Herakleios returned to Constantinople in triumph. The great enemy of Byzantium, the Persians, had at last been comprehensively defeated, and the power and prestige of the Byzantine state had been undeniably restored. The long war was over.

However, there was an event taking place to the south of both Byzantium and Persia that would change the known world for ever. In 629 the Islamic Prophet Muhammad had unified the Arab tribes of the Arabian Peninsula into a single force, with the intention of expanding their territory and converting all that they found.

At first the Byzantines did not take the Arabs too seriously. There had always been seasonal raids by various tribes into the Byzantine lands, after which they retreated back to their oases in Arabia, and skirmishes in which the Byzantines thought little of their defeats. But not this time. At the Battle of Yarmak in 636, a large Byzantine army was defeated, allowing the Arab forces to capture the whole of Syria and move on through Palestine. In 638 they took the holy city of Jerusalem itself. The long years of war between Persia and Byzantium had greatly depleted the armies on both sides, and the effects of the plague had not long abated. This paved the way for the fervent, mobile forces of Islam, and the Arabs surged through the lands of Persia, taking all before them. It was just ten years since Herakleios had returned to Constantinople as the all-conquering hero, but now virtually all the lands he had captured from the Persians had been taken by the Arabs. Egypt was lost to the forces of the caliph Umar, and Constantinople would receive no Egyptian grain for the next thousand years.

After the death of his first wife, Eudokia, Herakleios had remarried, choosing his niece Martina as his bride – a decision that the people found incestuous and difficult to accept. Her unpopularity meant that the people started to turn against the emperor as well. His unsuccessful attempts at religious harmony through the instigation of his compromised doctrine of Monothelitism had failed. Ten years earlier he had been heralded as the greatest of all emperors, but he now had to watch as his triumphs were undone by the marauding Arab armies. The mighty Herakleios, scourge of the Persians and restorer of the True Cross to Jerusalem, died in 641, a broken man.

Constantine III & Heraklonas

February – April 641 and April – October 641

Of Constantine III:

He was a sickly man, and grew sicklier every day.

SYMEON THE LOGOTHETE, *c.* 970

Constantine Herakleios (Constantine III) had been co-emperor for many years and now, through the insistence of his stepmother Martina, his younger half-brother Herakleios Constantine (Heraklonas) was also named joint ruler. Their short reign was doomed from the start. Constantine III holds the dubious distinction of ruling for the shortest time in the empire's long history: within just 100 days he had died of tuberculosis and set in train Heraklonas's demise. Behind the two of them sat Martina, who somewhat unfairly received the blame for her incestuous marriage to her uncle Herakleios. She was an ambitious figure who knew that, if she wanted to protect her children (she had given birth to at least ten with Herakleios, having been on campaign with him), she would have to have a hand in government. But joint rule was never going to be easy, and the untimely death of Constantine III simply added to Martina's troubles. Many believed she had poisoned her stepson, but there is no real evidence for this.

A general named Valentinos had been instructed by Constantine III to distribute 2 million gold *solidi* among the troops of the eastern provinces to support him in the event that his half-brother and stepmother should ever try to depose him. When Constantine III died, Valentinos took it upon himself to follow the will of the people and the Senate, marching with an army to Chalcedon, which lay just across the Bosphorus from Constantinople. He demanded that Martina and Heraklonas step down and crown Constans, the son of Constantine III and grandson of the revered Eudokia and Herakleios, as the true emperor. Despite the pleading of Martina and an agreement to make Constans II co-emperor alongside Heraklonas, Valentinos had the two arrested

HERAKLIAN DYNASTY

and banished. He was reluctant to kill a mother and child, so had them both disfigured, thus preventing them from ever ruling again (emperors were required to be physically intact). Martina was subjected to *glossotomia*, meaning that her tongue was cut out, while the poor 15-year-old emperor Heraklonas suffered the punishment of *rhinokopia*, or having his nose mutilated. The mother and son were sent to the island of Rhodes and never heard of again.

Constans II
October 641 – July 668

As they would not accept his heresy, he condemned many of the Orthodox to a life of torture and banishment, and confiscated their property. For these actions he was greatly hated by all.
THEOPHANES THE CONFESSOR, BEFORE THE END OF 814

Constans, nicknamed 'Little Constantine', came to the throne at the age of 11; despite reigning for twenty-seven years and sporting probably the most magnificent beard ever seen on a Byzantine coin, the name stuck. Constans's real name was Flavios Herakleios, but he was crowned Constantine, after his father. He grew up in what must have been a rather loveless and hostile environment – a background that was reflected in his character.

When he was a child, the senate ruled the government on his behalf, ably led by the patriarch Paul II of Constantinople, but when Constans turned 18 he took control of both the state and the army. Dominating his reign were the Arabs, who were relentlessly seizing Byzantine lands in raids and in open warfare. The Byzantines lost the province of Egypt definitively and permanently in 642. The Muslim forces under the very capable caliph Mu'awiya were accepting of their Christian prisoners and keen to learn many skills from them that they had not yet acquired for themselves. These ranged from administration to shipbuilding – an initiative that enabled the Arabs to build themselves a fleet to rival the Byzantine navy. After capturing a number of islands off the southern coast of Anatolia, notably Chios, Rhodes and Kos, Constans II decided to confront the Arabs personally, leading his fleet in a pitched sea battle known as the 'Battle of the Masts' in 655. However, the Byzantine navy was decimated, and Constans had to escape capture by disguising himself as a common sailor.

Fortunately for Constans, the Arabs had their own internal struggles. Following the murder of the caliph Uthman, the son-in-law of the Prophet Muhammad, Ali, was installed as the new caliph. Mu'awiya, an opponent of Ali, was forced to quit the fighting and return to Damascus to resolve the situation. He quickly concluded a peace treaty with Constans, ceasing hostilities on condition that a large tribute was paid to the Arabs on an annual basis. Having bought himself some time, Constans turned his attention to the Slavs, who were once again pillaging Byzantine territories in the Balkans and posed a constant threat to the capital itself. Here Constans was more successful, defeating them in significant numbers and even transporting thousands to the less populated lands of Anatolia. This forcible resettling of defeated foes within Byzantine territories was a practice maintained by subsequent emperors for many hundreds of years.

In religious matters, there is little evidence to show that Constans himself had strong beliefs, but he tolerated no deviation from the official doctrine. He tried to settle the ever-present Monothelite question by issuing an edict, the 'Typos', intended to halt all dispute by simply prohibiting its discussion: there was to be no more argument over whether or not Christ had two wills or one, or whether he was divine, human or both. But the Typos failed. Constans had infuriated many with his somewhat antagonistic approach: both Pope Martin and Maximus the Confessor, outspoken critics of this policy, were arrested and banished.

Constans suppressed any challenge to his rule, and could be brutal in his treatment of those who tried. His own family were not exempt: when his brother Theodosios was suspected of plotting

HERAKLIAN DYNASTY

against him, he had him killed. There are stories that Constans suffered from nightmares over this murder, perhaps the sign of a guilty conscience. Believing that he was unloved and misunderstood in Constantinople, he decided to move the capital of the empire back to Italy. He marched with his army through Greece and fought the Lombards in northern Italy, then headed south, stripping Rome and other cities of their treasures before finally moving on to Sicily, where he set up his court at Syracuse. The Byzantines still viewed Italy as part of their birthright and their homeland, and Constans knew that Constantinople was becoming too difficult to defend against the surging Muslim armies to the south and the Slavs in the north. He decided that Syracuse was to be his new capital and sent for his wife, Fausta, and their family to join him. It was a disaster. The people of Constantinople were so incensed that they refused to let the imperial family leave. According to one version of events, while Constans was lying in his bath in Syracuse, an attendant took a soap dish (or bucket) and crashed it down upon his head, causing the death of the 38-year-old emperor a few hours later. The dream of moving the Byzantine capital anywhere, let alone Sicily, was crushed forever. There was little mourning over the death of Little Constantine.

Constantine IV
September 668 – July 685

As his father lay murdered in his bath, the people of Constantinople welcomed the adolescent Constantine as the rightful heir to the throne, as a descendant of the Heraklian dynasty. The man behind the murder of Constans II was probably an Armenian general named Mezezios, who proclaimed himself emperor of the Romans while in Sicily and enjoyed the support of his own regiment. However, he was never taken very seriously back in the capital, and in Ravenna the exarch denounced him as a usurper, remaining loyal to Constantine. After just seven months, Mezezios was eventually killed, either by troops loyal to Constantine IV or perhaps even by Constantine himself.

As he assumed the role of emperor, a condition was imposed upon the 16 year old that he made his two younger brothers, Tiberios and Herakleios, co-emperors. This he duly did, in 668. The aim would have been to keep the family close and lessen the chances of any fraternal internecine struggle. For many years they co-existed peaceably enough, perhaps because there were greater problems for Constantine to deal with. The Arabs under the powerful caliph Mu'awiya were preparing to besiege Constantinople, and by 674 they had built a large navy that sailed to the capital and prepared to capture the glittering city. Once again, the land walls built by Theodosios and others were too well designed and well defended for the Arab armies to scale, and the vast Muslim army returned to its ships to continue the siege.

The most significant military advance of this period was the introduction of 'Greek fire'. A highly flammable compound developed by a Syrian refugee named Kallinikos, it could be hurled through pipes or with other weapons at enemy ships and could not be extinguished with water. The formula for this methane-based liquid remained a closely guarded secret for several centuries and provided the Byzantine navy with an advantage over its foes. This Greek fire caused havoc among the Arab fleet, even though it outnumbered the Byzantine navy, and destroyed its ships repeatedly.

The siege of Constantinople lasted several years. The Arab fleet wintered at Cyzicus on the Lycian coast and then set sail for Constantinople every spring. By 678, after years of constant setbacks, the Arabs were exhausted and were finally defeated in a large-scale land battle. Mu'awiya was forced to retreat, concede the lands he had previously captured and pay a tribute to Constantine of 50 horses, 50 slaves, and 3,000 pounds of gold.

The significance of this successful defence of Constantinople cannot be overstated. An Arab conquest of the capital would have exposed the West to formidable and disciplined Muslim troops.

        HERAKLIAN DYNASTY

Europe would almost certainly not have evolved as it did, and Christianity may have struggled simply to remain extant, as indeed was the case in lands that were conquered by Arabs elsewhere. The world order would have been dramatically different. Modern Europe's foundation can be traced back to Constantine IV, his use of the almost magical 'Greek fire', and the troops that returned from Sicily after the defeat of Mezezios.

With the Arab threat neutralized, Constantine IV turned his army towards the Slavs, who had been attacking Thessalonica. He succeeded to repel the Slavic armies, but they were not comprehensively beaten and maintained a hostile presence on Byzantine lands for many years.

Like his predecessors before him, Constantine IV too was confronted with the continuing dispute between Monothelitism and Orthodoxy. In 680 he convened the Sixth Ecumenical Council, in which church leaders were invited to debate the age-old issue of the nature of Christ. Over the course of eighteen sessions, in which Constantine presided but did not give an opinion, the council came to the decision to uphold the findings of the Council of Chalcedon back in 451. Orthodoxy had triumphed. This had been easier for Constantine to achieve than in previous centuries because the majority of Monothelites were now to be found in Syria, Mesopotamia and Egypt, lands controlled by the Umayyad caliphs. Nevertheless, it was an impressive achievement and allowed for some harmony within the church.

The Bulgars, a semi-nomadic tribe originally from Central Asia but now more settled in the Pontic–Caspian steppe, were once again invading the northern areas of the empire, so Constantine led his army to confront them in Moesia, in modern-day Romania. Before the battle could commence, the emperor was struck down with gout, an illness that had plagued him for many years, and he sought treatment and relief at a spa in Thrace. His own troops, misunderstanding his actions and thinking that he was running away from the Bulgar forces, panicked and fled. In the mayhem that ensued, Bulgar soldiers slaughtered many Byzantine men, and the whole Byzantine army was routed. Constantine was forced to make peace with Asparukh, the Bulgar chief, and agreed to pay him an annual tribute, allowing the Bulgars to settle in the northern lands of Moesia.

A beautiful mosaic of Constantine, his two brothers and his young son can be seen in the church of Sant'Apollinare in Ravenna. This portrait of an imperial family, very much in the style of Justinian the Great, was commissioned in happier times, before Constantine began to suspect his brothers of mounting a coup against him. Whether or not they were plotting we do not know, but in 681 he arrested both Tiberios and Herakleios and handed them the singular Byzantine punishment of *rhinokopia*, or disfigurement of the nose. This mutilation prevented the two brothers from ever ruling the empire. At the same time Constantine bestowed the title of co-emperor upon his 12-year-old son Justinian.

Constantine IV continued to reign until 685. Often ill, he had the young Justinian at his side, learning the ways of the court and how to manage an empire. Constantine died in his early 30s from dysentery in September that year. His defeat of the Arabs in 678 had almost certainly altered the shape of the Western world.

Justinian II Rhinotmetos
September 685 – November (?) 695 (*first reign*)

The last emperor of the great Heraklian dynasty began his reign in a relatively strong position. He was the fourth emperor in succession to take the throne as a teenager, in his case when he was about 16 years of age.

Justinian II was fortunate to inherit the peace treaty with the Arabs that his father, Constantine IV, had negotiated, which saved him the worry of attacks from the south. The empire had managed to retain most of its lands in central Anatolia; not only did this keep

     HERAKLIAN DYNASTY

the Arabs at bay, but it also allowed the system of administration units known as 'themes', established under Herakleios, to flourish. These divisions (of which there were four at the outset) provided military bases for the defence of the empire: land was given to smallholders in return for taxes and the provision of soldiers in times of need. Justinian II, in his very determined and organized way, continued this tradition, laid down by his father and grand-fathers before him. Were it not for his uncontrollable temper and natural tendency towards despotism, he may well have been a great ruler. Despite his undoubted piety, hard work and, at times, inspired leadership in matters of administration and reform, he was to make too many enemies to succeed for long.

Justinian's land reforms were in direct conflict with the ambitions of the aristocracy and, while the peasants enjoyed their smallholdings, they did not appreciate the punitive taxes that came with them. He embarked on lavish building programmes that mainly benefited the House of Justinian, constructing the *triklinos*, a huge dining room lavishly decorated with mosaics in the centre of the Great Palace. Resentment was building against Justinian II but he did not seem to care.

Justinian took religion very seriously, and was the first emperor to place a portrait of himself on the reverse of his coinage, reserving the obverse for an image of Christ. This was a concrete departure from paganism, and a signal to the world that Christ was the true ruler and the emperor merely his vice-regent and confidant on earth.

Justinian's devotion to religious matters reached its zenith with the Council in Trullo, also known as the Quinisext Council, which he convened in 692 and during which he confirmed the condemnation of Monothelitism and laid down rules and guide-lines concerning everyday morals as well as the running of the church. He enforced a ban on any festivals and rituals that had their beginnings in paganism. The Brumalia – wine harvests in honour of Dionysus in which men and women wore masks and cavorted about the streets – were all outlawed. University students were forbidden from performing in any theatrical productions. This clamping down on 'fun' in the name of religion contributed to the growing unrest and discontent with regard to Justinian's style of rule. His highlighting of differences between the Eastern and Western observances, such as allowing priests to marry and forbidding the Roman tradition of fasting on a Saturday, further annoyed the pope in Rome, who refused to comply. When Justinian demanded that he be arrested and brought to the capital for trial, the local militias of both Rome and Ravenna sided with the pope. It was no coincidence that at this point the Umayyad caliph Abd al-Malik decided to exploit the unrest within the Christian church by building the Dome of the Rock in Jerusalem and adorning it with the Qur'anic phrase 'He is God the One, God the Eternal. He begot no one, nor was he begotten.' This was a deliberate attack on the Christian belief of the Holy Trinity.

One policy Justinian had pursued to great effect was the mass displacement of subjects from one part of the empire to another. After a victorious battle in the Balkans against the Slavs, he moved some 50,000 people into Anatolia to act as a buffer between Byzantine lands and enemies in Armenia. This forcible migration of whole towns and villages was successful in quelling unrest and protecting the inhabitants of the empire's lands, and also contributed to multiculturalism within the bounds of the Byzantine Empire. Slavs, Bulgars, Avars, Khazars, Armenians, Greeks and of course Romans were all forced to live together over many generations – a diverse ethnic mix throughout the whole of Anatolia. They were unified through their Christianity, their loyalty to the emperor, and – eventually – by the fact that they shared one official language, Greek.

However, the many changes he imposed upon the aristocracy and his interference in ordinary people's lives resulted in a coup, and Justinian II was finally deposed. The man who led the rebellion was a general named Leontios, who decreed that Justinian should be subjected to *rhinokopia*. Like so many of his own victims, Justinian did indeed have his nose cut off, and was henceforward known to history as Justinian II Rhinotmetos ('Cut-Nose').

Justinian was banished to the distant Black Sea port of Cherson and supposedly prevented by his disfigurement from ever reigning as emperor again. His cruel mutilation and exile heralded what is commonly known as the 'Twenty Years of Anarchy', when no fewer than six emperors would rule, all but one of them ending their reigns either murdered or disfigured. Justinian would return with a vengeance that no one had anticipated.

TWENTY YEARS OF ANARCHY

(695–717)

Surrounded on all sides, the empire suffered a period of unrest until the Isaurian dynasty was established in 717. Justinian II returned to rule, despite his disfigurement (he was now known as 'the slit-nosed'), but with no lasting consequences.

Leontios

695–698

As the new emperor, Leontios, watched Justinian II's *rhinokopia* in the Hippodrome in front of the jeering crowds, he would never have suspected a similar fate would befall him within just three years.

Leontios was a nobleman and general, whose coin portraits reveal a portly, round-faced man. It is possible that he had been imprisoned by Justinian for losing a battle against the Umayyads and looked after by two monks, Gregory and Paul, who prophesied that he would one day become emperor. Upon his release he was ordered to protect his new theme, Hellas, in northern Greece. Leontios must have had some courage, as he took his troops straight to the prison where he had been held captive, released all the prisoners and eventually overthrew the emperor. In deference to Justinian's father, Constantine IV, under whom Leontios had served, he spared Justinian's life and sent him into exile in Cherson on the remote Black Sea coast.

It was a brief reign, dominated by the return of the plague and a decisive military defeat. The Arabs had started a long and

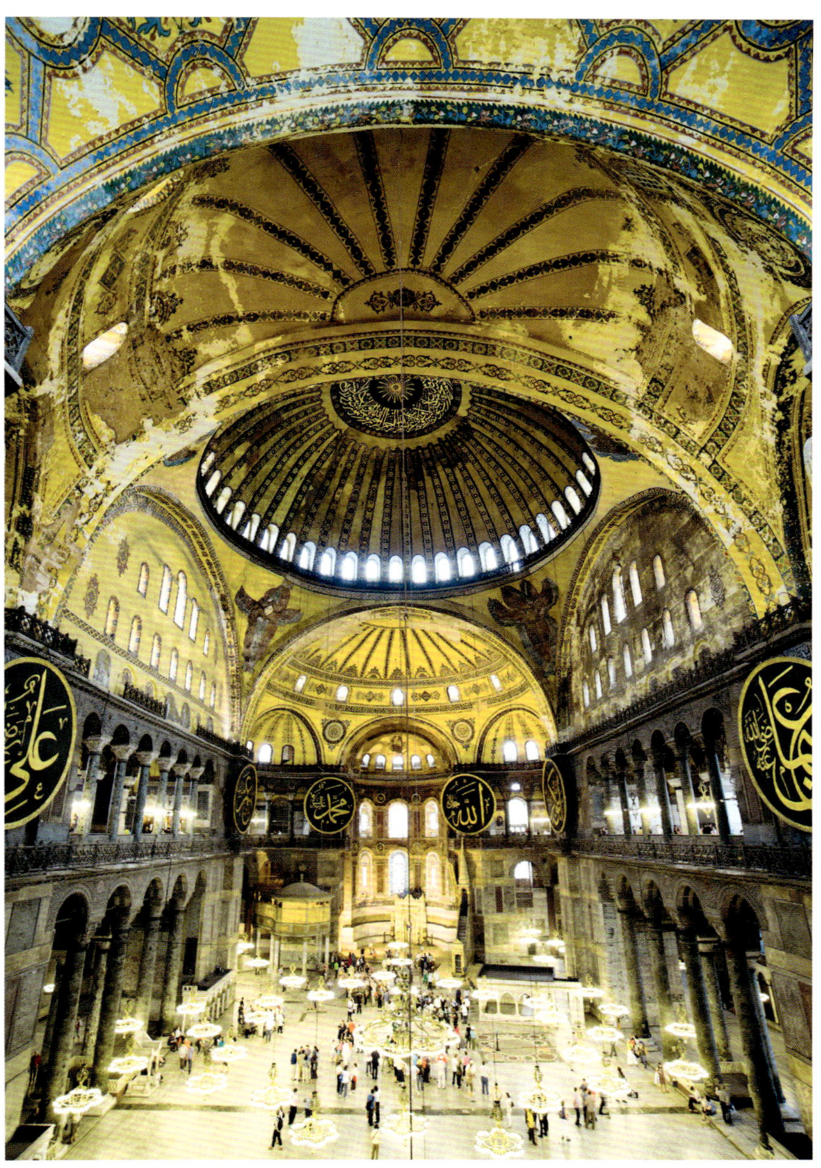

1   The interior of Hagia Sophia, literally the 'Church of Holy Wisdom', built by Justinian I in Constantinople after the Nika riots of 532.

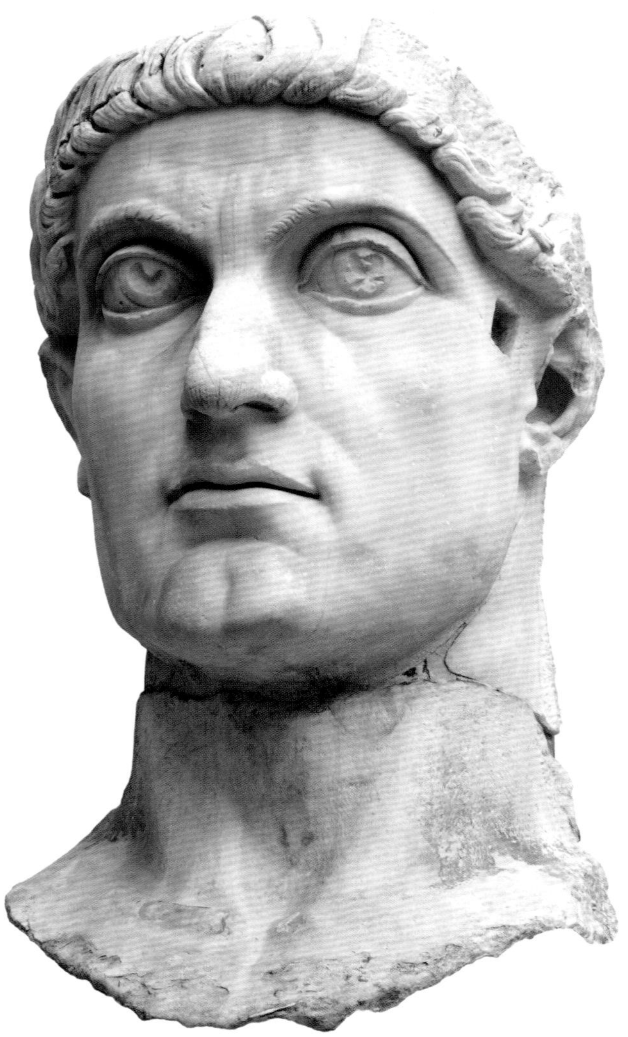

2 A colossal head of Constantine I, made to be the centrepiece of the enormous basilica begun by his defeated predecessor, Maxentius. Presumably constructed of marble (for skin) and bronze (for the clothing), the statue would have measured some 15 m (49 ft) high. There is no suggestion of Christian humility here: it would have resembled classical depictions of heroes.

3 Decorative silver bowl
from the mid-4th century
showing the triumph
of Constantius II. He is
depicted on horseback,
accompanied by an arms-
bearer and the goddess
Nike. The entire image is
subordinated to a single
idea: the desire to extol the
emperor and to emphasize
his godlike power, evident
from the golden halo
around his head.

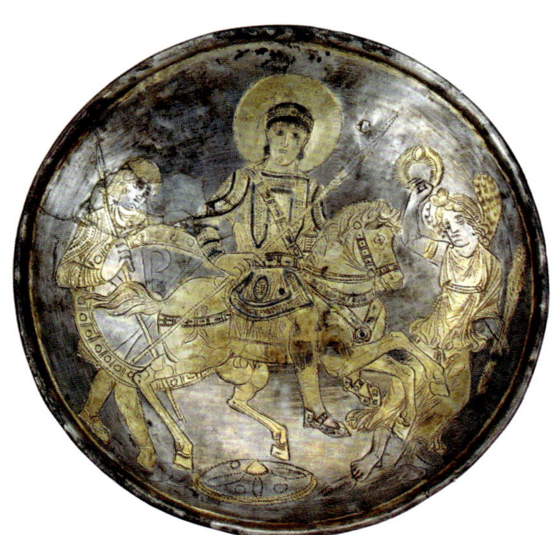

4 The *missorium* of Theodosios,
commissioned *c.* 388 to
celebrate the 10th anniversary
of his reign. The emperor,
flanked by the young *augusti*
Arcadius and Valentinian II,
hands a codex to an official.
The bountiful earth is
shown below.

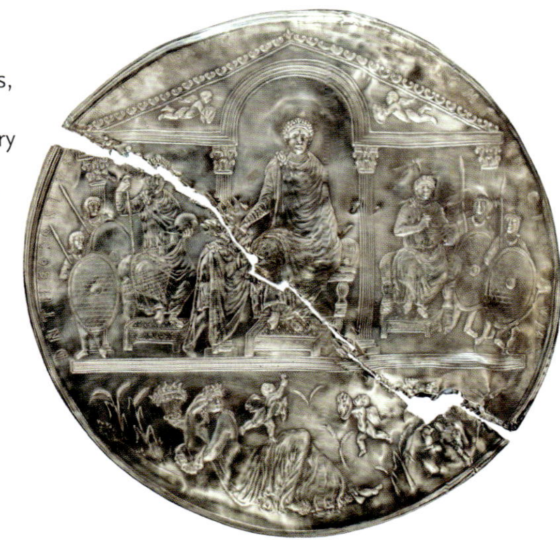

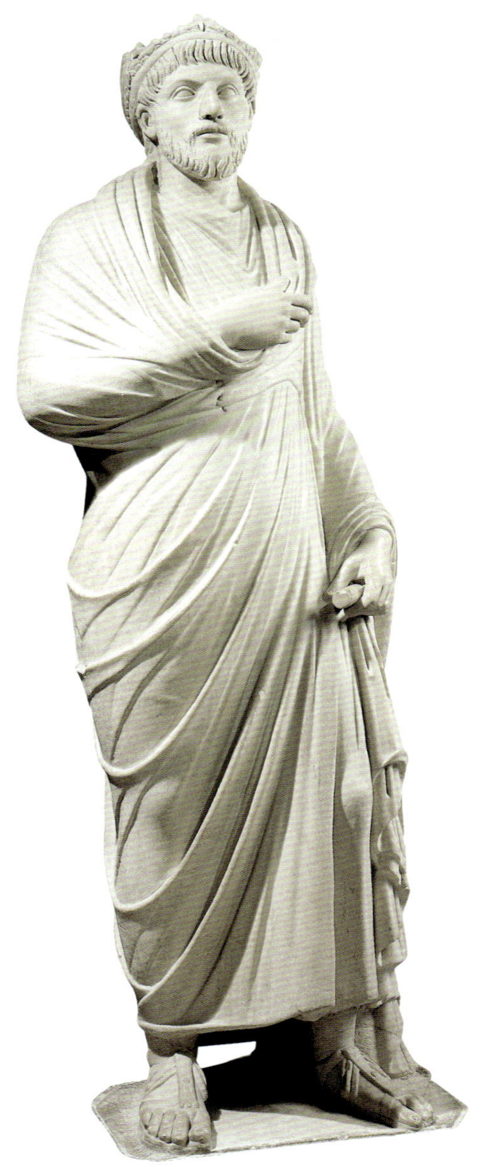

5 Full-length marble statue of Julian II, from the 4th century. Unlike any of his fellow emperors before or after, Julian is clad in the robes of a pagan high priest.

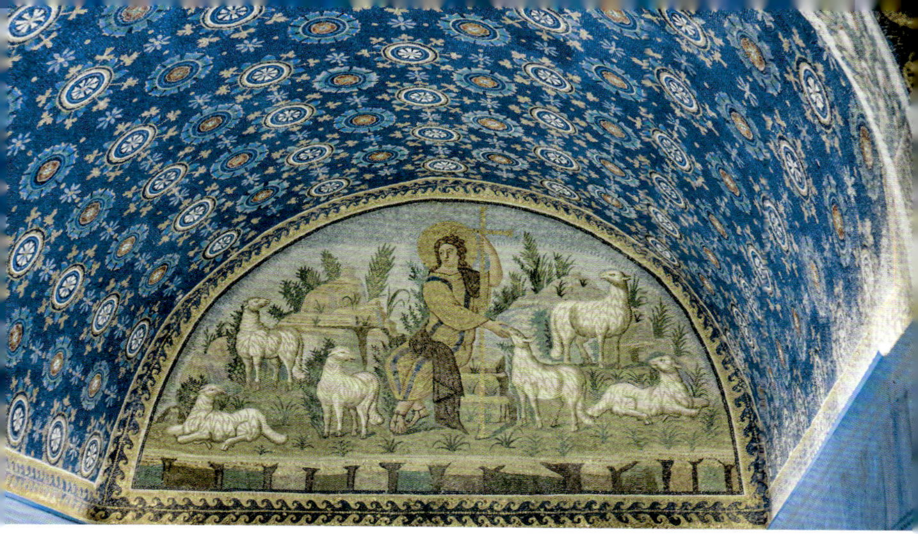

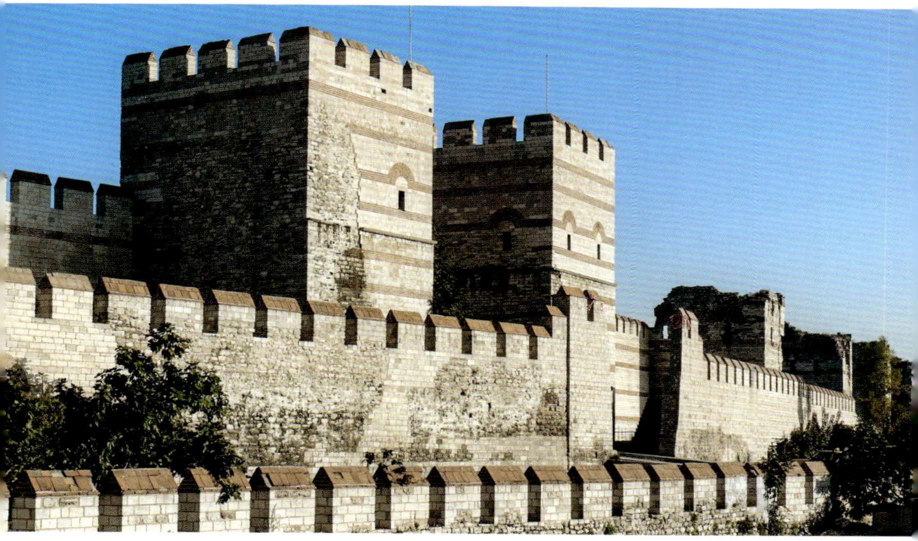

6 The Mausoleum of Galla Placidia in Ravenna, a masterpiece of Late Antique architecture and mosaic decoration, *c.* 430. Galla Placidia was the daughter of Theodosios I and the wife of the Western emperor Constantius III. This small chapel depicts Christ as the Good Shepherd: he is shown in the form of a young, beardless man, as was common in the early days of Christianity.

7 The 5th-century (and modern restoration) land walls of Constantinople comprised an inner wall around 11 m (36 ft) high, towers, a lower, outer wall, and a moat. They proved well-nigh impregnable until 1453.

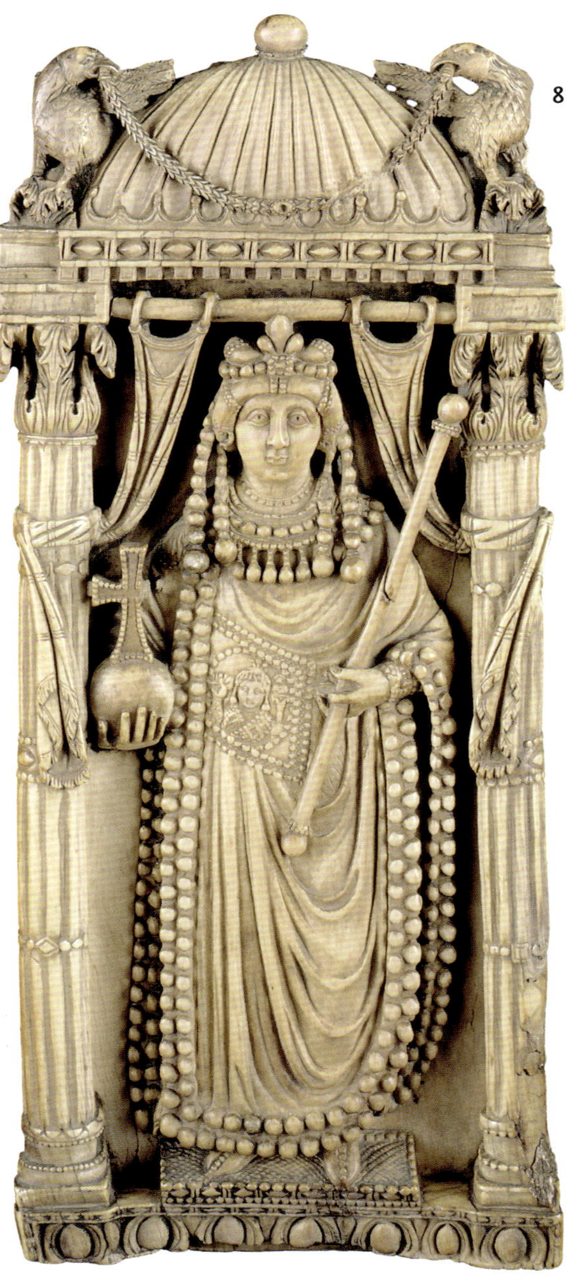

8 A 5th-century ivory panel of the empress Ariadne, who wears a portrait of her son, Leo, on her cloak. The boy is clad in a *loros*, a long ceremonial scarf, and holds the *mappa* (a red cloth), symbols of consular office.

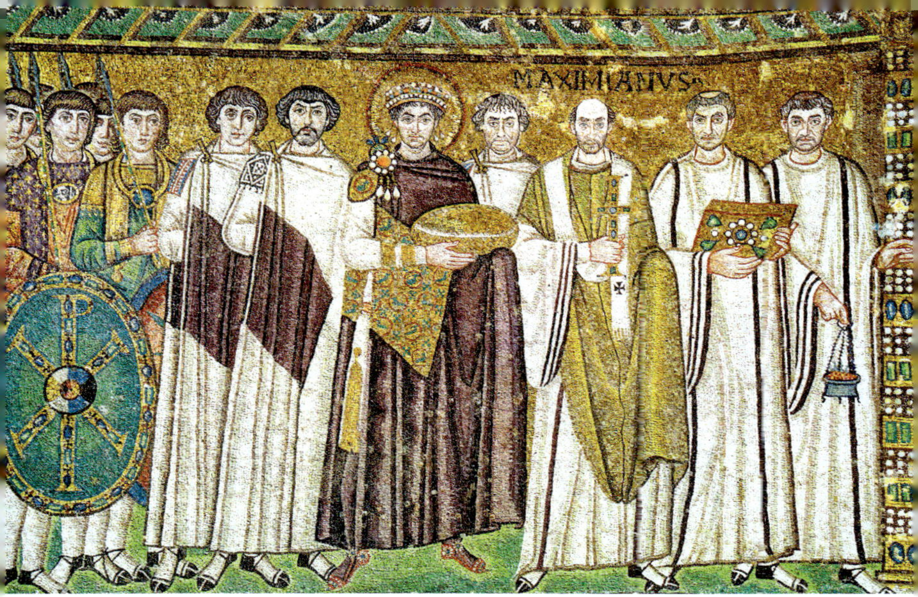

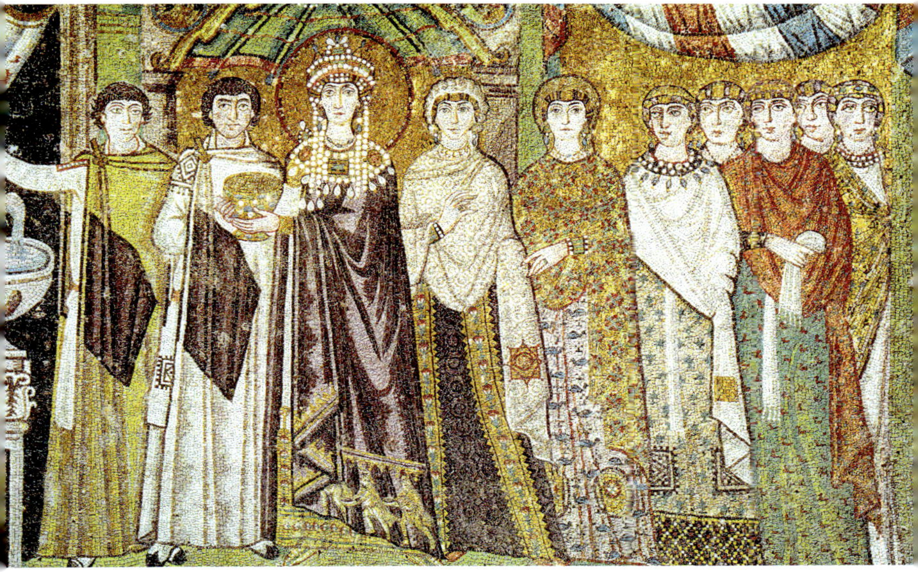

9, 10 Justinian, his court and Bishop Maximian (*above*), and Theodora with her retinue (*below*). These mosaics in the church of San Vitale, Ravenna, are some of the most famous images of Byzantine imperial power. Since neither Justinian nor Theodora ever visited Ravenna, these scenes must be understood as symbolic.

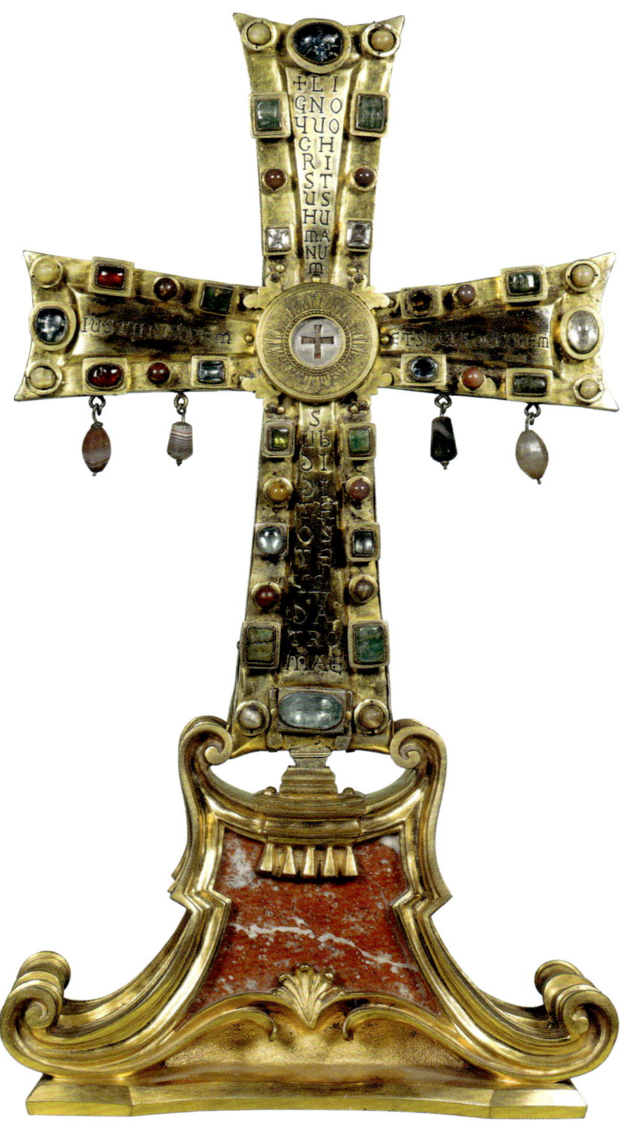

11   Probably given by Justin II to the people of Rome, this cross includes a relic of the True Cross and bears the inscription: 'With the wood with which offers Christ conquered man's enemy, Justin gives his help to Rome and his wife offers the ornamentation.'

successful onslaught on the North African coast and when they arrived at Carthage in 697, a Byzantine fleet was dispatched by Leontios to help the beleaguered city. The naval officer in charge of the fleet – a *droungarios*, or middle-ranking naval officer, named John Patrikios – realized that he could neither defeat the Arabs nor defend Carthage, and retreated to Crete for reinforcements and supplies. The fleet then mutinied on Crete and proclaimed the *droungarios* Apsimaros as emperor under the name Tiberios. Tiberios then returned to Constantinople, where he lay siege to the capital for several months. Leontios had never been fully accepted by many in Constantinople and was overthrown by Tiberios, with the help of the Green faction and many members of the aristo-cracy. His nose was severed, and he was locked up in a monastery in Constantinople for several years. When Justinian returned to power, Leontios was executed, and his body was believed to have been thrown in the sea. His reign was brief, bringing little benefit to the empire and much misery to Leontios himself.

Tiberios III Apsimar
February 698 – August 705

Having successfully overthrown Leontios, Tiberios was crowned by the patriarch Kallinikos in February 698. Previously it had always been the army that had provided emperors, and Tiberios was the first to have come from the navy. Unsurprisingly, one of the first things Tiberios instigated was a complete repair of all the sea walls around Constantinople to protect it from any naval assault.

The Umayyads were still raiding and attacking Byzantine lands, particularly in the south and east of Anatolia. As if this were not enough to contend with, the disfigured and exiled emperor Justinian was making his way back to the capital with a foreign army of Bulgars and Slavs right behind him. Tiberios decided that he could not survive against the forces ranging against him and chose to abandon his post and escape to Sozopolis in Bithynia. There he hid from Justinian's forces for several months, before being captured and taken to Constantinople. According to Theophanes the Confessor, he was dragged to the Hippodrome in terror, brought before the reinstated emperor, and untied next to the man he had mutilated and deposed three years previously: Leontios. In front of the vast crowd, the two ex-emperors were forced to lie prostrate in front of Justinian, who placed his feet on their necks for the duration of the first race; the crowd chanted: 'You have set your foot on the asp and the basilisk, and you have trodden the lion and the serpent.' After this humiliation they were sent to the Kynegion quarter to be beheaded – an ignoble end for two emperors who had claimed their thrones by violence.

Justinian II Rhinotmetos
705 – November 711 (*second reign*)

The return of Justinian II, now wearing a golden nose, ushered in a six-year period of terror and persecution. Where Justinian had shown promise as a young man on the throne, he was now consumed by a need for revenge and never ceased in his determination to find and kill all those responsible for his downfall.

Justinian's time in exile reads like a work of fiction. While in Cherson, the place to which Leontios had banished him, he was constantly problematic, acting as if he were still emperor and causing dissent among the governors. The authorities decided to send him back to Constantinople and let the court deal with him, but Justinian became aware of their plan and fled the city with his followers. He took refuge with the *khagan* of the Khazars, Busir, and plotted his return to the Byzantine throne. Busir was at first impressed with Justinian and his promise of riches from the great city of Constantinople, and so agreed to help him, even offering him the hand of his sister in marriage. Justinian accepted this gift and renamed his wife Theodora, probably in honour of his name-sake Justinian I's wife a hundred years before. Busir gave his sister and the exiled Byzantine emperor a house to live in on the Black Sea coast. When news reached Tiberios of his machinations, he bribed Busir to betray Justinian. Two assassins were sent to murder him, but Justinian discovered them and strangled them both with his bare hands. He then requisitioned a boat and set sail for Constantinople. A storm raged and the boat appeared as if it might sink. One of his companions asked Justinian to pray and promise to be merciful to his enemies if they all might be spared death in the storm. Justinian was reported to have replied, 'If I spare a single one of them, may God drown me here.' He survived.

Justinian then sought support from the king of Bulgaria, Tervel, once more with the promise of riches, and marched on Constantinople with a Bulgar army of many thousands of men. Thwarted by the great walls of the city, Justinian and a few brave soldiers crawled into the city by a viaduct and attacked any who opposed him. Tiberios fled, and the way was open for Justinian. He was the first emperor to regain his throne, despite the disfigurement that should have stood in his way. He was also the first to have an empress who had been born outside of the empire.

Justinian took up the duties of emperor as he had left them, organizing the administration to further suit him, laying out grand plans to retake Italy, defending the borders against the Umayyad armies, and reinstating the depiction of Christ on his coinage that the previous two emperors had removed. It is noticeable that in his new portrait there was no hint of his disfigurement, which went against the Byzantine ideal of what an emperor should be.

Justinian's persecution of past enemies continued unabated, and he treated any he suspected of disloyalty with unabashed cruelty. Preoccupied as he was with exacting revenge, Justinian was also concerned that the pope should agree with his edicts as put forward in the Quinisext Council some years before. When Pope Constantine visited Constantinople in 710, the emperor received communion from him, thus establishing a close personal tie with the church of Rome. Constantine would be the last pope to visit Constantinople until Pope Paul VI visited Istanbul in 1967.

The year 711 brought with it another uprising against the ever-unpopular leader, this time in Cherson, the place of his former exile. A fleet was dispatched to take back the city and execute the rebels, but the emperor's troops, led by their commander, Bardanes, changed sides, proclaimed Bardanes as emperor and set sail for the capital. Justinian tried to flee but was captured and executed.

So ended the second reign of the remarkable Justinian II Rhinotmetos, killed by an unknown assailant outside the walls of his capital. His 6-year-old son, Tiberios, was found hiding in the church of St Mary in Blachernae, dragged outside, divested of his collection of holy relics, stripped naked and killed. With this, the noble line of Herakleios had almost come to an end. It had started with such hope and vigour under the almost godlike figure of Herakleios of Carthage, and yet – despite a few notable exceptions, such as Constantine IV's defence of Constantinople against the Arabs – it had never again matched its early success. The Heraklian dynasty – Byzantium's first real dynasty – had ended in violence and shame, with the murder of a defenceless child.

Philippikos Bardanes
November 711 – June 713

Bardanes was an Armenian from Pergamum who had served in the army under Justinian II but fallen foul of his emperor. He was banished to Cephalonia before being recalled and sent on a mission to Cherson. Here, he claimed that he had a dream that an eagle protected him from harm, thus revealing his destiny to become emperor. On his coins an eagle was depicted on the tip of his sceptre in recognition of this premonition. He managed to ingratiate himself among the people of Cherson and the powerful Khazars who ruled the region, but his self-aggrandisement was brought to the attention of Tiberios II Apsimar, who swiftly had him arrested and imprisoned.

Upon the reinstatement of Justinian II, however, and his subsequent release, Bardanes quickly recommenced his intrigues to become emperor. The soldiers who had been sent by Justinian to attack Cherson finally rebelled against Justinian's cruel oppression. They joined forces with the troops of Cherson and their Khazar allies, and elected Bardanes as their new emperor. He changed his name to Philippikos, since he believed it sounded more appropriately regal, seemingly unaware that there had never been an emperor with that name.

Justinian was caught trying to flee Constantinople and executed by soldiers or confidents loyal to Bardanes. The new emperor, Philippikos Bardanes, promptly marched into the capital unopposed.

Philippikos's problems began when it was revealed that his religious beliefs were Monothelite in nature. The pope in Rome denounced him, and the Orthodox citizens of Constantinople, who must have thought that this controversy was behind them, were furious that their emperor had raised this heretical view once again. Despite their strong opposition, Philippikos installed John VI of Constantinople, whose beliefs aligned with his own, as patriarch.

In a climate of rebellion and murder, which were becoming commonplace in the capital, a group of conspirators plotted the emperor's downfall. When the powerful Tervel of Bulgaria camped outside the walls of the city, Philippikos called on troops from the theme of Opsikion to come to his aid and repel the fearsome Bulgars. Once they had succeeded, however, the troops from Opsikion agreed with the conspirators that Philippikos had to go. After a reign of less than two years, he was taken from his afternoon siesta and disfigured. The practice of *rhinokopia* had proved ineffective in deterring Justinian from regaining his crown, so it appears that a new form of mutilation was called for: blinding. Red-hot pokers were placed on Philippikos's eyes and he was banished to a monastery, where he was never heard of again.

Anastasios II Artemios
June 713 – 715

A civil servant in the treasury department named Anastasios was installed as the new emperor of Byzantium in June 713. He had changed his name from Artemios to Anastasios in honour of the emperor Anastasios I, who had also been a civil servant. Voted in by the members of the Opsikion theme and others in the senate, he quickly proved himself a competent administrator. There was intelligence that the Arabs were once again preparing to besiege Constantinople, and Anastasios II sprang into action, ordering the land walls to be repaired, the granaries fully stocked and the naval fleet upgraded. Closer to home, he rescinded all the decrees against Orthodoxy that Philippikos had instigated, and removed the patriarch John VI, replacing him with an Orthodox candidate, Germanus, in 715, thereby reopening relations with the pope.

Anastasios recognized the Umayyad forces as a real threat to the Byzantine lands and to Constantinople itself. When news reached him of the death of Caliph al-Walid, he organized an attack on their base at Rhodes. It would seem wise to strike at the enemy while they were in disarray from the death of their leader, but – inexplicably – the powerful leaders of the Opsikion theme decided against it. Perhaps Anastasios was more dynamic and decisive than they had bargained for but, whatever the reason, they moved against the emperor that they had helped install just two years previously. They called off the attack on Rhodes and sailed to Constantinople, where they laid siege to the capital for six months, proclaiming the reluctant Theodosios as their new emperor and waiting for Anastasios to surrender. Anastasios had just dispatched a highly

 TWENTY YEARS OF ANARCHY

competent general, Leo the Isaurian, to fight the Umayyads in Syria, and was now powerless to deal with his real enemy. Realizing that his time was up, Anastasios II Artemios resigned as emperor and was allowed to retire to a monastery, where he could have lived out his life in peace and tranquillity. However, some years later, when the same Leo he had sent to Syria became emperor, Anastasios was implicated in a coup against him, summoned from his monastery and executed. The mild-mannered civil servant had proved to be a very able statesman, but with no military experience or support from the army he was ousted within two years.

Theodosios III
715 – March 717

Theodosios III, known as 'the Reluctant', forms a somewhat comic footnote to the line of Byzantine emperors. According to Theophanes the Confessor, he was a local tax collector in the town of Adramyttion near the Aegean coast, quietly going about his business, when troops from the Opsikion theme came across him, asked his name and, upon hearing it was Theodosios, urged him to become emperor and replace Anastasios. Theodosios at first refused, wanting nothing to do with imperial power, but the soldiers insisted and marched towards Constantinople with their new leader at their head. The life expectancy of a new emperor was consistently decreasing; no middle-ranking officer would have willingly put himself forward to head a prospective coup at this time.

At some point, Theodosios managed to escape his captors and tried to hide in the mountains, but he was soon found. After hiding in Nicaea for many months Anastasios II finally surrendered and allowed Theodosios, now in Constantinople, to become emperor.

The first act of Theodosios III was to conclude a treaty with Tervel, probably ceding to the Bulgarians land stretching up to the borders of Thrace in return for their help and support against the inevitable attack from the Umayyads. It was at this time that Leo the Isaurian, the brilliant young commander of the troops from the Anatolikon theme, launched his own rebellion with the support of the Armeniakon theme and his colleague Artabasdos. Theodosios was delighted to vacate his post and retired to a monastery at Ephesus.

The reluctant emperor had at least managed to abdicate without losing his nose, his eyes or his life. He remained at his monastery in Ephesus for many years, and after he died his tomb came to be known as a place of pilgrimage, where miracles of healing took place. Known posthumously as St Theodosios, he was recorded as a good tax collector, an indifferent emperor, and by all accounts a virtuous monk. His abdication finally put an end to the twenty years of anarchy that had plagued the empire and paved the way for a new dynasty.

ISAURIAN DYNASTY

(717–802)

The Isaurians were remembered chiefly for the instigation of Iconoclasm, a strategy that sought to reconnect the people with God by prohibiting the worship of icons. This brutally enforced policy caused internal strife throughout the empire for a hundred years. The Isaurian dynasty was successful in defending the empire from its two principal external enemies, the Muslim caliphate and the Bulgars.

Leo III the Isaurian

March 717 – June 741

Born with the name Konan, Leo III was a peasant from Syria who joined the army of Justinian II on his campaign to regain the throne in 705 and quickly rose through the ranks to become *strategos* (a high-ranking army general) of the powerful Anatolikon theme under the emperor Anastasios II.

Having overthrown Theodosios III, the new emperor was immediately confronted with an extremely precarious situation. The caliph's brother, Maslama, had prepared for a great siege of Constantinople, amassing an army to cut the city off from the Thracian side and a navy to blockade the capital. Fortunately, Leo III was able to rely on his Bulgarian allies, whose forces attacked the Umayyads from the north, while the continued use of Greek fire against the Arab navy meant that the Muslim forces were repelled. Leo cleverly cut off the supply of provisions to the Umayyad forces and, with the arrival of the fiercest winter in living memory (the Black Sea froze over, and icebergs floated down the Bosphorus), disease spread among the Arab soldiers. They had to concede defeat. Again, if the Umayyads had won and taken Constantinople, the history of the West may well have been very different. Leo III had fought off the Arab onslaught of Constantinople for the final time, and they would never again attempt to capture the capital. When Charles Martel, known as 'the Hammer', halted the Arab advance at Poitiers in 732, the Umayyad dream of Islamic expansion was stopped, and the political map of the Mediterranean was now fixed for the next few centuries.

Domestically, Leo III undertook two major initiatives. First, he issued a recodification of Byzantine law, called the *Ecloga*, which incorporated many changes to existing legislature and was deliberately designed to help the poor rather than the rich and the clergy. It was more merciful than what had gone before, banning the death penalty almost completely, and revealed Leo's belief that he was responsible before God for the welfare and governance of his people. For perhaps the first time in Roman history, the law was written in a way that was intended for all people to understand. Women were more protected, thanks to the rewriting of divorce terms in favour of wives and the establishment of a long list of sexual crimes against women that were to be punished severely. There was a particular emphasis on mutilation as a punishment: it must be remembered that in Roman times most serious crimes would have been punishable by death. The people of 8th-century Byzantium would have interpreted these new laws as more humane and lenient than they had been before.

Leo's second most significant change was the introduction of Iconoclasm. This ban on the use of religious images was fiercely unpopular, but despite major opposition from many quarters Leo persisted. Quite why he embarked on this course is open to debate. There can be no doubt that, among the more ignorant, the veneration of images and icons had reached a level akin to superstition and idolatry, and that some of the monks who produced and distributed these images among their flock were exploiting

　　　　　　　　　　　　　ISAURIAN DYNASTY

their ignorance to their own advantage. Many people, particularly in the western provinces, adored their icons and believed in the power that they might possess. However, Leo had spent much of his time on the eastern frontiers of the empire, and as a native Syrian he would have seen how the soldiers of the east were more uncomfortable with such ideas. The Umayyads had been more successful in battles than had the Byzantines, and the Qur'an actively discouraged the use of images in any religious setting. Perhaps Leo hoped that the conversion of Muslims was more likely if Christianity also forbade the worshipping of icons. It was hard to differentiate between religious beliefs and superstition, and the 7th and 8th centuries had seen more than their fair share of natural disasters. Earthquakes, plagues, an enormous volcanic eruption in Santorini and the ensuing tsunami, variations in climate (the harsh winter of 717–718) and the failure of crops, were all seen as divine intervention upon the Byzantine state. Whatever the reasons for Leo's introducing the ban on religious images, the results were nothing but harmful to the political situation of the empire. The pope and the whole of the Western church completely rejected Iconoclasm as a concept, and the long-standing patriarch of Constantinople, Germanos II, even resigned. As an indication of how seriously he took the policy, Leo removed the image of Christ from the Chalke Gate of the imperial palace, but still the people defied him. He stopped short of persecuting those who rejected the Iconoclastic movement, the so-called *iconodules* ('servants of images'), but made it very clear that they were openly defying the wishes of their emperor and God's vice-regent on earth.

Leo III died in June 741. With his wife, Maria (about whom very little is known), he had a son who would become the future Constantine V. Leo III had pulled the empire from the brink of collapse and steered it away from the twenty-year period of anarchy that had preceded his reign.

Later historians, in their hatred of Iconoclasm, gave Leo III little credit for his reign, but with the benefit of hindsight it can be seen that the Byzantine Empire was very fortunate indeed to have had such a capable man take control at a crucial moment in its history.

Artabasdos
741 – November 743

Artabasdos had been a friend and compatriot of Leo III when they were both *strategoi* of their respective themes, Leo of the Anatolikon and Artabasdos of the Armeniakon. Together they had defeated the emperor Theodosios III and placed Leo on the throne, and it was clear that Leo's eldest son, Constantine, was destined to inherit the empire. Artabasdos, however, saw it differently.

Artabasdos was a powerful man in his own right, who had the entire Armeniakon theme at his disposal and had also married Leo III's daughter Anna. After Leo's death, Constantine V crossed Anatolia with Artabasdos to fight the Umayyads. Seizing this moment, Artabasdos challenged Constantine in battle and was victorious at Dorylaion. Constantine fled to Amorium, and Artabasdos marched into Constantinople, declaring himself emperor. His popularity was assured when he reversed his predecessor's policy of Iconoclasm and allowed the churches and the monks to restore their icons as they wished.

Constantine could not accept this situation and marched back to the capital to reclaim his crown. The two forces met in battle, and this time Constantine was victorious, prompting Artabasdos to flee to the castle of Pouzanes in Opsikion. Artabasdos could not hide for long, however, and was brought back to Constantinople. The usurper and two of his sons were taken to the Hippodrome and publicly blinded before being sent to the monastery of Chora, where they were to end their days. Artabasdos had seven other children whose fate is unknown, and his wife, Anna, erstwhile *augusta* and sister of Constantine V, was never heard of again.

Constantine V Kopronymos
June 741 – September 775

Thus he ended his life, stained as he was with Christian blood, with the invocation of demons whom he worshipped, with the destruction of the holy churches and those of true faith, including the slaying of monks and the desecration of monasteries; in all manners of evil he had reached a pinnacle not seen since Diocletian and the ancient tyrants. A filthy and bloodstained enchanter taking pleasure in evoking devils.
THEOPHANES THE CONFESSOR, 814 OR EARLIER

For Mary gave birth to Him just as my mother Mary gave birth to me.
THEOPHANES THE CONFESSOR, QUOTING CONSTANTINE V, 815 OR EARLIER

While Constantine was being baptized as an infant, it was rumoured that he defecated into the baptismal font, thus giving rise to his nickname of 'Kopronymos', the 'Dung-Named'. Few emperors have received quite such biased accounts of their leadership, for the reason that virtually all those who wrote about him were vehemently opposed to the defining feature of his reign, Iconoclasm. However, Constantine V was a lot more than an image-destroying zealot.

Having been crowned co-emperor at just 2 years old, Constantine V had spent all his life close to his father and subscribed to Iconoclastic beliefs. As a scholar, he wrote treatises on religious doctrine and intellectualized Iconoclasm, whereas his father, Leo III, had used it more as a political tool. As a successful military commander, Constantine won many battles against both the Arabs and the Bulgars, and increased the territories of his empire. And as a reformer of the legal system, he co-wrote the *Ecloga* with his father, which extended more rights to the people.

When Constantine was around 14 years old he married Tzitzak, a Khazar princess who changed her name to Irene when she became a Byzantine and tragically died giving birth to their son, the future Leo IV. In 741, when Leo III died, Constantine assumed the throne as his divine right and crushed Artabasdos's challenge. No mercy was shown to his brother-in-law, betraying a ruthless side to Constantine's character that would reveal itself increasingly as time went on.

Constantine never faltered in his belief that image worship was wrong and harmful to Christian society. The argument went to the very nature of Christ: since Christ was God, he could not therefore be represented in an image. Constantine convened a synod in Hieria in 754 that ratified this position, and the persecution of icon worshippers took hold. The walls of churches that bore images, whether in mosaic or paint, were scrubbed clean, and transportable icons were sought out and destroyed. Monasteries were particularly targeted as many were opposed to Iconoclasm and Constantine felt that they had too much power and wealth. This persecution accelerated to the point that monks and nuns were taken from their monasteries and forced to marry. Many fled to Italy, Rome in particular, to escape. The Iconoclast movement accentuated the differences between the Western church's attitude to images and that of Constantine's Eastern approach. When the patriarch Anastasios opposed Constantine's views, he was made to ride backwards on a donkey through the city streets and was ridiculed. Even holy relics were considered anathema; many were confiscated and destroyed. This ban on venerating images extended to the saints themselves: it was said that Constantine even forbad the use of the word 'saint'. According to rumour – or at least the accounts of later Iconodule historians who reviled him – he would refer to 'Sophia's' rather than 'St Sophia'.

As a result of Constantine's policy of Iconoclasm, combined with his prioritizing of the regions to the north and south of the empire, Byzantium's influence over Italy was at first ignored and then lost for ever. In Rome, Pope Stephen II rejected the notion that Constantine V could be of help against the invading Lombards, and

ISAURIAN DYNASTY

turned to the Franks and their king, Pepin the Short, instead. Pepin's son Charlemagne was eventually established as Roman Emperor in the West, and for the first time in its history the empire was irrevocably split in two. This did not seem to trouble Constantine V, who believed that it was more important to deal with the immediate threat from the Bulgars and the Arabs than argue with decadent Italy. He was fortunate that the great early leaders of Islam the Umayyads, had come to the end of their time, and that in 75c a new central administration and court had been set up under the Abbasids, who moved their capital away from Damascus and settled further east, in Baghdad. Their switch allowed Constantine to transport Christians from the borders of the Muslim lands to Thrace, where he needed help to counter the aggressive ambitions of the Bulgars. This left a large no-man's-land between the Byzantine border in the east and the western reaches of the Abbasids, making it difficult for the Muslims to plunder. Repeated attacks by the Byzantine forces against the Bulgars made them less of a threat, with the result that the empire was now relatively stable and prosperous. Constantine V gained some popularity by lowering the price of food in the capital and holding spectacles in the Hippodrome with brutal shows of strength. He had many captive Bulgars, including a chief, brought back to Constantinople in chains and thrown to the factions, where they were murdered in full public view.

Not everyone was an Iconodule. Many were fervent supporters of Constantine's Iconoclastic policy, particularly in the army, and life within the empire probably seemed safer and more prosperous than it had been for years.

Constantine's building works were extensive, mainly within the Great Palace in Constantinople, including the church of the Virgin of the Pharos ('lighthouse') and, perhaps most significantly, the Porphyra. This was a large room entirely lined with porphyry where all future emperors were to be born, giving rise to the term *porphyrogennetos*, 'born in the purple', which legitimized the hereditary nature of becoming emperor.

Constantine V died as he embarked on another campaign against the Bulgars in 775. He had suffered from ill health all his life and was possibly an epileptic, but this extraordinary man carried on to the very end, performing his duties as the defender of the empire. He left his third wife, Eudokia, their many children, and his first-born son and successor a stable government, a full treasury and secure borders. Later historians denigrated his rule, describing it as one of continuous terror, and recounted that his body was removed from the church of the Holy Apostles once Orthodoxy had been reinstated. However, at the time of his death he was acclaimed as a military leader and administrator. An indication of how much Constantine was admired is the fact that, when the great Bulgar leader Krum was threatening to invade the capital some twenty years after his death, soldiers and 'impious members of the foul heresy of the God-hated' would gather around his green marble tomb and try to awaken the spirit of their great deceased emperor.

Leo IV the Khazar
September 775 – September 780

The short reign of this sickly young emperor was marked by two events. First, he relaxed the Iconoclastic policy of his father, Constantine V. Monks and nuns were allowed to continue their way of life, people were not persecuted for holding Iconodule views, and many icons long thought destroyed miraculously appeared again. Second, he led a successful military campaign against the Abbasids and defeated them in Syria.

Leo IV was the first emperor to be *porphyrogennetos*, 'born in the purple'. His first year as emperor saw his two half-brothers, Nikephoros and Christopher, challenge him for the leadership, but by crowning his infant son, Constantine VI, as co-emperor and dealing firmly with his brothers' supporters he stamped the rebellion out quickly.

His wife, Irene of Athens, would have a major influence on the history of Byzantium. She was neither a princess nor an aristocrat, and the story went that she was chosen from a sort of beauty pageant known as a 'bride show'. Her beauty was often remarked upon, but it was her thirst for power that marked her out for the next twenty years.

Leo IV suffered from tuberculosis, and it was this terrible affliction that caused his death just five years into his reign, at the age of 30. He had been a kindly if ineffectual ruler and left his 9-year-old son Constantine VI in the care of his regent mother. He would not have foreseen the mix of personal ambition and cruelty that she would unleash on both the people of Constantinople and her own family.

Constantine VI the Blind
September 780 – August 797

Throughout the 780s, Constantine VI reigned but his mother, Irene, ruled. She exercised control over all matters of state and relied heavily on her chief minister, the eunuch Staurakios, to oversee the day-to-day running of the government.

When he was just 16 years of age, Constantine VI was made to oversee a Seventh Ecumenical Council (also known as the Second Council of Nicaea) that condemned Iconoclasm and sanctioned the veneration of icons. It was all the work of Irene and was popular with both the church and the people, guaranteeing her a special place in their affections. She also decided who should marry her son. Constantine VI had been betrothed to Rotrude, the daughter of Charlemagne, king of the Franks, in a diplomatic match to help unite the two halves of the Christian empire. For some reason, and probably on the initiative of the Frankish side, the engagement was called off, and a bride show was arranged to find a wife for Constantine. The winner was a beautiful young peasant named Maria, from Amnia in Paphlagonia, and the wedding duly followed. Unfortunately, the increasingly unhappy and unruly Constantine did not like his

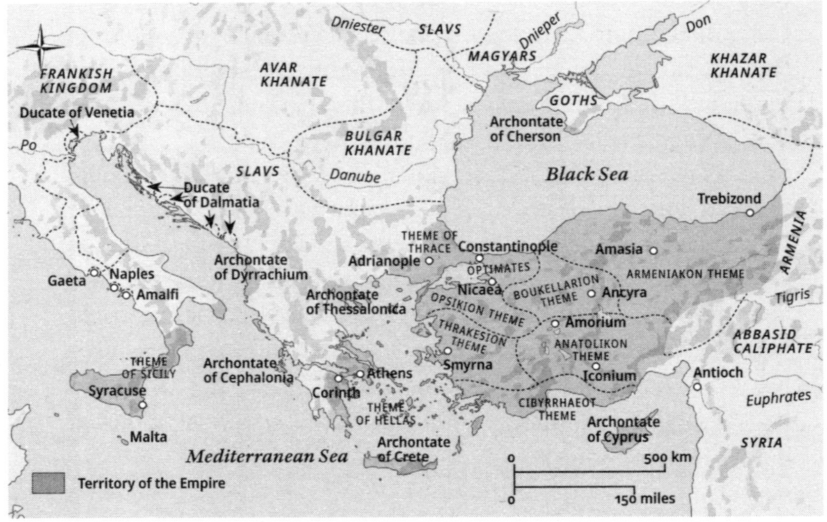

new wife, and preferred to carry on with a lady-in-waiting named Theodote. Eventually, Maria was sent to live in a monastery, whereupon Constantine VI promptly married Theodote – an act that the furious Orthodox clergy saw as a form of bigamy. Irene, ever scheming to maintain her own power, sided with the clergy and condemned her son for the marriage. The resulting feud was known as the 'Moechian Controversy' (from the Greek word for adultery, *moichos*) and cost Constantine what little popularity he had left.

Irene tried to formally acquire the title of empress but was overruled by Constantine and briefly stepped back into the shadows. During this time Constantine VI took to the battlefield, where he was woefully unsuccessful, suffering defeat at the hands of Kadram of Bulgaria in 792, at the Battle of Marcellae, and against the Muslims in the south. Faced with these setbacks and his ever-growing unpopularity, Constantine VI recalled his mother to the court to help him rule.

The emperor became increasingly cruel in his choice of punishments. When he suspected his uncle of staging a coup against him, he had him blinded and arrested his four other uncles, having their tongues cut out. This erratic and unpopular behaviour played into the hands of his mother, and in 797 she in turn had him arrested and blinded by her henchman. On the day he died there was a total eclipse of the sun, and the darkness was said to have lasted for seventeen days.

To compound this act of cruelty, it was said that Irene had her son confined for life in the small room in the palace where he had been born. His wife, Theodote, reportedly volunteered to be incarcerated with her husband, but from that moment on nothing was ever heard of the emperor again. The final irony was that he was buried in a monastery his mother had founded, that of St Euphrosyne.

Irene

August 797 – October 802

Irene the faithful emperor.
IRENE'S SIGNATURE ON OFFICIAL PRONOUNCEMENTS,
c. 800

The remarkable Irene Sarantapechaina, better known as Empress Irene of Athens, first appears in history when she was brought to Constantinople by the emperor Constantine V, on 1 November 768, to marry his son Leo IV. She was barely 15 years old, and Leo was just 18. It is unclear why Constantine V chose a young Athenian orphan from a good but undistinguished family to be the wife of his son and the next empress consort, a mystery that has led to stories of her being chosen in a 'bride show'. There can be little doubt that Irene possessed exceptional beauty, but she also had a rampant craving for power. This was a woman who would stop at nothing, including giving the order to blind her own son.

Irene was the first woman to become sole empress of the empire in her own right. There had been others who had ruled as regents for their young children, but none had been crowned empress alone. She had been the empress consort to her husband, Leo IV, from 775, and then empress regent from his death in 780. It would have been customary for her to step down once her son had come of age, but she did not, and Constantine VI seemed disinclined to force her. It is telling that, on coins issued during her reign as regent, she had her portrait and name placed on the obverse, and her son Constantine on the less important reverse. This was a woman who wished to stamp her imperial authority wherever she could.

It was Irene's sympathy for the Iconodules that kept her popular; her wish that the veneration of icons should be restored was ratified at both the two church councils of 786 and in Nicaea in 787. Irene was constantly looking for an opportunity to take control of the empire for herself, and the increasingly Iconoclastic position taken by Constantine gave her that chance. Intriguing with bishops and courtiers, Irene plotted against her son and gave orders that he should be arrested. Despite fleeing to the Anatolikon theme, Constantine VI could not escape her agents, who caught him and brought him back to the Great Palace in Constantinople where he was blinded on the orders of his mother. It may have been so brutal that he died a few days later; in any case he was never heard of again.

Irene could now rule alone. She occasionally chose to call herself *basileus*, not *basilissa*, thus removing the element of femininity from her title. Once in control, Irene was a disaster. She placed her two chief ministers, the eunuchs Staurakios and Aetios, in positions of power, but they proceeded to plot and scheme against one another rather than run the empire. The monasteries and the monks, always the cornerstone of her power base, were given more autonomy and tax exemption, and the population of Constantinople, who had been paying high taxes under previous emperors, were also exempted from the municipal tax. In a highly theatrical but

　　　　　　　ISAURIAN DYNASTY

seemingly effective manner, Irene would ride through the streets of the capital throwing handfuls of money to the people.

Throughout her life as empress consort, empress regent and now *basileus*, Irene had maintained close relations with the powers in the West. As Muslim forces were threatening the strength of the Byzantine Empire in the south and east, and the Bulgars in the north, Theophanes the Confessor proposed that she offer her hand in marriage to Charlemagne. Despite her genuine anti-Iconoclastic views being more in alignment with the church in Rome than that in Constantinople, Charlemagne refused. The crowning of Charlemagne as Holy Roman Emperor by the pope on Christmas Day 800 was a significant moment for the Byzantines. There had only ever been one Roman Empire, and it was theirs, centred on Constantinople and ruled by their emperor. Now there were two heirs to the great Roman world, and at this point the West looked stronger than the East. The dream that there would be one Christian empire, ruling over all of Christendom, had been broken for ever. The two sides – who differed in their language, culture, politics and religious beliefs – would never be reunited.

When Irene's end came, it came swiftly. A coup was arranged, led by her chief finance minister, Nikephoros. With the backing of many patricians and others in government who could no longer tolerate her inept leadership and the disastrous state of the empire, Irene of Athens was removed from office and banished to the island of Lesbos. Fortunate not to have been tortured as she had tortured her own son, nor killed like many usurped emperors before her, she spent the rest of her life engaged in menial tasks to eke out a meagre existence. She had led an extraordinary life, shaped by her ambition and cruelty. The restoration of Orthodoxy would always ensure her a place in the hearts of many Byzantines, but she had also presided over the empire's decline in both size and power, and played no small part in the damaging split between the Christians of the East and those of the West.

NIKEPHORIAN DYNASTY

(802–813)

The Nikephorians' short period of rule was generally unsuccessful. The dynasty included an emperor who died in battle, one who ruled for only a few months before dying from wounds received in the same battle, and Michael I, who upon hearing that Leo V was marching on the capital ran away to a monastery. The empire was left in a highly precarious position.

Nikephoros I
October 802 – July 811

Here is the list of the ten horrible misdeeds of Nikephoros.
THEOPHANES THE CONFESSOR, 814 OR EARLIER

As chief finance minister under both Constantine VI and Empress Irene, Nikephoros was a far more knowledgeable economist than many Byzantine emperors. Once in power, he immediately set to work improving the state of the empire's accounts, which meant raising taxes. The church and monasteries were required to contribute more, the people were taxed at a higher rate than they had been for many years, and members of the aristocracy were forced to underwrite the taxes due from peasants and farmers on their estates. Unsurprisingly, these policies conspired to make Nikephoros deeply unpopular with some throughout his nine-year reign. Xenophobic rumours spread that he was of Arab descent; they were almost certainly untrue, but are nonetheless an indication that he was viewed with suspicion and never accepted as emperor by the people. Almost as soon as he was installed, Nikephoros had his son,

Staurakios, marry Theophano, a relative of the empress Irene, in an attempt to legitimize his family's imperial credentials.

Nikephoros forcibly moved thousands of Christians to repopulate areas of the empire that were not sufficiently 'Byzantine' and change the local ethnic mix. This rebalancing of the population was crucial, introducing a Greek element among the Slavs who had settled in large numbers in the Balkan peninsular. The move was necessary, to restabilize the economy and put the empire back on its feet, but at the time it further cemented Nikephoros's reputation as an uncaring and distant leader and was deeply resented.

On the military front Nikephoros was less assured. He had had no military training but as emperor saw it as his duty to lead his troops into battle. Unfortunately, he was up against a great Muslim leader in Harun al-Rashid, who defeated him in the Battle of Krasos in 804 and humiliated him again when he invaded Cappadocia, forcing Nikephoros to capitulate land and pay a large annual tribute. To compound the humiliation, Harun made Nikephoros and his son Staurakios pay a personal tax of three gold pieces to the caliph himself.

On the western front, Nikephoros I concluded a treaty with Charlemagne, which he grandly termed the 'Pax Nikephori', but refused to recognize him as Holy Roman Emperor – a slight that resulted in war over Venice and its territories. The conflict concluded with Byzantium maintaining control over Venice and Istria, but conceding Rome and Ravenna, probably for ever, to the Franks.

The only sphere in which Nikephoros had some success was his campaign against Bulgaria and its chief, Krum, invading the country on two occasions and both times emerging victorious, even sacking the capital, Pliska. His treatment of the defeated populace was brutal, however: he rounded up all the children of the conquered cities and beat them to death with millstones. The chronicles of later historians are not necessarily to be trusted, but there can be little doubt that Nikephoros was not magnanimous in victory.

After his defeat, Krum tried to make a peace treaty with Nikephoros, but the arrogant and victorious emperor refused to negotiate and pursued him into the mountains, where he intended to annihilate the Bulgars once and for all. This was a terrible mistake: the entire Byzantine army set up camp in an area that could not be easily defended, and the opportunistic Krum attacked the Byzantines as they slept. It was a massacre, and the Byzantine army was destroyed. Nikephoros was slain on the battlefield, the first emperor to die in battle for 400 years. In retaliation for Nikephoros's previous atrocities, Krum had the Byzantine emperor decapitated and his skull lined with silver, to be used as a goblet. For years to come, visiting Byzantine dignitaries were forced to drink from the skull of their former emperor.

Despite the good he had achieved through his reorganization of the tax system and the administration of the empire, Nikephoros was criticized by his people and later historians (Theophanes made a list of 'ten horrible deeds of Nikephoros'), and came to a brutal and ignoble end.

Staurakios
July 811 – October 811

The brief and tragic reign of Staurakios was the fault of his father, Nikephoros I, who had allowed the Byzantine army to be destroyed. His father dead, the badly wounded Staurakios was taken to Adrianople along with other senior members of the government who had survived the massacre, notably his brother-in-law Michael Rangabe and the *magistros* Theoktistos. After a brief discussion, they all concluded that Staurakios should be proclaimed emperor, and they set off, with Staurakios in a litter, to Constantinople.

Up to this point Staurakios had lived a fairly normal life for the son of an emperor. He had been proclaimed as co-emperor in 803

      NIKEPHORIAN DYNASTY

when still a boy, after an attempted coup by Bardanes Tourkos had been crushed. The teenage Staurakios was married to Theophano, a relative of the empress Irene, who had been selected for him by his father at a bride show. Although they had no children, they appeared to be happy together.

When the severely wounded emperor had reached Constantinople, there were immediate calls for clarity as to who should succeed him. The general consensus was that Michael Rangabe, brother-in-law to Staurakios and a senior and respected figure at the court, was the obvious candidate, but there was some initial reluctance on Michael's part to take the throne by force against his weak and dying relative. Staurakios favoured his wife, Theophano, as successor. After all, Irene had reigned in her own right, so why not Theophano? However, resistance to this idea was strong, and even his sister Prokopia was opposed to it. Fearing that Staurakios could die at any moment, and that an uprising and general chaos could ensue with the lack of an agreed and established heir, Michael Rangabe acted with general consent in proclaiming himself emperor in the Hippodrome.

Upon hearing the news, Staurakios at first accused the patriarch Nikephoros and his close friend, the domestic of the schools, Stephen, of treachery, asking them to blind Michael, whom he had always disliked. But they persuaded the now former emperor that they had saved his life, not betrayed him. Staurakios, who could see that his position was hopeless, agreed to abdicate, and gave Michael Rangabe his blessing as the heir to his throne. Staurakios was taken to the monastery of Braka, where he died of gangrene within a few weeks. After a short and brutal experience as emperor, Staurakios was still a teenager when he died.

Michael I Rangabe
October 811 – July 813

Michael was in the prime of life, with a round face and skin the colour of wheat; with black hair and a manly beard, handsomely styled.
SCRIPTOR INCERTUS, FIRST HALF OF THE 9TH CENTURY

Handsome he may have been, but Michael I Rangabe was a weak ruler. He was possibly the wrong choice to succeed Staurakios, but he had taken on the role of emperor at a terrible time for the Byzantine state, since the army's defeat by the Bulgar king Krum had been catastrophic. To the south, the only thing keeping the powerful Abbasid forces at bay was a huge and damaging annual tribute to Harun al-Rashid.

Ill-equipped to cope, Michael turned to those around him for guidance and was drawn into internal conflicts among clergy and politicians alike. In the vain hope of securing the goodwill of his people, he gave back the taxes that Nikephoros I had so carefully raised, thus emptying the treasury of the surplus that had started to build up. He allowed the church to hold sway once more in matters of both religious doctrine and government policy. He fell under the spell of the powerful abbot Theodore the Studite and reduced the authority of the patriarch Nikephoros. The emperor's attitude to the West also changed: where Nikephoros had refused to acknowledge the religious supremacy of Charlemagne in any way, Michael I capitulated and formally recognized the imperial status of 'Charles the Great'. In 812 the Byzantine delegates in Charlemagne's capital, Aachen, finally acknowledged him as *basileus*. The admission that there existed a second empire represented a profound capitulation on behalf of Byzantium, which could no longer claim to be sole heir to the heritage of ancient Rome. The Byzantines had always seen themselves as Romans; if they were not, then what were they? Perhaps the most immediate issue for Michael was the Bulgarians and their triumphant king, Krum. Although the Bulgarians' own forces were depleted from several years of warfare with the Byzantines, militarily they were now in a more powerful position. Krum seized the initiative and demanded draconian peace terms. The hapless Michael I prevaricated, and Krum invaded and captured important towns on the Black Sea coast, including Mesembria. According to Theophanes the Confessor, he found stores of gold and silver that the Byzantines had been hiding, and also captured a large quantity of flame-throwing weapons for launching Greek fire. The small advantage that the Byzantine navy had enjoyed for years had been lost.

Many around Michael, including the patriarch Nikephoros, urged him to accept the peace terms offered by Krum, but he was still in thrall to the forceful and stubborn abbot Theodore the Studite, who recommended taking the fight to Krum. The two armies met on the plains outside Versinikia near Adrianople, and conflicting reports blame either Leo the Armenian or the emperor himself of serious military incompetence. The result was a comprehensive victory for Krum and his army.

The woeful and humiliating leadership of Michael I Rangabe led him to abdicate as soon as he heard that the retreating Leo the Armenian had declared himself the new emperor. Michael retired to a monastery. His wife, Prokopia, became a nun, and Leo ordered Michael's sons to be castrated and sent to monasteries. Ironically, one of his sons, Ignatios, was to become a highly respected patriarch of Constantinople and gained the respect of many in the capital. Michael I Rangabe had left the empire in a worse position than he had found it, and the immediate future looked bleak.

NON-DYNASTIC RULER

Leo V the Armenian
July 813 – December 820

He was noticeably small but thick-set and muscular, handsome,
with a full beard and much hair, and a voice booming like a lion.
SYMEON THE LOGOTHETE, *c*. 970

Leo V, a military man through and through, had served under the
rebel general Bardas Tourkos before deserting him as he attempted
a coup against the emperor Nikephoros I. The new emperor,
Michael I Rangabe, offered Leo the prestigious job of governor
of the Anatolikon theme. After the Byzantines' disastrous defeat
at the hands of the Bulgarian army at the Battle of Versinikia, and
despite doubts over his role in the fray, Leo led a rebellion against
Michael I and had himself installed as emperor.

Leo began his rule by telling a number of lies. First, to the patriarch Nikephoros he declared his devotion to Orthodoxy, a claim
that directly contradicted his upbringing as an Iconoclast and
belied his intention to restore Iconoclasm as soon as he was able. He
then agreed to negotiate a peace with the Bulgar leader, Krum. The
Bulgarian army was camped outside the city walls of Constantinople
and, although they could not penetrate the city's defences, they
were a terrifying force, in full view. Krum came unarmed to discuss
the terms of their treaty with Leo V in person, but the untrustworthy
Leo had him ambushed. Krum managed to escape, and in retaliation
wreaked havoc in the surrounding towns and countryside, destroy-
ing everything and everyone he came across. Krum marched to

Adrianople and sacked the city, taking all the citizens back across the Danube into Bulgaria as slaves. Just one year later Krum marched up to the walls of Constantinople again, but fate intervened: fortunately for Leo V and the Byzantines, Krum dropped dead of a cerebral haemorrhage on 13 April 814. His successor, Omurtag, had different ambitions and wanted to strengthen Bulgaria's borders to the north and west of the country; he subsequently agreed terms for a thirty-year peace between the Byzantines and the Bulgars. Omurtag swore his oath on a bible presented by Leo V, whereas Leo V swore on a stack of dead dogs topped by a sword. This agreement gave Leo V breathing space to attend to the other parts of the empire that were in dire need of attention. He was in luck once again when his other main adversary, the great Arab leader Harun al-Rashid, died suddenly, leading to internal strife among the Muslim leadership that dissuaded them from advancing into Byzantine lands for several years.

The relative calm on his borders allowed Leo V to pursue his ambition for the restoration of Iconoclasm. He deduced that the military disasters of the last few years were due to a slackening in the empire's Iconoclastic beliefs: Constantine V and Leo III, both Iconoclasts, had been successful in battle, whereas the softer Iconodule beliefs of both Nikephoros and Michael I had led to military disaster. Leo employed the considerable talents of John Grammatikos, at this point a high-ranking cleric, to argue the case for a second wave of Iconoclasm, at the same time banishing both the Orthodox patriarch Nikephoros and the great abbot of the Studite monastery, Theodore. On Easter Sunday 815, Leo V installed his friend Theodotos Melissenos as the new patriarch, a man with strong Iconoclastic views.

Leo also appointed friends to senior military positions. Michael the Amorian and Thomas the Slav, both old army friends and supporters, were made senior governing generals. This was a mistake on Leo's part, since Michael would go on to mount a coup against his old compatriot. Shortly before Christmas Day in 820, Leo uncovered the plot to assassinate him and had Michael thrown in prison to be killed the next day. Michael's supporters broke him out of confinement and proceeded to hunt down Leo V and kill him. It was a brutal end to a deceitful man who had some success in strengthening the borders and improving the empire's finances but was denigrated for trying to restore Iconoclasm.

AMORIAN DYNASTY

(820–867)

The Amorian dynasty was also known as the 'Phrygian' dynasty, named after the area of Anatolia from which they came. The Amorians continued the unpopular policy of Iconoclasm, consolidating the second wave of this divisive dogma. It worsened relations with the West, and ended only when the regent Theodora, mother of the 2-year-old emperor Michael III, renounced it for ever. Wars with the Abbasids continued to plague the empire, but as Michael grew older and assumed control, he strengthened the empire's military capabilities, which unknowingly paved the way for the great period of the Macedonians.

Michael II

December 820 – October 829

The reign of evil will afflict the earth, When Babylon is by a dragon ruled, A Stammerer with too much love of gold.
JOHN SKYLITZES, QUOTING AN ANCIENT ORACLE,
SECOND HALF OF 11TH CENTURY

Born about 780 in the Phrygian city of Amorium to humble parents, Michael belonged to a Judaeo-Christian sect known as the Athinganoi, of whom there were many in Phrygia and Cappadocia. Regarded with suspicion by the more orthodox Christians, his beliefs were held against him even when he became emperor. Born with a speech impediment, and possibly a very pronounced lisp, he was known as 'the Stammerer'. He spoke with a heavy accent, and was most probably illiterate, and sneered at by the sophisticated elite of Constantinople. It was said of him that 'you could read a book in the time it took him to write down his name'.

Before Michael reached Constantinople, he followed the path of many of his kinsman by joining the Byzantine army. While a young officer, he formed friendships with two men that were to play a vital part in his life – Leo the Armenian, the future Leo V, and Thomas the Slav – and all three served under the command of General Bardanes Tourkas. There was a story that they were summoned to the general's table for supper, where all three were each offered the hand of one of his daughters. Although this came as a surprise to all of the young army officers, it was because the general had had a dream that one of them was going to become emperor. Such tales abound in Byzantine reports and were probably apocryphal, but both Leo and Michael did marry the general's daughters. Thekla, Michael's wife, was the mother of his only son, Theophilos. The same story relates how the three officers were also told by a soothsayer that two of them would become emperors, while the other would make an unsuccessful attempt at the throne. When Leo did indeed become emperor, it was believed that Michael had plotted against Leo to become the second emperor of the prophecy.

The emperor at that time was Michael Rangabe. Leo called upon the help of his friend Michael to overthrow Rangabe and promote himself to the throne, becoming Leo V. Michael was rewarded by being given command of a corps in the imperial bodyguard, the *excubitores* – a very prestigious job.

It did not take Michael long to become jealous of Leo V. Remembering the prophecy made just a few years earlier, he decided to plot against him. It is possible that Leo V had also divorced his wife, Michael's sister-in-law, by this point, and had married a woman named Theodosia, with whom he had children; no doubt there was personal resentment.

Michael's plot to kill Leo V was discovered the day before Christmas 820. Leo V's response to his betrayal was to condemn his erstwhile friend to die by being shackled to an ape and thrown into the furnace that heated the imperial baths. As it was Christmas Eve, the wife of Leo V, Theodosia, persuaded her husband to delay his execution until after the religious holiday. That night, Michael managed to rouse his supporters into acting on his behalf. Dressed as church choristers, they entered Hagia Sophia, initially mistaking the patriarch for Leo V, who was wearing a similar fur hat. This mistake gave Leo time to grab a large cross with which to defend himself – but to no avail. First his arm was cut off, and then his head. The conspirators threw his dismembered body into the public latrine before hauling it out to put on display in the Hippodrome. Once freed, Michael had all four of Leo's sons castrated (one of whom died in the process) and banished them, along with their mother, to the Princes' Islands.

Michael II's coronation happened in the early morning on the day of his release from prison; unable to remove the manacles from his legs, he was inaugurated while still in chains – an honour he alone holds among the Byzantine emperors.

The third of the three young officers, Thomas the Slav, decided that he would rebel against Michael II and began inciting the people and the commanders of the themes to rise up in rebellion against this recent usurper and despot.

Michael II had reinstituted Iconoclasm, which was still hated by much of the populace as well as substantial parts of the clergy, so Thomas had little trouble in raising a serious force against his old compatriot. Thomas also visited the Abbasid court in Baghdad, where it is generally accepted that he received the backing of the caliph Ma'mum (r. 813–833), the son of Harun al-Rashid. He then declared himself emperor of the Romans, was crowned in Antioch (a city controlled by the Arab forces, so therefore with the tacit blessing of the caliph), and fought many successful campaigns against his old friend. The rebellion and eventual civil war were significant, since many saw Thomas as attempting to side with the people against harsh taxes and general neglect under the unpopular and radical emperor. With a large force and a substantial naval fleet, he nearly succeeded in overthrowing Michael. He besieged Constantinople for about a year from the end of 821, before the Bulgarian army under the *khan* Omurtag came to Michael's aid and forced Thomas to flee. Michael II finally managed to destroy Thomas's ships moored in the Sea of Marmara with the use of Greek fire.

When Thomas was eventually captured he was brought back to Constantinople to face his erstwhile colleague, who stamped his imperial purple boot on his neck, a time-honoured sign of the death penalty, and ordered his hands and feet to be cut off before he was impaled on a stake. Michael II was tireless in his pursuit of Thomas's accomplices and had many hunted down and killed, including Thomas's son, whom he also had impaled. These were brutal times.

Thomas the Slav's revolt against Michael II had nearly succeeded. It had forced the emperor to deploy resources in defence, which weakened the army and navy and in turn led to an inability to defend territories from Arab attack, notably in Crete in 824, and three years later in Sicily, where territories were lost after much fighting. The Aegean became the home of Arab pirates who interrupted trade throughout the Eastern Mediterranean.

Despite being an undisputed Iconoclast, Michael II wanted the controversy to end and ordered the persecution of the Iconodules to stop, even recalling the most notable opponents of Iconoclasm, the patriarch Nikephoros and Theodore the Studite. As the Iconodules reintroduced images to the churches and appealed to the pope for help, Michael revealed his sterner character and had the pope's messenger, Methodios, beaten and imprisoned. Although he wished persecutions to stop, he never went as far as to formally restore the veneration of icons.

The clergy had always been ill disposed towards Michael II the Amorian, who, like other Iconoclasts before him, was painted in a poor light. He was, however, an able administrator, and after quelling the civil war against Thomas the Slav started to rebuild the military in preparation for the inevitable fight against the Muslim Arabs.

When Michael's wife, Thekla, died, he married again, which caused some controversy, as he picked Euphrosyne, the daughter of Constantine VI and Maria of Amnia, who was a nun. However, to some extent it did legitimize his regal credentials, and his son, Theophilos, succeeded him in a smooth transition of power, with no political unrest at all. He died relatively peacefully in his own bed, the first emperor to do so for over fifty years.

Theophilos
October 829 – January 842

From the beginning, he was determined to bring ruin and destruction on all those who had taken part with his father in the murder of Leo.
JOHN SKYLITZES, SECOND HALF OF 11TH CENTURY

When Theophilos began to go bald, he ordered that no Roman citizen should wear his hair longer than the neck, while alleging that this was done to restore ancient Roman hairstyles.
THEOPHANES CONTINUATUS, 10TH–11TH CENTURIES

Most probably an adolescent when his father Michael II died, the young Theophilos had been well prepared for the role of Emperor of the Romans. Unlike his father, he had been given the best possible education under the supervision of the great intellectuals of his time, including the leading Iconoclast John Grammatikos. This tutor and mentor was to have a profound effect on Theophilos and the empire, principally because he was the last of the great Iconoclast thinkers, and his young pupil was utterly seduced by the brilliant teacher's philosophy. Theophilos is significant because he was the last emperor to promote the policy of Iconoclasm.

As a young man, Theophilos was something of a romantic. Despite spending much of his adult life fighting the Arab armies, he was fascinated by the Muslims and the famous tales of the court of Harun al-Rashid in Baghdad. His admiration for the culture, sophistication and opulence of the Abbasid court was no secret; indeed, when he embarked upon his extensive building plan for his several palaces, he copied elements of Islamic architectural and decorative design. It was said that he imitated the behaviour of Harun al-Rashid by disguising himself as a common man and walking among his people to hear the truth of what they were saying. On one occasion a woman stopped him in the street and claimed that the emperor's brother-in-law was building a house next door to her own that blocked out all the light in her garden. Theophilos looked into the matter and, on discovering that she was telling the truth, had his brother-in-law flogged and confiscated his house.

Theophilos could also be cruel and ruthless. Some sources report that, upon ascending the throne, he promised a reward to all those who had aided his father in deposing Leo V, summoning them to court, where they were instantly put to death. He acted thus to distance himself from their treacherous acts, even if they had helped his cause.

It is as a patron of the arts and architecture that Theophilos is best remembered. Within a vast new palace he created the Triconchos, a construction with three apses supported by giant porphyry columns, marble-clad private quarters, sections for his many daughters in white Carian marble, and a gold roof atop a hall of green Thessalian marble. This was an emperor who loved opulence and was unabashed in showing off his wealth and exotic taste. He was fascinated by mechanical devices, which were produced by an army of craftsmen working in the palace. Elaborate toys were to be found throughout, including one described as a golden plane tree complete with jewelled birds and animals that moved and made noises at the emperor's command.

Theophilos's marriage was arranged by his stepmother, Euphrosyne, who had organized a bride show in 830. These parades were not uncommon in the 9th century; the empress Irene, Euphrosyne's grandmother, had introduced them to court some

AMORIAN DYNASTY

fifty years earlier. Theophilos picked the young Theodora, but in so doing overlooked one of Byzantium's most intriguing and intelligent women, the poet Kassia. Having been disregarded, she entered into a monastery and spent her life writing poetry, hymns and the music to accompany them, some of which are still sung in the Orthodox church today. With the exception of a boy, Constantine, who tragically died in infancy, Theophilos's children with Theodora were all girls. The couple waited twenty years before the redoubtable Theodora finally gave birth to a boy who lived, Michael.

Throughout Theophilos's reign there were constant battles with the caliphs in Baghdad, at first Mamun and, after his death, Mutasim. Theophilos himself had some early successes, which he celebrated with enormous pomp and extravagance back in the capital, but each time he was attacked once more and lost more than he gained. A particularly humiliating defeat took place in the city of his father, the important and prosperous city of Amorium, which had strategic as well as symbolic significance. The Muslim armies defeated Theophilos's army outside the city walls and then lay siege. Theophilos was fortunate to escape with his life and hurried back to Constantinople, but the citizens of Amorium did not fare so well. Once the walls had been breached, Mutasim and his forces burnt many Christians alive as they sought refuge in the great church, and many more were massacred or enslaved. A group of high-ranking officials were forced to march to Samarra, where they were to become slaves to the Muslim court. The legend states that only forty-two people survived the ordeal of transportation, which took nearly seven years to complete; when they arrived at the banks of the Tigris, they were offered freedom if they renounced Christianity and embraced Islam. Every one of them refused and were beheaded where they stood. These unfortunates are known today as the Forty-Two Martyrs of Amorium.

After the loss of Amorium, the caliph Mutasim sent a fleet of forty ships to attack Constantinople in 842, but they encountered a tremendous storm and all but seven of them were destroyed.

Mutasim had died a few days before this catastrophe, and indeed Theophilos, suffering from dysentery, died a few days later, still in his thirties. He left as heir his infant son Michael, and in his last days established a council of regency, chief among them his loyal wife, Theodora, to run the empire until his son's coming of age.

There was a change in the Byzantine world when Theophilos died, as Iconoclasm as an imperial force died with him. For decades the mood of the people had been moving against the Iconoclasts, and there was a tangible longing for the old images. Even his wife was well known to have had icons in the palace, and his great minister of finance, Theoktistos, instantly reverted to his old ways of icon veneration when Theophilos died. A complex character, Theophilos was capable of great cruelty but also possessed real ability in administering the empire and was a patron of the arts and a genuine intellectual. However, nothing, it seems, defines his life as much as the fact that he was the last Iconoclast emperor.

Michael III
January 842 – September 867

The untimely death of Theophilos left the empire in the hands of his 2-year-old son, Michael. His boy's mother, Theodora, immediately assumed the regency and promptly set about ruling on her son's behalf. The early story of the reign of Michael III is thus the story of his mother and the collection of people she gathered around her to help. These included the eunuch Theoktistos, who was the *logothetes tou dromou* – in effect her chief minister and right-hand man – and Bardas, her brother, a distinguished army commander and later her de facto co-emperor.

Theodora, who today is revered as a saint in the Eastern Orthodox church, was instrumental in restoring the veneration of icons. The importance of the defeat of Iconoclasm cannot be overstated: it was as significant for the religious and cultural life of the empire as was military success to its political expansion, and represented the victory of the Greek outlook over the Asian. Now and for ever after, Byzantium was a Graeco-Christian empire halfway between East and West. The removal of Iconoclasm was handled very effectively by re-affirming the decisions taken at the Second Council of Nicaea in 787, deposing the arch-Iconoclast patriarch John Grammatikos, and electing Methodios I to the post instead. The Eastern church still celebrates this episode on the first Sunday in Lent as the 'Triumph of the Orthodox', and commemorates Theoktistos as a saint.

The 'blessed' Theodora became increasingly dependent on the ambitious Theoktistos, to the point that she ousted her brother Bardas from his position of power and would listen only to the capable eunuch. He was a brilliant politician and personally led the Byzantine navy in successful attacks on the Arab forces in Crete, reclaiming the island for the Byzantines in 843 (albeit not for long). But, as was so often the case in the early Middle Ages, he was also capable of great cruelty and barbarism. He sacked the port of Damietta in Egypt in 854, capturing some 20,000 people, and when he was made aware of the massacre of the Christians at Amorium retaliated by executing many of the Muslim prisoners. His most brutal legacy was one also supported by Theodora: his persecution of the Paulicians (a Christian sect that disagreed with many fundamental Orthodox doctrines) can be read only as an act of genocide.

Theoktistos's neglect of the young Michael III, however, would prove his undoing. Some sources claim that Theodora had always treated her son with disdain and even cruelty, and Theoktistos simply went along with it. Michael was denied a formal education and was barely literate, instead being encouraged to drink and spend his young teenage years carousing with friends, going on hunting expeditions and driving chariots. When he turned 15, his uncle Bardas, who had been sidelined by both his sister and Theoktistos a few years previously and who had made it his business to stay close to the young emperor, convinced him that Theoktistos and his mother were plotting to have him killed so that they could rule the empire alone. Perhaps the final straw was when Michael, who had fallen in love with a commoner called Eudokia Ingerina, was told to ignore her and attend a bride show arranged by his mother. Here he was ordered to marry another girl, Eudokia Dekapolitissa, instead. Michael III immediately recalled Bardas and ordered him to remove Theoktistos and his mother from the palace. This Bardas did with glee, sending his sister to the Gastria monastery and murdering the unfortunate Theoktistos on his saint's day, 20 November 855.

Thus ended the life of one brilliant leader, as another stepped in. The more talented Bardas, who proclaimed himself *caesar* in 862, continued the work of Theoktistos for ten years and surpassed it, enjoying military successes against the Arabs in the East that culminated in the Battle of Lalakaon in 863. Bardas established the influential School of Magnaura, which taught philosophy, grammar, mathematics and astronomy, and introduced intellectuals such as Leo the Mathematician to the court. In a deliberately provocative move, he also made Photios the new patriarch – a man whose views on the nature of Christ were at odds with those of the pope. This appointment was of great significance: it was Photios who instigated and presided over the irrevocable split between the Eastern and Western churches – a conflict that has subsequently been called the 'Photian schism' – even as it contributed to a surge in confidence in the empire on all fronts.

Michael III and Bardas jointly appointed two brothers from Macedonia, Methodios and Constantine (later St Cyril), as the chief missionaries to the Bulgarian court with a view to converting the nation to the Eastern Orthodox religion, both as a religious necessity but also as a way of keeping the pope and the Western church out of the sphere of influence of the Byzantine Empire. It appears that the brothers were first sent to the court of the Khazars, in the Crimea, where they successfully converted them to Christianity. Subsequently, in 862, they were sent to the court

     AMORIAN DYNASTY

of the Moravian king Rastislav, and once again succeeded in converting an entire nation. This they did by translating the Bible into what became known as Old Church Slavonic, so that the populace could understand it, whereas the pope had refused to permit the Bible to be translated from Latin. This gave the brothers a great advantage, allowing them to connect with both the Moravian clergy and the common people. They even devised a new alphabet to reflect the Slavonic language more closely, known as the Glagolitic alphabet, in more modern form known as the Cyrillic alphabet. Methodios and Constantine managed to keep Rome on side and, indeed, were received by Pope John VIII. Their work in Bulgaria, Serbia and Moravia undoubtedly facilitated the spread of Christianity from the Balkans to Russia.

It is at this point in Michael's story that one individual emerges who went on to have a profound effect on the empire. Michael had formed a close relationship with a groom in his stables called Basil and had become increasingly in thrall to him. He even encouraged the marriage between Basil and his own mistress, Eudokia Ingerina. However, unbeknownst to him, Basil possessed an unparalleled ambition and, despite his humble beginnings, had his eye on the throne.

Basil understood the threat that Bardas posed to his objective and attacked him violently, killing him in the process. Michael accepted Basil's claims that Bardas was conspiring behind his back, but Basil did not stop there, and ultimately arranged for Michael to be murdered in his bed. A new Byzantine dynasty was born.

As a personality, Michael III was undoubtedly flawed, but – surprisingly – he left the economy in a very good state, annual revenues having risen to 3.3 million *nomismata*. Iconoclasm was finally at an end, and the conversion of the Slavic nations was well under way, enabling the religious and political influence of Byzantium to extend through the Orthodox Christian church. Paradoxically, although he made his viper-like confidant Basil marry his long-term and undoubtedly adored mistress Eudokia Ingerina – perhaps to keep her close – it was she who would give birth to the future emperor Leo VI, and many believed the father of Leo VI to have been Michael III himself. Thus the next great period in Byzantine history, the Macedonian dynasty, may not have been Macedonian at all, but in truth a continuation of the short Amorian line, of which Michael III appeared to be the last.

Michael III was much maligned by near-contemporary historians because Basil I and the Macedonians wanted to cover up their part in his brutal murder and erase his successes from the historical record. However, it was under his authority, albeit it largely managed by Theoktistos and Bardas, that Byzantium was set on a course that would make it the most powerful empire in the Western world for many decades to come.

MACEDONIAN DYNASTY

(867–1056)

The Macedonian era is seen as the second golden age of Byzantium. It was founded by an unlikely usurper, Basil I; having murdered his predecessor, he became a patriarchal figure (he was more likely Armenian than Macedonian) who established the second-longest reigning dynasty in Byzantium's extensive history. The Macedonians initiated a renaissance in art, literature and architecture; and the territorial expansion that culminated under Basil I's great-great-grandson Basil II ('The Bulgar-Slayer') was greater than it had been since the 7th century. The Byzantines were the dominant power in Europe and the Near East throughout the 10th and 11th centuries.

Basil I
September 867 – August 886

No family was ever so favoured by God as the Macedonians –
a surprising thing when one remembers that it was a family rooted in
the ground by murder and bloodshed. Yet that plant took root, and
sent out such mighty shoots, each bearing imperial fruit, that
no other can be compared with it for beauty and splendour.
MICHAEL PSELLOS, EARLY 1060S

Basil I, founder of the Macedonian dynasty that was to rule Byzantium for 200 years, symbolizes the paradox of the Byzantine Empire itself. A violent and cruel man, uneducated and illiterate, he established a dynasty and a government that oversaw the return to the empire of much of its former glory, both military and intellectual. He took the crown by stealth and brutal murder, and in reality was more likely to have been from Armenia than Macedonia. His great dynasty was thus probably not really Macedonian at all. His successor, Leo VI, was quite possibly the illegitimate child of his predecessor, Michael III, a man he had befriended and murdered, and it is possible, therefore, that his descendants were a continuation of the Amorian dynasty that had ruled before. Whatever the truth, Basil was undeniably a force of nature.

With unknown but certainly humble origins, Basil was possessed of two extraordinary qualities: enormous physical strength, and an ability to train any horse he encountered. He would defeat champion wrestlers in competitions and later slaughter men with his bare hands, but it was his almost magical ability to tame horses that drew the interest of the fickle emperor Michael III.

There are many versions of the story, but it seems plausible that Michael III was given a magnificent white stallion that was wild and seemingly unmanageable. When somebody suggested that they let their talented groom, Basil, attempt to tame it, Michael witnessed his powers at first hand. Basil took the horse's bridle in one hand and stroked its ear with the other, whispering all the while. The horse was instantly tamed, and Michael hired Basil on the spot as his chief groom.

There was also a story that, when he first arrived in Constantinople, Basil was in the vicinity of the church of St Diomed when the abbot walked out and called Basil's name, having not seen him and having no knowledge of him. Basil answered the call and entered the church, where the abbot looked after him. This episode was later cited as a portent of Basil's greatness.

Michael III, known by later historians – without much evidence – as 'Michael the Drunkard', quickly fell under the spell of his new friend, promoting him through the ranks of the palace. He even gave him the most favoured position of *parakoimomenos* ('one who sleeps nearby') so that they were virtually inseparable. There is a later inference, again unfounded, that they were homosexual lovers, but in any case Michael certainly enabled Basil to thrive at court. He even made Basil divorce his wife, Maria, with whom he already had a son, Constantine, and marry Michael's mistress, Eudokia Ingerina, who also bore him a son, Leo. Bizarrely, Michael then made his own sister, Thekla, live in Basil's household – a strange *ménage à quatre* that continued for several years. Upon Michael's death, however, Thekla fell in love with a nobleman called John Neatocomites, only for Basil to send him to a monastery and force Thekla to be confined to her house, where she eventually died. The nature of Basil's relationship with his second wife is unclear, but she bore him two more sons after Leo – Alexander and Stephen, born in 870 and 867 – and four daughters, Anna, Anastasia, Helena and Maria, all of whom became nuns.

In the world of court politics, Basil also worked ruthlessly to secure the throne. He recognized Bardas, the brother of the emperor Michael's mother, Theodora, as a threat to his ambitions and so poisoned Michael's mind against him, insisting continuously that Bardas was plotting against him to take the throne for himself. Bardas heard of this dangerous conspiracy against him and confronted the two of them in person. Both Basil and Michael signed a document assuring Bardas that it was untrue. However, when they were all preparing for an expedition to invade and reclaim Crete from the Saracens, Bardas was set upon and murdered, with or without the direct involvement of Basil. Michael was stunned but ultimately complicit: choosing to believe Basil, he wrote to the patriarch explaining that Bardas was conspiring against him and that he had therefore ordered his immediate execution. On returning to Constantinople, Michael sat in Hagia Sophia and in front of all assembled nobles read out this proclamation: 'The *caesar* Bardas plotted against me to slay me, and for this reason induced me to leave the city. Had I not been informed of the conspiracy by Simbatius and Basil, I should not be alive today. It is my will that Basil, the high chamberlain, who is loyal to me, who has delivered me from my enemy and who holds me in great affection, should be the guardian and manager of my empire and should be proclaimed by all as *basileus*.'

In just nine years Basil had come from obscure stable-boy to co-emperor; now he just needed to rule alone. So, in 867, a year after being honoured by Michael, he attended a banquet, got Michael 'the sot' drunk, and then had him murdered in his bed. The empire was finally his alone. This illiterate peasant, who spoke poor Greek and was violent by nature, became a ruler who established a lasting dynasty and re-established Byzantium as the most powerful empire in the world. He achieved an astonishing amount in a relatively short time. He instituted a reform of the entire legal system not attempted since the time of Justinian, publishing both the ambitious *Procheiron* (handbook [of the law]) and the *Epanogoge* (or *Eisagoge*, introduction [to the law]), which would last for centuries. His armies were also stronger than they had been since Justinian; they destroyed the Paulicians, and had the Saracens in retreat in the Latin West, as well as the Persian East. Both the Bulgarians and the Serbians were converted to the Orthodox church and, with the aid of Photios, he had demonstrated to the pope in Rome that Byzantium was the higher religious force.

Basil extended the territories under Byzantine control to a degree that was never surpassed. He restored and repaired the great buildings of the capital as well as the wider empire, and built a glorious church, the Nea, the like of which had not been seen since Hagia Sophia itself, thus reaffirming Byzantium's status as the greatest city on earth. (Not a stone of the church remains today, but contemporaneous descriptions reveal it to have been a magnificent building, decorated with extreme opulence.)

Basil adored his son Constantine, but loathed Leo, who was rumoured to be Michael III's son, and regularly tormented and abused him. Basil was told that Leo was planning to kill him and had secreted a sword in his boot ready to strike Basil down. As he was riding near his father, Leo gave him his sword, and Basil, in the belief there was a political conspiracy, had Leo arrested and thrown in prison. He even wanted him blinded but was persuaded otherwise by Photios the patriarch. Leo was, in fact, completely innocent of the charge and eventually released.

Basil's end mirrored his beginning, with a death that was bloody and violent. It was probably ordered by Leo. Basil spiralled into depression after the premature death of his favoured son, Constantine, and lost all interest in governing his empire, believing, according to the prevailing psychology of the times, that tragedy was divine retribution for the murders he had committed to obtain the crown.

Finally, in the summer of 886, while out hunting, the 74-year-old emperor went after a large stag on his own as the rest of his party rested; he became entangled in the antlers of the stag, fell from his horse and was dragged 26 km (16 miles). The party saw the emperor's rider-less horse return and went in search, only to find him half dead and still attached to the stag. A guard cut him loose, but when Basil regained his wits he instantly ordered the guard be executed because he had dared to raise a sword against the sovereign. The emperor was carried home where, suffering from internal bleeding, he clung on for nine agonizing days, eventually dying on 29 August. It is not inconceivable that this incident was a story designed to cover up the fact that his death was ordered by Leo and carried out by Leo's future father-in-law, Stylianos Zautzes, who just happened to be present. For all his great achievements, Basil died by violence, just as he had risen through violence; his end was lamented by few.

Leo VI
August 886 – May 912

This emperor was much given to study, particularly the effects of astronomical phenomena. He set verses to music for singing in church, verses of great sweetness. He was a devoted reader of Archimedes, more so than anyone at that time.

JOHN SKYLITZES, SECOND HALF OF 11TH CENTURY

On the death of his father, Basil I, Leo immediately had Michael III reburied with full imperial honours, giving rise to the rumour that Michael was indeed Leo's real father. He also removed the redoubtable 70-year-old patriarch Photios, replacing him with his own 16-year-old brother, Stephen, and promoted Stylianos Zautzes – the father of his mistress, later his wife, Zoe – to the newly created rank of *basileopator* (a chief aide of sorts).

Leo VI's reign was solid, if unremarkable, but for the complexities of his own succession. His childhood had been tough, as the man believed to be his father despised him, and even imprisoned him for a few years. When he finally became emperor, Leo was too eager to assert himself and clumsily stumbled into wars with the Bulgars, resulting in an embarrassing defeat at the hands of the Bulgar leader Symeon, following which Leo was forced to pay large sums of tribute money to keep the Bulgars at bay. While he was occupied with this war, the Arabs attacked, sacked and destroyed Thessalonica, the second city of Byzantium, slaughtering thousands before they withdrew.

Despite these setbacks, Leo – a genuine intellectual and scholar – was known as 'Leo the Wise' or 'Leo the Philosopher'. He wrote political orations, theological treatises and liturgical poems. He continued the work his father Basil I started, attempting to codify all the existing Byzantine laws, which resulted in an impressive collection known as the *Basilika*.

Beyond his intellectual pursuits, the dominating feature of Leo's life was his inability to father an heir. He had been married as a boy of just 15 to Theophano, but his austere and devout wife gave birth to only one daughter, Eudokia, who died as an infant before 895 and was shortly followed by her mother. Leo then married Zoe, his long-standing mistress and daughter of his chief advisor, Stylianos, who had previously given birth to two daughters, Anastasia and Anna, born out of wedlock and so not fully recognized by the church. Zoe died after only a year of marriage. It is not inconceivable that Leo truly loved Zoe, since she had been his chosen mistress for

     MACEDONIAN DYNASTY

many years, and he crowned their daughter Anna *augusta*. However, he needed to marry once more to provide a son and heir – meaning that he was obliged to go against the church's teaching that a man could be married legally only twice. Leo married Eudokia Vaiana in 900, with whom he had an infant son, Basil, born soon after. Before the church could object, she suffered the fate of his previous two wives, dying unexpectedly after just one year, along with the child, leaving Leo without a wife once more.

Rather than continuing to antagonize the church, Leo took a mistress known as Zoe Karbonopsina ('Zoe of the coal-dark eyes'), who four years later bore him a son, the future Constantine VII. Nicknamed 'Porphyrogennetos', meaning 'born in the purple', he was born in the porphyry-lined room reserved only for emperors. Leo's task was now to legitimize his son in the eyes of the church, to which end he agreed to abandon Zoe if the boy was baptized. The patriarch of Constantinople, Nikolaos Mystikos, agreed to these conditions, and the infant Constantine was baptized in 906. Leo then went against his word, married Zoe, and proclaimed her *augusta*. The patriarch was of course outraged, but Leo cleverly played upon the rivalry between the Eastern and Western churches, appealing to Pope Sergius III in Rome to legitimize his son. This the pope duly did, as much to anger the patriarch of Constantinople as to favour Leo. Constantine VII was crowned co-emperor in 908 at the age of just 3. Leo VI had been made co-emperor alongside his brother Alexander, but since Alexander had no interest in affairs of state it appears he led a life of little consequence within the palace walls; he was never called upon to take part in government during Leo's lifetime.

The seemingly endless task of finding an heir had finally been accomplished. However, when Constantine was barely 7 years old, Leo was struck down with a debilitating disease that would end his life.

Leo VI the Wise was not the son of his father – literally as well as figuratively. He possessed none of the dynamism and personal strength that had allowed Basil to forge a dynasty from nothing. However, he was a good leader and an honest man. He left the empire stronger and more powerful, and through his intellectual pursuits established a code of law that lasted for centuries. He was adored by the populace and had taken the task of continuing the Macedonian line very seriously, angering the church in the process. On his deathbed, the story goes, Leo looked up, saw his disreputable brother Alexander, said, 'Behold, evil times after thirteen months,' and then died.

Alexander
May 912 – June 913

The emperor Alexander's former way of life was nothing but decadent. His passions were hunting and other licentious practices, for he knew nothing of the behaviour worthy of an emperor, preferring to indulge himself in debauchery and immorality.
JOHN SKYLITZES, SECOND HALF OF 11TH CENTURY

Alexander, brother of Leo VI and co-emperor since 879, was a disaster for the empire. A drunken, debauched hedonist, he had only one guiding principle: to undo everything his brother had done. He removed all of Leo's appointments in crucial roles of state and church and installed his own followers. He moved into the imperial apartments, discarded his wife and son to make room for his concubines, and made plans to have his young nephew, Constantine Porphyrogennetos, castrated at the age of 7 or 8. Fortunately, Alexander was also stupid, and those in proximity found ways to distract and outwit him. Zoe, the imperial widow and mother of the young co-emperor, successfully persuaded Alexander that harming the infant could enrage the populace and that, as the child was sickly, he would probably die of natural causes soon anyway.

The reign of Alexander coincided with the arrival of Halley's Comet, which the unremittingly superstitious population took as a bad omen caused by Alexander's dreadful behaviour. After one particular bout of revelry and drunkenness, the emperor was met by the emissaries of the Bulgar leader Symeon, who asked for their tribute to be paid, as agreed with Leo VI. Alexander sent them away with insults and a refusal to pay anything. On hearing this, Symeon prepared for war and mobilized the army.

Alexander's thirteen months were soon up. According to the historian John Skylitzes, after a typical night of drinking, Alexander began 'haemorrhaging from his nose and his genitals' and one day later was dead. He had bequeathed the throne to Constantine, his 7-year-old nephew, and had arranged a council of seven men to act as regents. Dead at the age of 42, he had split the church even further, angered the populace and begun a war with the Bulgars that the empire could not afford.

Constantine VII Porphyrogennetos
June 913 – November 959

He was as erect as a cypress tree, broad-shouldered, affable, kindly to all, and yet quite shy, fond of the banquet and fond of the wine, charming in his manner, and generous with gifts and assistance.
THEOPHANES CONTINUATUS, *c.* 944–61

The long and complex reign of Constantine VII can be read as the story of intellect triumphing over brute force. Constantine was first and foremost a scholar and author, whose most famous surviving work describes the ceremonies that were prevalent in Byzantine court life throughout the 10th century, the *De Ceremoniis*. He also wrote a detailed biography of his grandfather Basil I, the *Vita Basilii*, which was designed to extol the virtues of the Macedonian dynasty rather than find an objective truth.

Constantine VII was thrust into the political fire at the tender age of just 7 years old and, under the instructions of the dying emperor Alexander, he was surrounded by a group of people who were to act as regents until he came of age. (In fact, he would have to wait until his 39th birthday to become the unchallenged and genuine ruler of the empire.) So, once again, it was his mother, Zoe Karbonopsina, 'she of the coal-dark eyes', who controlled the destiny of both the young Constantine VII and, indeed, the entire state, just as Irene had with Constantine VI, and Theodora with Michael III before her. Although there was some religious resistance to the idea of an uncanonical fourth wife of an emperor giving birth to a legitimate heir, the fact was that Leo VI and Zoe had insisted on bringing Constantine into the world in the royal purple birthing room, which legitimized his credentials in the minds of the populace and saw them eventually accepted by all.

Alongside Zoe in the early years was the patriarch Nikolaos Mystikos, who was the de facto leader of the regents. Mystikos was an able politician but was forced to make peace with the hated Symeon of Bulgaria, whose army was camped outside Constantinople and who cleverly sued for advantageous peace terms rather than try to scale the impregnable walls of the city. Zoe eventually took sole charge of the state, reversing some of this demeaning settlement, which included the engagement of her son to Symeon's daughter. However, she was unable to calm the powerful Bulgarians, and her chosen general, Leo Phokas, was defeated in battle against them. This setback undermined Zoe's position as the people's favourite and opened the way for another leader of the regency to emerge, the heroic admiral Romanos Lekapenos. In 919 Romanos appointed himself as *basileopator* and then, in 920, as *caesar*, and for twenty-four largely successful years he was in charge of the empire while Constantine VII, although co-emperor in name, had to wait until 944 before he took sole control.

After thirty-nine years of waiting in the wings, Constantine VII finally came to power. He had successfully removed a threat in the form of Romanos's ungrateful and stupid sons, and proved to be a capable and benevolent ruler for the remaining fifteen years of his life. Married to the daughter of Romanos Lekapenos, Constantine

     MACEDONIAN DYNASTY

had many children, including Theodora, who was to marry the future emperor John I Tzimiskes. It was the birth of Constantine's son, Romanos, in 938 that was of most significance: Constantine had him named as co-emperor at the age of 7, to ensure the clear direction of the dynasty.

Constantine's time in the shadows had been spent productively, pursuing literary and artistic interests. He was a skilled painter, collected a variety of artworks and books, and wrote several important works himself. He kept the company of scholars, and was diligent in his approach to the ceremonial aspects of being emperor. His political duties he took no less seriously, and through a combination of good judgment and the continuation of many of Romanos's policies – most notably issuing further legislation against the alienation of peasant holdings – as well as a shrewd ability to choose highly successful army generals, such as Nikephoros Phokas and Bardas Phokas, the empire flourished under his leadership.

In the east, themes and cities were retaken from the Arabs, and on the diplomatic front Constantine VII was particularly active, initiating cordial relationships with both Otto I of the Holy Roman Empire and the caliph of Cordoba, Abd ar-Rahman III. Perhaps most significant was his relationship with Olga of Kiev, regent of the Kievan Rus' people, who visited Constantinople in 957, was eventually baptized a Christian and had Constantine VII as her godfather. There were rumours that he had fallen in love with the Russian princess, but that she spurned his advances by pointing out how unsuitable it would be for a godparent to have a relationship with his goddaughter. Nevertheless, it helped pave the way for the conversion of the Rus' to Christianity, which would serve Byzantium well in the centuries to come.

Despite his unlikely start as an unhappy and ungainly child emperor, with a domineering and ambitious mother and surrounded by political intriguers, Constantine VII was an intellectual and a careful and astute leader. He proved to be a great emperor, distributing wealth among the peasant holdings, reclaiming territories long lost from the empire's control, and leaving to posterity a body of literary work that was among the most valued of the 10th century. In a typically thorough manner, he organized the continuation of the Macedonian dynasty by preparing his son, the future Romanos II, for the role of emperor, and died peacefully in his bed surrounded by his family. The only shadow cast on his exemplary life was the unsubstantiated rumour that he had been poisoned at the end by his ambitious daughter-in-law, who went on to play a significant role in the politics of the court.

Romanos I Lekapenos
December 920 – December 944

The Lord Romanos, the emperor, was a common illiterate man, and not from among those who have been brought up in the ways of the palace and have followed the Roman customs from birth; nor was he of imperial and noble stock, and therefore in most of his actions he was too haughty and despotic.
CONSTANTINE VII, *c.* 950

Romanos I Lekapenos was born of humble stock to an Armenian family that had enjoyed a momentous rise to prominence. His father, the extraordinarily named Theophylact the Unbearable, had saved the life of the emperor Basil I in battle and had been rewarded with a place in the imperial guard at the palace in Constantinople. The young Romanos was thus brought up close to the seat of power at the imperial court. Little is known of him from the period of his rise through the ranks of the military, but he had become the admiral of the fleet by 917. He served well under Leo VI and avoided the humiliation of defeat by the Bulgarian forces in the early years of the century. When Zoe could not deal with the Bulgarian forces massing on the frontiers, popular opinion allowed the successful commander to take charge of the empire in order to restore order and confidence. He did so carefully, without harming or even insulting the noble Macedonian family, and by stealth had himself named at first as *magister*, then *basileopator*, then *caesar*, and was finally crowned as co-emperor with Constantine VII in December 920. This subtle consolidation of power earned him the nickname 'the gentle usurper'. He soon crowned his own sons, Christopher, Stephen and Constantine, as co-emperors, although never placed them above Constantine VII. He made his other son, Theophylaktos, the patriarch in 933; and, most significantly, he married his daughter Helena to Constantine VII. This was a marriage that would last happily for the rest of their lives, and led to Romanos I becoming the grandfather of the emperor Romanos II.

Romanos I Lekapenos was admired throughout his lifetime but not adored, and never eulogized. He was a successful and efficient statesman and a largely triumphant military commander, yet he seems to have been something of an introvert, steely in nature but not charismatic. Other than the rather stylized portraits of him to be found in the 12th-century illuminated manuscript of the *Chronicle* of John Skylitzes in Madrid, the only contemporary image we have of him is that on his coinage, where he appears as an ill-tempered old man with a large beard.

In his dynamic years, however, Romanos accomplished a great deal. He established a stable and efficient civil service and, most importantly, supported smaller landowners against the growing power of the aristocratic families that were beginning to deprive the state of much needed men and revenues. This may have been partly a result of a popular uprising in Bithynia led by a man named Basil 'the copper hand'. Something of a minor revolutionary, Basil had previously attempted a rebellion, for which he had been arrested and punished by having his hand cut off. Upon returning home, he had a copper hand with a sword attached. When he tried a second peasant revolt, he was once again arrested, and this time tried and burnt alive in Constantinople.

On the diplomatic front, Romanos was very successful, making peace with the Bulgarians after Zoe had soured relations with them. In the east he sent the brilliant general John Kourkouas to defeat the Abbasids in Mesopotamia. Kourkouas also besieged the important city of Edessa and assured his place in Byzantine history by retrieving one of the most important of holy relics, known as the Mandylion. This was a piece of cloth reportedly given by Christ to Abgar, the king of Edessa, when he became ill. According to legend, when the image of Jesus's face on the scarf was brought to the king he was instantly cured. The Mandylion remained in Edessa until Kourkouas brought it back to Constantinople, where it was paraded around the streets as an *acheiropoieton* – an image not made by human hands – before being kept in the palace. The image showed that Christ was a man, with human features, thus supporting the teachings of the Council of Chalcedon and representing a defence for the worshipping of icons. The style of the face resembled the image known as Christ Pantocrator, which came to be the standard representation of Christ in the church; copies of it are found in almost all Orthodox churches today.

Despite his successes, Romanos was devastated by the death of his son Christopher in 931. From this moment on he was inclined to restore the throne to its legitimate emperor, Constantine VII, who was of higher status than his two remaining sons.

In rather typical Byzantine fashion, Stephen and Constantine organized a coup against their father, having him arrested and sent to a monastery on the Princes' Islands, with a view to deposing the rightful heir. Constantine VII seized his moment and led a counter revolt in which they were both arrested and banished, joining their father in his monastery.

Romanos ended his days as a monk and died peacefully in June 948 – a man somewhat broken by events, but one who had emerged from very humble beginnings to accomplish great things. His reputation was, understandably, panned by Constantine VII as soon he took the throne, but Romanos's reforms, and his diplomatic and military successes, speak for the quality of the man who had ruled the empire for twenty-four years.

 MACEDONIAN DYNASTY

Romanos II

November 959 – March 963

*When he ascended the throne, he proved himself a reasonable
and rational man, a benefactor to his subjects; but then certain
depraved confidants, who were ruled by their stomachs and their
sexual appetites, inveigled themselves into his inner circle and
corrupted him.*

LEO THE DEACON, AFTER 995

*He did nothing but behave in a debauched fashion, always in the
company of vain young men who frequented prostitutes, wantons,
actors and comedians.*

JOHN SKYLITZES, SECOND HALF OF 11TH CENTURY

Romanos, who was approximately 20 years old, sat by his father's
deathbed with his mother, Helena, and five sisters, and realized that
he would very soon be ruler of the empire. He was, after all, the
great-grandson of Basil I, the grandson of both Romanos Lekapenos
and Leo VI, and the son of the dying emperor Constantine VII. He
had a mixed reputation: according to some, he was a fun-loving,
good-time prince who played too much polo, was out hunting night
and day, and was overfond of drinking.

Romanos was tall, handsome and built like his father. At the tender
age of just 14, he was married off to Bertha, an illegitimate daughter
of the king of Italy, Hugh of Provence, who died within a few years.
Romanos then fell hopelessly in love with a totally unsuitable woman,
Theophano. She was to become a major figure in the Macedonian
dynasty, marrying two emperors, having an affair with a third, and
giving birth to two more. This daughter of a Peloponnesian inn-
keeper was named Anastaso but assumed the name of Theophano
once she became empress. She was described by all who saw her as
quite the most beautiful woman of her age, with the historian Leo
the Deacon writing that she surpassed 'all the women of that time in
beauty and in the grace of her body'. She was, however, as ruthless

and ambitious as she was attractive, and for the whole of Romanos's brief reign she dominated him. They married in 956, and almost immediately she made the hapless Romanos send his five sisters, kicking and screaming, away from the palace to a number of different convents. Romanos II remained utterly devoted to Theophano, even as she took complete control of their lives. Management of the affairs of state, neglected by the emperor, was left to the capable eunuch Joseph Bringas.

It was the appointment of some extraordinarily capable military men that secured the expansion of the empire: the brothers Leo and Nikephoros Phokas, and John Tzimiskes, all of whom were highly successful generals who were also somewhat manipulated by the beguiling Theophano.

Their military victories were extraordinary. In 960 Nikephoros invaded Crete with 3,000 ships carrying over 50,000 men. After a long and arduous siege that lasted the entire winter, he was successful in capturing Candia and removing the Muslim forces from the island. Many had tried to take back Crete but until now none had succeeded. It was not, however, the most noble of conquests. There were tales of massacre and butchery on a scale that surprised even the medieval mind. Women and children were raped and killed, the elderly and infirm were systematically murdered, and the few who did survive were sold into slavery and sent far away. The wealth of the city was plundered and sent back to Constantinople. It was claimed that Nikephoros had tried to halt the slaughter, but not even he could contain the savagery of his men. According to Leo the Deacon, writing in the late 990s, Nikephoros himself introduced the grim practice of catapulting the decapitated heads of his victims into cities to act as a terrifying spectacle and encourage them to surrender. During this period, there was great intellectual debate, religious discourse, artistic brilliance and acts of kindness and chivalry. But there were also occasions, such as the sacking of Crete, when men acted with a callous disregard for life on an epic scale.

 MACEDONIAN DYNASTY

Evidently these men had recognizable human attributes – they had families of their own, and had known the love of their parents and siblings – and yet they were capable of stabbing a 3-year-old child and his mother for no apparent gain. Was this a religiously inspired cleansing? Did these men suffer mental trauma as a result? There is certainly no account of this. It remains a phenomenon if not exclusive to the Middle Ages, then definitely commonplace at this time.

After his victory, Nikephoros took his army to join his brother Leo in the eastern provinces and defeated all in his path. The great Arab leader Saif-ad-Daulah, who had been a thorn in the side of the Byzantines with his annual raids and seizing of territory, was chased from his sumptuous capital of Aleppo, and from this moment on Nikephoros was known as the 'Pale Death of the Saracens'.

During these years, Romanos remained in the capital doing very little of note except fathering two children, Basil II and Constantine VIII, who he named as co-emperors in 962. He presided over the triumphant return of Nikephoros to the capital as the all-conquering hero, showering him with praise and gifts in front of the people.

Suddenly, on 15 March, as Nikephoros was campaigning in central Anatolian lands of Cappadocia, Romanos II contracted an illness and died. There were rumours that Theophano had poisoned him, but this seems unlikely, as it would have put her and her two young sons in great danger. It was now the turn of the beautiful and ambitious Theophano to step up and to act as regent to the two princes, and in this she knew she needed a strong and powerful ally. She made her choice, sending a message to Nikephoros Phokas to return to the capital and meet her at once.

Nikephoros II Phokas
August 963 – December 969

He is a grotesque man, dwarfish, with a fat head, and mole-like owing to his small, beady eyes, deformed by a short beard that is wide and thick and greying, disgraced by a scrawny neck ... and his complexion is like that of an Ethiopian whom you would not like to meet in the middle of the night.
BISHOP LIUDPRAND, c. 970

Few Byzantine emperors enjoyed such a spectacularly successful military career and yet failed to win the hearts and minds of their subjects. Nikephoros Phokas was a man beloved by his soldiers, who nicknamed him 'the Morning Star' and willingly followed him into battle wherever he led them. When he received a secret message from the empress Theophano upon the death of her husband Romanos II in 963, asking him to hasten back and to help protect the two princes of the Macedonian line, Basil and Constantine, Nikephoros wasted no time at all in coming to her aid, either through a keen sense of duty or as a result of Theophano's powers of persuasion.

Hailing from a family of distinguished generals, Nikephoros and his brother Leo, together with his nephew John Tzimiskes, dominated the military establishment throughout the reigns of Constantine VII and Romanos II, and helped to expand the territories of the empire in many directions. After the death of his first wife, Nikephoros appears to have shown no interest in women until his summons from Theophano. In matters of religion Nikephoros was highly devout and especially dedicated to the cult of the Mother of God. He was interested in holy Christian relics and sought to bring examples back to Constantinople from wherever he could find them. He wore a hair shirt under his tunic and slept on a leopard-skin rug given to him by his uncle, who was reportedly a saint. Nikephoros was a vegetarian, which was unusual among his class: vegetarianism was normally only practised by certain monks and aesthetes. These hard-line religious beliefs and practices were often at odds with the patriarch and sections of the clergy, whose withholding of support made his task at court ever more difficult. He unsuccessfully tried to convince the church that soldiers killed in battle against Muslims should be treated as martyrs. In 963 Nikephoros married the widow Theophano, outwardly to protect the two young princes from any unscrupulous usurper. There seems to have been no intimacy between the two, who could not have been more different in their personalities and behaviour. Their partnership also complicated Nikephoros's relations with the church, since some of the clergy, including the patriarch Polyeuktos, were opposed to the marriage on the grounds that, as he was already godfather to Basil and Constantine, in the eyes of the church he could not be their mother's husband. In the event either Theophano insisted that the marriage should go ahead or it was deemed necessary by the clergy. Nikephoros dutifully obliged.

Soon after the marriage, Nikephoros began campaigning against the enemies of the empire once more, firstly in Cilicia and then into Syria. Later, in 968, he annexed the Armenian state of Taron, then turned his attention to Tripoli and put Antioch under siege. His great friend the monk Anathasios seems to have been one of the few people whose company he enjoyed and who shared his religious views, and when Anathasios moved to Mount Athos to start a monastery it was Nikephoros who largely paid for it. Nikephoros claimed that soon he would retire and spend the rest of his days in the Great Lavra monastery, which is still standing today. It was not to be.

Later historians often use powerful women at court as scapegoats for any wrongdoings that occurred. In this case, available sources allege that Theophano, having achieved what she wanted from Nikephoros – that is to say, the certainty of her sons' succession and her continued domination of the palace – started to grow tired of her warring, over-religious husband and began to look elsewhere for pleasure. She did not look far, and soon started an affair with

Nikephoros's nephew, the handsome and dashing John Tzimiskes. It was a short time later that a plot was hatched to get rid of the charmless emperor and replace him with the charismatic John. On the night of 11 December 969, a group of conspirators broke into the emperor's chambers and assassinated him as he lay sleeping.

He was mourned only by his soldiers; the clergy had had enough of his antagonistic ways, the people had grown tired of the extra taxes he had instigated in order to fund all these military victories, and the power within the palace, Theophano, had moved on to a seemingly more exciting chapter. A truly great general but too clumsy a politician to survive for long, the taciturn Nikephoros certainly left the Byzantine lands in a better place and it was somehow fitting that the inscription on his sarcophagus read 'You conquered all but a woman'.

John I Tzimiskes
December 969 – January 976

I am sure that in this life and in the earthly domain there are two established orders: priesthood and imperial rule.
LEO THE DEACON, *c.* 995,
QUOTING THE EMPEROR JOHN TZIMISKES

He created a new paradise, from which flowed the four rivers of justice, wisdom, prudence and courage … Had he not stained his hands with the murder of Nikephoros, he would have shone in the firmament like some incomparable star.
CONSTANTINE MANASSES, MID-12TH CENTURY

The manner in which John Tzimiskes acquired the throne would cast an unwelcome shadow across his otherwise brilliant career. The sheer brutality of the murder of his emperor, his erstwhile friend and his uncle was never forgotten. According to the chronicler Leo the Deacon, who differs in several details from John

Skylitzes, the story went that John sat on the bed of Nikephoros as a blow struck his uncle across the face. He was then dragged to the feet of John, who cursed him, kicked him virtually to death and pulled out lumps of his hair and beard, before somebody ran him through with a curved sword. John then calmly walked to the Chrysotriklinos, the throne room of the palace, where Theophano and her two young sons were waiting, and was proclaimed as the new emperor.

However, there was one element that Theophano and John had not considered. The patriarch Polyeuktos, always a thorn in Nikephoros's side, required certain conditions to be met if he was to allow John to enter Hagia Sophia and be crowned emperor. The first was that he had to rid himself of his immoral and evil mistress, Theophano, and never see her again. Second, all his co-conspirators were to be named and punished for their part in the assassination of the previous emperor. Third, and most important for the patriarch, John was to undo all the legislation put in place by his predecessors concerning the confiscation of church lands and taxes that disadvantaged the church. Only the ever-trusted eunuch Basil, who had served both Nikephoros and Romanos II before him, was to stay in post.

All of these conditions John adhered to completely, and so it was that one of the most extraordinary women of the Byzantine world disappeared from history. Theophano had married two emperors, had an affair with a third, and had fathered two boys who would both become emperors in time. She left cursing and screaming at both John and the patriarch, and was carried off to a remote part of Armenia, where she remained until her son Basil brought her back to Constantinople after the death of John Tzimiskes.

Despite John's questionable past behaviour, he was quickly adored by the people and all who dealt with him. Tall, handsome, clever and surprisingly kind, he embodied a perfect change from his unfortunate predecessor, and would go on to be one of the greatest of Byzantine emperors. Brilliant in battle, skilled in diplomacy and generous in victory, he elevated the empire to a position of power and pre-eminence that it had not enjoyed since the time of Heraklios.

John quickly married one of Romanos II's sisters, Theodora – a union that, in the honoured Byzantine tradition, connected him completely to the ruling Macedonian line. He repealed most of the unpopular laws instigated by Nikephoros, lowering taxes for the poor and ending the persecution of the Jacobite Syrian church. He was not too proud to build on the successes of Nikephoros, further strengthening the position of the monks at Mount Athos, and regularly gave money and help to the poor, the sick and the needy. The behaviour of this emperor was exemplary.

Further afield, John resolved two diplomatic issues in a short space of time by securing truces: one with Otto II, the Holy Roman Emperor, to whom he married off his niece, and one with the great Russian ruler Prince Svyatoslav, which was more pressing. Svyatoslav had invaded most of the lands north of Thrace and had subjugated the Bulgarians to his rule. Leading a vast army, he was poised to attack Byzantium and take control of the city, leaving the Byzantines with Anatolia alone. But John was too smart for him: relying on a brilliant combination of diplomacy and military tactics, he defeated the Russian forces and, after a face-to-face meeting with the Russian prince, agreed a peace with him. The Russians were sent back to beyond the Danube. Next, John defeated the Bulgars, stripped them of all imperial rights and effectively ruled them from Constantinople. He could now claim control of vast swathes of the European mainland.

In 975 John set off with his victorious army to lead another highly successful campaign. He marched from Antioch through Homs, Baalbek and Damascus into Palestine, conquering all before him. Only Jerusalem was overlooked: it would have delayed his plans and was of no strategic importance.

This was to be John's last campaign. While on his way back he developed a terminal disease, possibly typhoid, and barely made it back to the capital in time to receive the last rites. He nonetheless managed to donate two extraordinary relics to Hagia Sophia: the sandals that Christ wore in Jerusalem, and the hair of John the Baptist. He finally succumbed to his illness on 10 January 976.

John was the most brilliant of generals and an exemplary emperor, his only stain being the vicious murder that had got him into power in the first place. Building on the success of the man he had brutally kicked to death just six years before, he established the empire as the dominant force in the known world. He was mourned by friends and foe alike.

Basil II Bulgaroktonos
January 976 – December 1025

Basil's character was two-fold, for he easily adapted himself both to the crisis of war and the calm of peace. He was a villain in wartime, and an emperor in peace.

MICHAEL PSELLOS, EARLY 1060S

The reign of Basil II marked the highpoint not only of the Macedonian dynasty, but indeed the whole of the medieval Byzantine Empire. There were periods of glory and strength among the many reigns that followed, but never would the might of the empire's army, the extent of its territories or the influence of the Orthodox church be matched again. To many historians, the death of Basil II in 1025 marked the beginning of the long, slow decline over the next four centuries that ultimately led to the Ottoman Conquest of 1453. (This view would seem unfair, since the empire continued to flourish until the 12th century.) But the fact remains that, for almost fifty years, Basil II ruled supreme as a true autocrat, highly involved with all aspects of the state: its government, its military and its church. It was a time when the empire enjoyed great power.

It was not, however, an easy start. His father, the rather ineffectual Romanos II, had died when Basil was just 5 years old, and he and his younger brother, the future Constantine VIII, were left with their mother, the redoubtable Theophano, to look after them. It was their great-uncle, the eunuch Basil Lekapenos, the trusted *parakoimomenos*, who assumed the role of father figure and true guardian of the future emperors.

A childhood spent in idle pleasure, his ceremonial duties a mere formality, Basil would have learned little of the ways of statecraft and government before the death of John Tzimiskes in 976. However, as soon as he became emperor, at the age of 18, there emerged two rival contenders for the throne, both of them very capable generals from powerful families and both equally hungry to hold supreme power: Bardas Skleros, the brother-in-law of Tzimiskes, and Bardas Phokas, a nephew of Nikephoros Phokas. In truth, Skleros's uprising was aimed more at the eunuch Basil than the young Macedonian prince, as it was the eunuch who controlled the government and had done so since the time of Romanos I Lekapenos. The eunuch Basil cleverly turned to Bardas Phokas for help against the powerful Skleros, who was marching towards the capital and defeating all the imperial forces in his way. Accepting a proposal put forward by the eunuch, who hoped to protect the young emperor, the two titans met, and in true medieval style fought in single combat in front of their armies. There are differing accounts of their fight, but it is possible that Skleros broke the established rules of engagement, striking Bardas Phokas on the head with his sword before his opponent was ready. Stunned but not wounded, Phokas returned the assault, and Skleros retreated, frightened and humiliated, whereupon the two armies fought and the forces of Phokas emerged victorious. Skleros retreated to the court of the caliph in Baghdad. For the moment, Basil II was safe.

In 985, Basil had a dispute with his great-uncle, doubtless the result of resentment that had been brewing for many years. Basil II had now fought wars, witnessed the machinations of power and experienced life as emperor: now he wanted it all for himself. Basil Lekapenos, trusted servant of the imperial throne for so long, was now in the way of the new emperor's ambitions and had to be moved aside. Basil II dismissed his erstwhile protector, banishing him from the capital and sending him into exile, where he died shortly afterwards. The new Basil II – tougher, more single-minded – had emerged.

Another uprising had begun, this time more organized and powerful than before. It was led by the same two pretenders, Bardas Skleros and Bardas Phokas, but this time they had joined forces and, what is more, had enlisted many powerful aristocratic families to join them. Fortunately for Basil, the galloping ambition of Phokas meant that he soon turned on his compatriot Skleros, proposing himself as sole emperor and suggesting that Skleros be left in control of Anatolia and remain subservient to him.

The only course of action for Basil II was to seek outside help. He courted the Russian prince Vladimir, promising him the hand of his sister Anna Porphyrogennete in marriage should he come to the aid of the empire and convert his subjects to Orthodox Christianity. The prince of Kiev duly agreed, and so for the first time in the long history of the Byzantine Empire a princess born in the purple was married to an outsider. Desperate times called for desperate measures; and although many felt this was a step too far, Basil had managed to protect his own precarious position, extend the empire's territories and further the influence of the patriarch, all in one bold move. The only unwilling party was his younger sister, who would have seen Vladimir as a barbarian; nevertheless, in 989 she found herself married to him, in the Crimea. The arrival of the Russian troops, all 6,000 Varangians, enabled Basil to defeat Bardas Phokas, and these soldiers would go on to form the basis of the famed Varangian Guard, who remained loyal to successive emperors for centuries.

After thirteen hard years of almost continual internal fighting, Basil II was, at last, unopposed and in total control of the empire.

His alliance with Russia meant that Byzantium had secured its northern borders and extended its reach and influence over an unprecedentedly vast area. The religious and cultural development of Russia was now firmly under Byzantine supervision.

The tireless Basil now turned his attention to the troublesome Fatimid caliphs in the south-east. He marched with his army down to Aleppo and lay siege to the city. In the year 1000, he signed a ten-year truce with the caliph Al-Hakim, which enabled him to leave the area and concentrate on wars with other territories, notably the Khazars around the Black Sea, the Georgians in the east and, most consistently and significantly, the Bulgars to the north. Over the next twenty years Basil fought the great Bulgar leader Samuel and his son Gabriel, which absorbed his time and plundered his resources, but he was determined to end the threat that his troublesome neighbours had posed to the empire for so long.

Basil's campaign culminated in the Battle of Kleidion in 1014, when he defeated Samuel's main army and took 15,000 prisoners. He then decided to have 99 out of every 100 men fully blinded and sent back home, led by one one-eyed man. It is said that, when Samuel saw the thousands of blind men returning, he suffered a stroke and dropped down dead. Despite the resistance of the Bulgar forces, spurred on by Basil's excesses of cruelty, the country was finally defeated and became a vassal state to the Byzantines. The victory gave Basil his nickname, *Bulgaroktonos* or 'The Bulgar-Slayer', and to this day, unsurprisingly, he is hated by the Bulgarians. Further successful conquests in Georgia, Armenia and even southern Italy all added to the glory of the Byzantine Empire in the last few years of Basil's extraordinary reign.

During these years of continuous war on nearly all fronts, Basil did not neglect his duties of state. Foremost among his concerns was a desire to curtail the power of the landowning aristocracy, and to help the condition of the peasant farmers and soldiers under their control. This he did by passing laws and tax reforms to help the populace, notably the so-called *allelengyon*, which obliged the wealthy to cover the tax arrears and underspends of the poor. It made him unpopular with the aristocracy, but Basil had long since stopped caring about what people thought of him and pursued these laws to the full. The value of this form of taxation to the treasury was enormous, keeping it in a financially strong position for years.

Basil's attitude to women is curious but perhaps mirrored his attitude to people in general, in that he showed no personal interest in anyone at all throughout his life. He appears to have had no close friends and to have incited little affection in the people he served so well, despite making large donations to the church, particularly on Mount Athos, and passing decrees that protected rural religious foundations. The flowering of the Macedonian renaissance occurred under his aegis, and yet Basil typically preferred to be on campaign rather than attend the arcane rituals of the Byzantine court or mix with its effete intellectuals.

Basil eventually died while campaigning to recover Sicily, on 15 December 1025. Allowing his seemingly weak-willed brother, Constantine, to succeed him was one of his few errors in what was otherwise the longest and most successful reign of any Byzantine ruler in the preceding seven centuries.

The view that this greatest of emperors had of himself is perhaps best summed up by the words inscribed on his tomb in the church of St John the Theologian at the Hebdomon Palace, outside the city walls. It ran as follows:

From the day that the King of Heaven called upon me to become emperor, the great overlord of the world, no one saw my spear lie idle. I stayed alert throughout my life and protected the children of the New Rome, valiantly campaigning both in the West and at the outposts of the East. O Man, seeing now my tomb here, reward me for my campaigns with your prayers.

Constantine VIII

December 1025 – November 1028

A man of listless character, with no desire for power; he was
physically strong, but mentally weak.
MICHAEL PSELLOS, EARLY 1060S

The monk, politician and historian Michael Psellos paints a picture of Constantine VIII – often unfairly regarded as the man who oversaw the beginning of the decline of the Byzantine Empire – at the age of 65, riddled with gout, clueless as to his responsibilities, weak-willed and petty-minded. Even if, contrary to the view of later historians, Byzantium would remain strong for many decades to come, Constantine was a man who had spent a lifetime within the privileged world of the imperial palace indulging his epicurean appetites, eating fine food, drinking wine and carousing with friends. He had been afforded every opportunity to fulfil at least some of the obligations of being a co-emperor for the previous sixty-two years, and yet he managed to achieve nothing. History's perception of him has not been kind. Perhaps the greatest mistake Basil II made was not fathering an heir, thus allowing the great Macedonian dynasty to be overseen by his younger brother, a living catastrophe.

Yet when, in 962, the 3-year-old Constantine and his elder brother were crowned co-emperors alongside their father, Romanos II, his future looked full of promise. Even after his father's untimely death, he grew up under the protection of his ferocious and mesmerizing mother, Theophano, and two extraordinary men who shared both his mother's bed and the throne itself, Nikephoros Phokas and John Tzimiskes. Yet Constantine showed no interest at all in affairs of state or military matters. He accompanied Basil II on one campaign in 989, but that was the first and last time Constantine took military command – despite his claims to have killed Bardas Phokas personally, according to Psellos.

Constantine married Helena, an aristocrat and daughter of Alypius; the marriage seemed to work for Constantine as he never divorced, had three daughters and was able to fulfil every indulgence while Helena turned a blind eye. His daughters went on to be significant figures in the story of Byzantium, but for the next fifty years Constantine himself accomplished nothing except the art of eating and drinking like a glutton.

Worse still, on the death of Basil in 1025, Constantine displayed a cruel and sadistic nature that had not been in evidence before. According to Psellos, who would have wished to portray Constantine in a negative light compared to Basil, once the role of emperor was thrust upon him, Constantine's weak character caused him to panic, and he lashed out at those around him he believed disloyal or those whom he simply disliked. Blinding was his preferred punishment: he had the eyes of hundreds of people put out for trivial misdemeanours. Torture became commonplace in the dungeons of the palace.

Constantine replaced senior officials with his life-long drinking companions, who were totally unsuited to their tasks, and bowed to pressure from powerful aristocratic landlords, reversing the land laws that Basil had so effectively put in place to help the peasants.

After Constantine had been emperor for only three years, his health had deteriorated to such a degree that it was obvious his end was near. He needed to marry his daughter to a suitable candidate for emperor. The more studious and intelligent of his daughters, Theodora, was hated by her elder sister, Zoe. The apparently spoilt and petulant Zoe had previously been betrothed to the German Otto III, the Holy Roman Emperor, in her early twenties, but upon her arrival in Italy she discovered that he had died and was sent back to Constantinople. Constantine now chose a dull but respectable person named Romanos Argyros, a 60-year-old court official. Doubtless those around Constantine VIII believed Romanos would be easy to manipulate. Three days before his death, Constantine VIII summoned Romanos and his wife, Helena, to his chambers and served him an ultimatum: either he divorced his legitimate wife instantly, married the emperor's daughter Zoe and was proclaimed emperor, or he would be blinded and retired to a monastery. Before Romanos could answer, he was saved by Helena, who immediately cropped off her hair and prepared to enter a monastery, thus ensuring her husband kept his sight and inherited the empire. Three days later Romanos Argyros was married to Zoe, and just three days after that Constantine VIII died in his bed.

Romanos III Argyros
November 1028 – April 1034

A belief in his own sagacity and a concern with things beyond his own intellectual limits led him to commit mistakes on a grandiose scale.
MICHAEL PSELLOS, EARLY 1060S

Romanos III Argyros was born in 968 to an aristocratic land-owning family and lived and worked mostly in Constantinople. Before becoming emperor he held a number of positions in the judiciary and civil service, most notably as one of the judges at the Hippodrome, and eventually as the eparch of Constantinople, the equivalent to mayor. He married Helena, who bore him as many as six children, and lived a somewhat unremarkable but comfortable life as a landowner and government bureaucrat until Constantine VIII called him to his deathbed and put forward the famous 'proposal' that he should marry his daughter and become emperor, or be blinded and retire to a monastery. It was widely believed that Constantine had wanted the esteemed retired noble-man Constantine Dalassenos to marry Zoe, but a close friend of Romanos named Symeon intercepted the emperor's summons to Dalassenos, who therefore never appeared. Romanos, virtually invisible until this moment, was thrust into the limelight.

   MACEDONIAN DYNASTY

Romanos and Zoe were married on 12 November 1028, just three days before the death of Constantine VIII. Romanos III Argyros was crowned emperor at the age of 60, and the problem daughter Zoe Porphyrogennete, now aged 50, was finally married and, what is more, co-regent.

Psellos informs us that almost immediately Romanos began to show delusions of grandeur. He likened himself to Marcus Aurelius and wanted to be known as a 'philosopher king'. Nobody took it seriously, so he decided to be a military genius like his other hero, Trajan, and to lead his army personally into battle. This resulted in a disastrous defeat at the hands of the Mirdasids of Aleppo: against the advice of his generals, who counselled against battle at all, he encamped his troops in a waterless site and left them open to attack near Antioch. It was an unmitigated disaster: hundreds were killed, and Romanos scuttled away to save his skin. He was fortunate in having the brilliant general George Maniakes close at hand, who did achieve military victories elsewhere, but the populace correctly attributed none of this subsequent success to Romanos. Like Constantine before him, Romanos repealed more of the popular egalitarian laws that taxed the landowners, instead looking after his own kind and placing more financial burden on the serfs. He even confiscated wealth from Zoe, thus alienating her and angering the people in one stroke. He showered monks with gold, commissioned churches to be built, including the grand and expensive St Mary Peribleptos, and spent a considerable sum restoring the church of the Mother of God at Blachernae with silver and gold. While work was being carried out there, an icon painted on wood was discovered, which subsequently became a very popular and much copied iconic form of the Virgin.

Zoe's younger sister Theodora allegedly attempted several insurrections against Romanos and was eventually tonsured by Zoe, banished from the palace and incarcerated in a convent. Having left much of the administration of the state in the hands of the capable but self-serving eunuch John, he gradually lost control of the tools of government and distanced himself further from the people, spending ever more money on expensive, self-aggrandizing building works.

John introduced his brothers into the orbit of power, including the very young and handsome Michael of Paphlagonia, who was to be the cause of Romanos's ultimate undoing, as he and Zoe became lovers. Romanos III made the fatal mistake of ignoring his wife, forgetting that all his power derived from his marriage to her and the association with the royal bloodline. The populace still had enormous affection for the Macedonian dynasty and always held both Zoe and Theodora in high esteem.

In his final weeks Romanos became mysteriously ill. Zoe had been flaunting her affair with Michael under her husband's nose and, although he confronted both John and Michael about it, they assured him (both swearing on holy relics) of their innocence. The couple were almost certainly poisoning Romanos using hellebore, and in the last few weeks of his life he lost his hair, suggesting that the poison was taking effect. Michael and Zoe ultimately grew impatient and arranged for him to be strangled and drowned in his bath.

The patriarch Alexis was summoned to the palace; he was horrified to see the near naked corpse of Romanos III, before a door was flung open to reveal Zoe and Michael seated on thrones waiting to be confirmed as joint emperors.

Romanos had greatness thrust upon him and was never capable of carrying it effectively. Michael Psellos, the great intellectual giant of the period, who met him when he was a young man at court, had little good to say about him. His marriage to Zoe had elevated him to the role of emperor, and it was she who was the cause of his death.

Michael IV the Paphlagonian
April 1034 – December 1041

I cannot fail to applaud his fear of Zoe, lest he too should be involved in calamity, like Romanos.
MICHAEL PSELLOS, EARLY 1060S

The end of the great Macedonian dynasty established by Basil I in 867 was now in sight. The empress Zoe, daughter of Constantine VIII and niece of Basil II, along with her monastic younger sister, were the last of the Macedonian bloodline to survive. Zoe had just murdered her first husband, the emperor Romanos III, after starting an affair with the dashing young Michael of Paphlagonia, and married him immediately, making him Michael IV. When they started their affair, Michael was around 19 years old and Zoe was 53.

Born into a family of peasants in Paphlagonia, an area today in northern Turkey bordering on the Black Sea, Michael had at least four older brothers and one sister; two of the brothers were eunuchs, John and Constantine, and the other two, George and Niketas, were 'bearded men'. Before Michael was attached to the imperial court, he and his family were money changers and quite possibly forgers of coins. The family was clearly upwardly mobile, and it was his older and influential brother John who ultimately enabled Michael to become emperor. Paphlagonia was an area famed for its supply of eunuchs to the palace of Constantinople. It was not uncommon for parents to have their sons castrated so that they might have more chance of obtaining important positions at court. This may seem brutal to our modern sensibility, but eunuchs were much admired and appreciated in the early Middle Ages, and the practice of castration was not seen as very different from sending a daughter to the court to marry upwards.

As one such successful eunuch, John had become the trusted confidant of the emperor Basil II and was given the prestigious position of *orphanotrophos*, an official role running the main orphanage in

Constantinople, before being made *protonotarios*, effectively Basil's chief of staff. John the Orphanotrophos introduced all his brothers to the court, and it was he who singled out his dashing youngest brother Michael to become the lover of the empress Zoe.

Michael was described as handsome and charming, and his seduction of the spoilt, sexually frustrated and unhappy Zoe seemed to have happened very easily. Ignored by her husband and still childless, Zoe was desperate for an heir. However, she seemed to ignore the fact that she was already over 50 years old and obviously incapable of becoming pregnant. John and Michael between them, using false witnesses and playing on omens and superstitions, preyed on her desperation and made her believe it was possible to have a child and that her exciting affair with the young Michael could last for ever. And so the plot to murder Romanos III was hatched.

Whether it was Zoe or Michael who actually carried out the murder or whether, more likely, they simply arranged for it to happen, we cannot tell, but the fact that they were married the next day, on Good Friday, 12 April 1034, suggests that they were certainly complicit. In order for them to marry so quickly, John had contacted important dignitaries all over the empire stating that Romanos III had decreed that Michael should marry his widow and become emperor. Nobody seems to have objected except Constantine Dalassenos, the elderly statesman who (according to Psellos) asked the question, 'Why, when there are so many excellent men of distinguished families and noble birth, a vulgar threepence-a-day man should be preferred above all others?' John moved quickly to neutralize him, banishing him from the capital. The marriage was authorized and performed by the patriarch Alexis I, who was initially horrified but, when given 50 pounds of gold for the clergy and 50 pounds of gold for himself, was only too happy to oblige.

As soon as Michael IV became emperor, life did change for Zoe, but not for the better. First, Michael revealed that he was epileptic. His condition would worsen throughout his life and eventually lead to severe dropsy (edema). Second, he was instantly afraid that Zoe would do to him what he had witnessed her do to her first husband. To prevent this from happening he banished her to the *gynaikeion*, a remote part of the palace reserved for women, had all her eunuchs and close staff dismissed, and put her under the supervision of his brother John the Orphanotrophos.

Portents were taken very seriously at this time, and at the eleventh hour of Easter Day, soon after Michael had been crowned, there was a hailstorm so violent that crops and trees were destroyed, houses collapsed, and a small famine ensued the next year. On the following Sunday there was a falling star so bright that people believed it to be the sun. It was at this point that Michael succumbed to his worst epileptic fit, and people began to believe that he was possessed by a demon.

When Michael was struck by dropsy, there were continuous earthquakes, frequent flooding and an outbreak of quinsy (an infectious disease that swells the tonsils and throat) so terrible that 'the living were unable to carry away the dead'. It culminated with a large earthquake that killed thousands and virtually destroyed the city of Smyrna. People attributed these disasters to the vile way in which Michael IV had become emperor. He seemed to be racked with guilt over his involvement in the murder of Romanos III, and turned more and more to the church for some kind of absolution, donating money to every priest, making endowments to monasteries and even paying people to enable him to become godfather to their children.

Much of this time Michael resided in Thessalonica, where he frequented the holy tomb of the martyr Demetrios, trying to atone for his sins and sampling every cure for his epilepsy that he could find. But nothing worked, and he simply became worse. Psellos maintained that he was a wonderful man, honest, pious and generous, and were it not for his illness would have been considered as one of the finest of all emperors.

Michael left two lasting legacies. He achieved a peace treaty with the Fatimids of Egypt that lasted thirty years and meant he could concentrate on the north and the east in terms of territorial defence and expansion. And in Bulgaria during his last year, he led an army and defeated Deleanos and Ibatzes, two insurgents who had been leading rebellions against the empire for some time, and brought them back to the capital in chains. There were also many internal rebellions against Michael in the last years of his reign, mainly aimed at the increasing influence and behaviour of his brother, who held the real power, but through a combination of diplomacy, politicking, bribery and force he prevented any of them from being successful.

On 10 December 1041 Michael finally succumbed to his illness and died. John the Orphanotrophos, ever the politician, had prepared the way for succession by inviting the imperial couple to adopt the son of his and Michael's sister as their son. The nephew of the dying emperor, Michael V Kalaphates, became the new Emperor of the Romans. Like Michael IV before him, he too was a teenager.

Michael IV died a somewhat defeated and tragic figure, plagued by guilt and hindered by an incurable affliction, his boyish good looks ruined by disease. He nevertheless left the empire in fairly good order and, other than the way in which he took the throne, seemed to possess a strong sense of morality. Fittingly, he refused to see his wife even on his deathbed, and must have associated her closely with the murder of his former emperor. His epilepsy struck him down while still only in his early twenties; had he lived longer, he may well have continued to restore the empire to its former glories.

Michael V Kalaphates
December 1041 – April 1042

The emperor was overwhelmed by the situation and his dreadful misfortune ... and continued to howl and cry aloud.
MICHAEL PSELLOS, EARLY 1060S

Chosen to follow in the footsteps of his uncle Michael IV by his powerful uncle John, perhaps in conjunction with his adoptive mother Zoe, Michael Kalaphates at first seemed a promising choice. Brought up among the elite, he was well educated, a capable administrator and a man of action. Zoe made Michael swear an oath over a sacred relic, the hand of John the Baptist, that he would obey her as his sovereign lady and mother for as long as she lived. The ceremony took place in the church of the Theotokos at Blachernae, and at the same time she banished John the Orphanotrophos from the city and stripped him of all his power. Michael V decided to test the people's loyalty to him and to Zoe by organizing a public procession on Easter Sunday from the palace to the church of the Holy Apostles. He wore the imperial diadem, decked himself out in the finest purple robes and paraded through the city. As he passed by houses and buildings, the people cheered and welcomed him as their emperor. He foolishly took this to be a sign that the people loved him and as confirmation that they no longer needed the bloodline of the Macedonian Zoe to flow through the veins of their new emperor. This proved to be a big mistake.

On returning to his palace, Michael arranged for a large reception; that night, he summoned Zoe and banished her to the Princes' Islands, saying she must become a nun. He demanded that she be tonsured and asked for her hair to be brought to him as proof. The next morning, with all the people assembled in the forum, his proclamation was read out: 'Because Zoe has shown herself ill disposed to my rule, she has been banished by me, and Alexios her like-minded accomplice has been expelled from the church. As for you, my people, if you maintain your favourable disposition towards me, you will acquire great honours and benefits, living an untroubled and quiet life.' But a voice from the crowd cried out: 'We don't want a cross-trampling caulker for emperor, but the original and hereditary mother Zoe.' At that point a massive riot broke out and took hold of the entire city. The people also decided that Theodora, the sister of Zoe, should be brought out of her nunnery and proclaimed co-empress. Michael gave up and went to hide in the monastery of Stoudios to devote himself to a religious life. But the rabble continued to pursue him and eventually dragged him out. Zoe was inclined to banish him and forgive, but Theodora was not. She ordered that Michael be publicly blinded and then banished to the monastery of Elegmoi in Bithynia. He had reigned for four months and five days, and it had been an unmitigated disaster. Now it was the turn of Zoe and Theodora, the last remaining survivors of the Macedonian dynasty, to try to rule the empire together. This was always going to be problematic, however: they had loathed each other for forty years.

Zoe Porphyrogennete
& Theodora Porphyrogennete
April 1042 – June 1042

The elder, Zoe, was quicker to understand things, but slower to articulate them. With Theodora ... it was just the reverse in both respects. To put it quite candidly ... neither of them was equipped to govern.
MICHAEL PSELLOS, EARLY 1060S

Zoe Porphyrogennete was the middle of three daughters born to Constantine VIII and Helena in 978, and she reigned as empress from 11 November 1028 until her death in 1050. Uniquely among empresses, she ruled alongside five different people: three husbands,

Romanos III, Michael IV, and Constantine IX; her adopted son, Michael V; and her younger sister, Theodora. Yet her life was not a happy one, and the circumstances of her upbringing and her peculiar role in the empire undoubtedly shaped the fickle, petulant, spoilt-child personality that was to define her, both during her lifetime and after her death. To the people of Constantinople, she was known as 'Mother', and throughout nearly all of her long and troubled life she enjoyed a level of affection and loyalty among them.

Zoe's elder sister, Eudokia, was badly scarred after contracting smallpox as a child and was packed off to a convent at an early age. Zoe's younger sister, Theodora, described as very plain, spent most of her time hidden in the women's quarters of the palace with Zoe, or in various monasteries.

Little was written about Zoe until she was in her early twenties and offered as a bride to the Holy Roman Emperor Otto III. This arrangement would have seemed a glamorous and exciting way out of her privileged but humdrum life, so when the marriage was called off it must have been difficult for the young Zoe. The three girls were thus confined to a life within the walls of the palace or in the church. This was not so unbearable for Eudokia (as far as we know) or for Theodora, but to Zoe, evidently more headstrong and distracted, this must have felt like purgatory. She hated Theodora, the more thoughtful, quiet and disapproving younger sister with whom she was forced to spend time.

Zoe remained in this state of limbo until Basil II died in 1025, making his brother Constantine VIII sole emperor. Zoe accepted Romanos Argyros as her husband, and on 12 November 1028 they were married in the imperial chapel. Three days later Constantine VIII was dead, and Zoe was at last 'queen' of the palace. One of the first things she did was to banish Theodora to the Petrion monastery, where she forced her to take religious vows.

Zoe's marriage to Romanos III was short-lived, and short on love, and finished when she fell for the young Michael IV, whereupon the two conspired together to murder Romanos. The marriage to

Michael IV was also a disaster, as he soon tired of her and had her banished back to the women's quarters. Zoe adopted Michael V, only to be banished by him to a monastery on one of the Princes' Islands. When he proved himself to be an inept and foolhardy ruler, the mob forced Theodora and Zoe, as the last in line of the much-loved Macedonians, to rule jointly. Since Zoe's hatred of Theodora meant that they could not cope with ruling together, Zoe found a third husband, a charming older lover named Constantine Monomachos, whom she married on 11 June 1042, making him Constantine IX.

Michael Psellos, the extraordinary chronicler of this age, devotes much time to Zoe and the fascinating contradictions of her character. She loved to spend the money her brilliant uncle Basil II had accumulated during his reign, but she was not concerned with replenishing the state coffers. She did not really spend it on herself, however, preferring to wear plain white robes rather than the bejewelled gowns she could have chosen. She became an expert in making perfumes, and because she hated fresh air always had her apartments scented with her own concoctions. Despite never finding true love, she allowed her third husband, Constantine IX Monomachos, to keep his mistress in the palace, and somehow this *ménage à trois* seemed to work. As Zoe passed into her late sixties and early seventies, Psellos writes of her becoming obsessed with a particular icon that she carried around with her everywhere and would talk to at length. An extraordinary and generally unhappy life had come to its end. Theodora would be sole empress – but not just yet.

Constantine IX Monomachos

June 1042 – January 1055

*Taking no interest in the responsibilities of power, but seeking
recreation in a multitude of pleasures, he was preparing the healthy
body of the empire for a thousand maladies destined to attack it in
the years to come.*

Michael Psellos, early 1060s

Constantine IX Monomachos had lived a full life before he was summoned back to Constantinople from his place of exile in Mytilene.
He was there because his father, Theodosios Monomachos, an official at the court of Basil II, had been suspected of conspiring against
the crown and had been banished, along with his family. To complicate matters further, the emperor Michael IV had suspected his wife
of having an affair with the handsome Constantine, sending him
away from the capital a second time. The young Constantine had
married twice, his second wife being a niece of Romanos III, and
now, presumably, that he was back in favour he was asked yet again
to return to Constantinople to help fix the mess caused by the joint
rule of the aged sisters Zoe and Theodora. Constantine accepted the
offer of marriage without hesitation. Despite the fact that both parties had been married twice before, the patriarch Alexius I granted
them a dispensation. Zoe and Constantine were duly joined in matrimony on 11 June 1042. The next day, Constantine IX was crowned
co-emperor alongside Zoe and Theodora.

Constantine was a charmer. He had enticed the aged Zoe to
pick him as her third husband, and he apparently delighted many
at court with his generosity, easy manner and good looks. He
even slept with no security and the door to his quarters unlocked,
claiming that God alone had chosen him to be emperor, and it was
God alone who protected him.

The tragedy of Constantine IX was that he never grasped the
qualities a good emperor was supposed to possess. He acted the

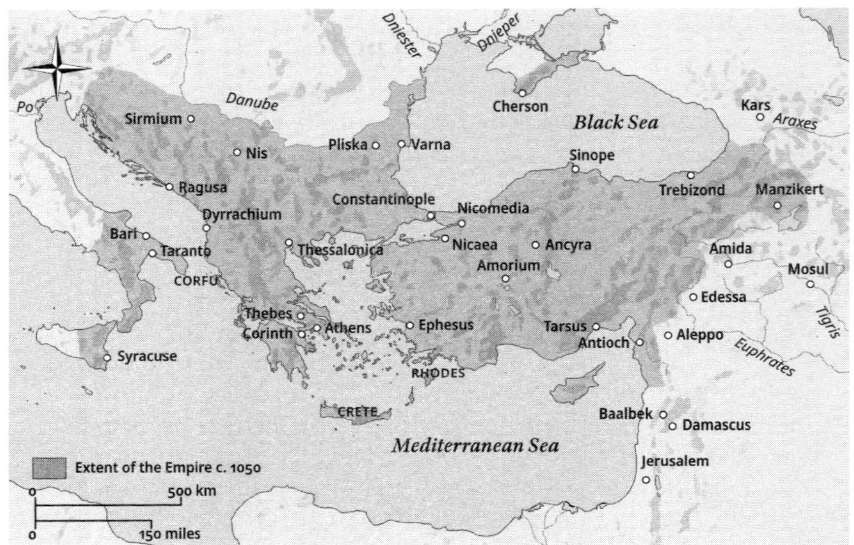

part during his entire reign rather than actually living it. Oblivious to the empire's slow but inevitable disintegration, he lived a life of pleasure and largesse. There were aspects of daily life that flourished under him: it was a brilliant time for the intellectuals at court, and Constantine was surrounded by extraordinary men, foremost among them Michael Psellos, known as 'Consul of the Philosophers', but also the patriarch and philosopher Constantine Leichoudes; John Mauropous, the great political and religious poet; and John Xiphilinos, a historian and a dominant figure at the court. Artists, too, found favour, as buildings were refurbished or built from scratch across the length and breadth of the empire. Constantine began extensive repairs to the church of the Holy Sepulchre in Jerusalem, which had been badly damaged by the caliph Al-Hakim bi-Amr Allah three decades earlier. No expense was spared in these endeavours, and life seemed privileged and

   MACEDONIAN DYNASTY

splendid, both in the capital and in the other major cities of the empire. But it was coming at a great cost.

Two major setbacks during these years had a long-lasting and damaging effect on the empire, and by neither issue did Constantine IX seem to be concerned. First, the great Byzantine army that had been built up by Basil II and that had dominated the arena for so long, began to be dismantled. This was the continuation of an earlier policy that had been accelerated owing to Constantine's anti-military instincts; he favoured his own class, and friends who all came from the civil landowning aristocracy. The number of peasant-soldier small landowners gradually declined as the wealthier barons bought up all available lands, thus eroding the base of soldiers who could be called up in times of war. This in turn meant that there was more dependence on foreign mercenaries to fight on behalf of the empire. Varangians from Russia, Normans from Italy and France, and Anglo-Saxons from England all joined at great expense and with little genuine loyalty.

The Kievan Rus', a league of North European peoples, attacked Constantinople in 1043 but were repelled with the use of 'Greek fire'. Constantine then followed the time-honoured tradition of diplomatically solving such problems through intermarriage, this time marrying off a female relative to the Russian prince Vsevolod I of Kiev, thus ensuring the end of these particular hostilities.

Peace was short-lived elsewhere, however, as Constantine sought to annex Armenia, thereby exposing him to the Seljuk Turks, a group of Turkic nomads who would eventually cripple the empire. In 1047 Constantine's nephew Leo Tornikios – who according to Psellos 'reeked of Macedonian arrogance ... his disposition was crafty and his mind was perpetually open to revolutionary ideas' – decided to rebel against his uncle and marched to Constantinople. Leo was eventually captured and blinded and presumably died, as he was never heard of again. The constant fighting weakened the imperial troops and allowed another group of Turkic nomadic peoples, the Pechenegs, to flood into the area and occupy it for many years. The Seljuks also took advantage of the turmoil and attacked. The Byzantine forces had met their match, and in a battle at Ardzen, in the east of Anatolia, the town and its 800 churches were sacked and destroyed, with the loss of some 150,000 people.

The second disaster of Constantine's reign was the further break-down in relations between the Western and Eastern churches, which had lasting repercussions. Relations with the West never fully recovered, just as new and old enemies were gaining strength. The cause of the schism was the same unresolved debate that surrounded several questions of religious doctrine: the so-called 'Filioque controversy', which touched on the origins of the Holy Spirit; the nature of the Holy Trinity; and differences in liturgical practice such as the use of leavened or unleavened bread. The refusal on both sides to agree to any kind of compromise or understanding led to the leader of each church excommunicating the other. During this period Constantine IX was trying to unite forces to fight the Normans, who had taken over the whole of Sicily and southern Italy, but the Christian alliance that he so needed was impossible.

Perhaps the way that he managed to keep his mistress, Maria Skleraina, at court the whole time he was emperor offers an insight into the mind and world of Constantine. Zoe seemed to turn a blind eye to the affair, and Maria even acquired the title of *sebaste*, meaning 'venerable'. Charm allowed Constantine to thrive at court, but could not help the empire strengthen its hold on its territories. He died in 1055.

Theodora Porphyrogennete
January 1055 – August 1056

Everyone was agreed that for the Roman Empire to be governed by a woman instead of a man was improper ... But one must also say that in everything that followed, the empire flourished and its glory increased.
MICHAEL PSELLOS, EARLY 1060S

                    MACEDONIAN DYNASTY

The aged spinster Theodora, last surviving descendant of the great founder of the Macedonian dynasty, Basil I, came to the throne aged over 70, opposed by some and adored by many.

Theodora had spent years living as a nun before fate beckoned her back to the centre of power with the overthrow of Michael V and the insistence that she share the throne with her hated sister Zoe. She was the junior empress in this arrangement, and her throne was even placed a few paces behind Zoe's at state occasions. This situation could never continue, and when Zoe chose her third husband, Constantine Monomachus, to marry her and become emperor, Theodora remained out of the way within the palace. She was there when Constantine died in 1055, finally becoming sole empress.

Theodora always commanded the loyalty of the people of Constantinople, and this, combined with her strong will and sense of entitlement, made her a force to be reckoned with from the moment she began to rule alone. Immediately she removed many of the senior officials she believed had opposed her, among them the leader of the European forces, Nikephoros Bryennios, and, more significantly, Isaac Komnenos, the successful commander of forces in Anatolia. She clashed with the patriarch Michael Kerularios, perhaps on account of her appointment of clerics to the church, as he refused to believe that a mere woman had the right to act in this way.

Psellos claims that Theodora was a competent ruler, efficient and decisive, promulgating laws, dismissing the church's attempts to dethrone her, and generally being a proactive and worthy empress. She would not, however, engage in the important question of who was to succeed her. Only when she was struck down with appendicitis, at the age of 77, would she agree to having the elderly patrician Michael Bringas anointed as her successor.

The hapless and unsuitable Bringas was to rule for one more year as part of the Macedonian line, with Theodora, the last direct descendant of that great dynasty, ending what had clearly been considered by many as the apogee of the Byzantine Empire.

NON-DYNASTIC RULER

Michael VI Stratiotikos
August 1056 – August 1057

A simple and uncomplicated man who, from childhood, had been occupied only with military matters and knew nothing about anything else. He was already over the hill and entering the age in which it is better to be retired.

JOHN SKYLITZES, SECOND HALF OF 11TH CENTURY

Little is known of Michael Bringas until he was chosen by Theodora's ministers to be the next emperor. He was already elderly, and although he was called *Stratiotikos* (meaning 'warlike', but only because he had been a finance minister in the service of the military), he was more commonly known as Michael 'the Aged'. He was childless and unmarried, and must have seemed a perfect choice for puppet emperor to the powerful court eunuchs and Theodora's trusted adviser Leo Paraspondylos, who wished to run the empire in his own way.

Michael VI was not quite the pawn his ministers had hoped for, but he was at best ineffectual. He helped his friends and cronies take high positions in government, managed to alienate many hardworking officials and, most dangerously of all, insulted the generals Isaac Komnenos and Katakalon Kekaumenos. This was a grave error of judgment that led to his eventual downfall, and followed the pattern that Constantine IX had set in favouring civil authorities over the military. In this case, the entire military establishment came together and joined forces with Komnenos to pronounce him emperor on 8 June 1057. Michael VI could not tolerate this challenge and sent his own forces to do battle with Komnenos outside Nicaea. There had been many coups in the history of Byzantium, but this was a violent and deliberate step towards civil war. The battle did not last long, and the emperor's forces were defeated easily.

Michael VI's short and impotent reign had lasted barely a year, and brought two glorious centuries of Macedonian rule to a final and definite end. His abdication also ushered in a different type of leader that had been missing from the empire for too long: a strong soldier, from a rich and powerful family, who was politically astute enough to see the dangers that were surrounding the empire and also had the drive to do something about it. A new dynasty, that of the Komnenoi, was going to bring radical change to the capital.

KOMNENIAN DYNASTY

(I: 1057–1059)

The Komnenos family produced five emperors who ruled the empire for over a hundred years, with a brief interlude, at the end of the 11th century, when the Doukas family were in power. The Komnenoi stabilized the economy, strengthened the military and, most famously, dealt with the Crusaders who invaded their lands during the First, Second and Third Crusades. Communication with the West was greatly increased, both politically and culturally. Through the efforts of Manuel I, Byzantine influence spread through the Roman Catholic West, with Byzantine art, culture and political thought significantly affecting the development of Western art and philosophy.

Isaac I Komnenos

September 1057 – December 1059

He was so gracious and pleasant on one occasion, and yet on another – why, even his face changed, his eyes flashed, and his brow, to put it metaphorically, hung threateningly over the clear light of his soul like a dark cloud.

MICHAEL PSELLOS, EARLY 1060S

It is telling that Isaac Komnenos decided to portray himself on his coins with a drawn sword instead of holding a *labarum*, the imperial standard, as was more traditional. He was the first emperor ever to do so, and it was a statement of intent: 'I am a soldier, and this is the time of the soldier-emperor.' The son of Manuel Komnenos, a high-ranking and wealthy commander of the east under Basil II,

Isaac was put under the care of the emperor in the monastery of Stoudios along with his brother when his father died in 1020. The boys' mother had died when they were very young, and they were educated by the best tutors and taught the rudiments of military life. They both joined the Hetaireia, a division of the imperial body-guard, at about the age of 20. This institutionalized childhood, spent in an environment devoid of women, run on either monkish or military lines, must have shaped the young man into the slightly charmless, irascible, yet driven character he would later become.

Isaac married a princess, Catherine of Bulgaria, in 1025; he was 18 and she was 15 years old, and he seems to have been content with her. Catherine, who was later made *augusta* when Isaac took the throne, had two children with him: a son, Manuel, who died as a teenager, and a daughter, Maria.

Isaac was reluctant to rebel against his reigning emperor, but had been twice slighted by the remnants of the Macedonian line. Theodora had dismissed him from his job as commander-in-chief of the east, and had him replaced by one of her cronies, a eunuch named Theodore. He was once more publicly insulted when her successor, Michael VI Stratiotikos, asked him to resume his role but without restoring the privileges and money that had originally been taken from him.

With the help of other generals and members of the military aristocracy, among them Nikephoros Botaneiates, Romanos Skleros and Michael Bourtzes, Isaac gathered his army and went into battle against the forces loyal to Michael VI, defeating them on 20 August 1057 at the Battle of Hades. Immediately Michael pan-icked and sued for peace, sending his brilliant group of courtiers, Leo Alopos, Michael Psellos and Constantine Leichoudes, to offer Isaac the position of *caesar* and a promise that he would inherit the throne. According to Psellos, Isaac agreed, but in the interim, before Michael learned of his acceptance, a crowd of both digni-taries and the common people started to rebel against Michael VI, demanding that Isaac be made emperor immediately. The balance of power was tipped in Isaac's favour when the powerful and popular patriarch Michael Keroularios demanded that Michael step down, accept tonsure and retire to a monastery. This Michael did, and Isaac was proclaimed emperor on 1 September 1057 in Hagia Sophia by the patriarch himself.

Isaac's tenure as emperor was marked by hard work and ceaseless activity, mainly connected with reforms of the army and the civil administration. Psellos remarked that, on the day Isaac was crowned emperor, he did not even change his clothes but went straight to work in his headquarters.

Feeling indebted to Keroularios, Isaac broke with centuries-old tradition and transferred his authority over church affairs to him, on the understanding that the patriarch would not interfere with matters of state. Isaac was probably influenced in his decision by his lack of interest in the church and an obsession with sorting out the civil bureaucracy and restoring power to the army and the military aristocracy. Although people disagreed with this policy direction, Isaac devoted all his energy to his reforms, undoing many of the actions of his predecessors. He cut salaries from the civilian nobility, confiscated privileges, reclaimed land that had been handed out as favours, and was generally unrelenting in his pursuit of funds for the army he so desperately wished to build up. He might have been successful if he had not then begun to interfere with the church, confiscating their lands and re-appropriating gifts. The strong-willed patriarch Keroularios felt this was a betrayal of their previous agreement; since he had been acting as though he were on an equal footing with the emperor, even trying on the imperial purple boots that only the emperor was supposed to wear, Keroularios publicly attacked the emperor's actions. This was too much for Isaac. Mindful of the patriarch's popularity within the walls of Constantinople, he waited until Keroularios had left the city on a visit to a monastery before having him arrested. Keroularios was then tried by a hastily arranged synod and condemned as a virtual heretic. Before the

     KOMNENIAN DYNASTY

synod could formally pronounce the removal of Keroularios from his position, however, he contracted a sudden and fatal illness and died on 21 January 1059. Isaac then gave the role of patriarch to Constantine Leichoudes.

Isaac was also active on the borders of the empire, trying to subdue the Georgians and the Armenians and to manage the growing threat represented by the newly established Seljuk Turks. He led the army into battle himself on the northern borders with Bulgaria, and managed to defeat or come to terms with the Hungarians and the Pechenegs. On his return to Constantinople, Isaac was out hunting when he was caught in a terrible storm. Reports claim that he was struck by lightning and fell off his horse. Many took this as a bad omen. Isaac fell ill with pneumonia and was rushed back to Constantinople.

Despite the protestations of his family, he selected Constantine Doukas as his successor, on 22 November 1059. Doukas had married Keroularios's niece, Eudokia Makrembolitissa, some years before. Despite the fact that he was a high-ranking official from a famous and wealthy family, it was a strange appointment.

Isaac did not succumb to his illness, and in fact lived on for another year as a monk at the monastery where he had spent his childhood, Stoudios, in the south of the city. He had seen the problems of the empire – the weakening of the army, the vulnerability of its borders, the fiscal mismanagement – and had started to do something about it, but a premature death left his potential unfulfilled.

DOUKID DYNASTY

(1059–1081)

The Doukas family's brief period of rule was one of military defeat and territorial loss. The Seljuk Turks marched relentlessly through Anatolia, famously defeating the Byzantine army at the Battle of Manzikert in 1071. To the north, the Serbs invaded most of the empire's lands in the Balkans, and in Italy the Normans removed the Byzantines from Italy altogether. It was only the marriage of Irene Doukaina to the talented young general Alexios Komnenos that saved the empire from potential collapse.

Constantine X Doukas

December 1059 – May 1067

He was delightful with his children, joining gladly in their games, laughing at their baby-talk, often romping with them.

He took a peculiar pleasure in my company. No one else had the same calming influence upon him. If I failed to present myself to him several times a day, he would complain about it and fret.
MICHAEL PSELLOS, MID-1070S

Constantine X Doukas was never suited to being an emperor. He had spent most of his life in comfortable privilege: he came from a distinguished and wealthy family, and married into another when he took Eudokia Makrembolitissa, the niece of the great patriarch Michael Keroularios, as his second wife. Little is known of his first wife, the daughter of Constantine Dalassenos, with whom he had no children.

Constantine Doukas first appears in the records as the victim of another clear-out of the nobility by John the Orphanotrophos during the reign of Michael IV. He was accused of supporting a rebellion and faded from view until the ailing Isaac I named him as his successor. With his second wife, Eudokia, he had many children: sons Michael, Andronikos and Constantius, and two daughters, Anna and Zoe. He was known as a scholar and a great orator, although he appears to have been something of a pedant in debate, loving nothing more than lengthy arguments on obscure points of philosophy and law. He was universally recognized as being a decent, charming man, who had few enemies and little stomach for the tougher side that went with the role. Unfortunately, this was not the time for a gentle and kindly emperor: the barbarians were gathering at the gates.

Constantine X curried favour with his class by reinstating those who had been banished by Isaac I, bestowing gifts on those members of the civil aristocracy that he favoured and, most baffling and damaging of all, ignoring the military divisions and starving them of funds that Isaac I had set in place.

Early on in Constantine's rule there was an attempted coup against him, successfully squashed by his more dynamic brother John, but it showed up his fragile grip on power. Revealingly, Constantine X never sentenced anyone to death during his reign, and never had people blinded or disfigured as was common during these times. The flip side was his lack of attention to military matters and the acceleration of the army's demise. Court life was undoubtedly cultured and pleasant under Constantine, but on the borders of the empire the danger was fast becoming tangible. Not only were the traditional enemies of Byzantium building up their forces and giving rein to expansionist ambitions, but there were new, more vigorous foes appearing on all fronts.

In 1064 the Seljuks appointed a new sultan, Alp Arslan: he was an ambitious, brave and war-like figure who would create havoc for the eastern provinces and make serious inroads into the Anatolian heartland of the empire. Owing to his very strict Orthodox beliefs, Constantine had increasingly singled out, discriminated against and persecuted the Monophysites, who held different views on the nature of Christ. A large part of Armenian Christians were Monophysites, however – a fact that influenced the fall of Armenia to the Seljuk Turks. Why fight for an empire that refused to accept your beliefs? Another separate group of Turks, the Oghuz, were raiding parts of Bulgaria, Macedonia and Greece, and found the underequipped and demotivated Byzantine troops to be no match for them. The Normans, who were ravaging the few remaining parts of Italy that were still under Byzantine control, presented a similar challenge to the new emperor.

Time took its toll on Constantine. By 1066, the aged emperor could see that he would not recover from an illness that had lingered for nearly six months. He summoned Eudokia and made her promise that she would never marry again, thus ensuring a smooth transition for his sons, at this stage too young to reign by themselves. As is fitting, this most temperate of emperors died peacefully in his bed with his family around him, the last to do so for many years. He had been unsuccessful in all but his personal relations with family and friends. The empire he was to place in the hands of the future Romanos IV was weaker and more vulnerable than it had been since the time of Phokas, four centuries earlier.

Romanos IV Diogenes
January 1068 – August 1071

For the most part he was a hypocrite and a show-off.
MICHAEL PSELLOS, MID-1070S

In one aspect, Romanos IV Diogenes was exactly what the empire needed at its darkest hour. He was a nobleman from the distinguished family of Diogenes, which owned half of Cappadocia, and

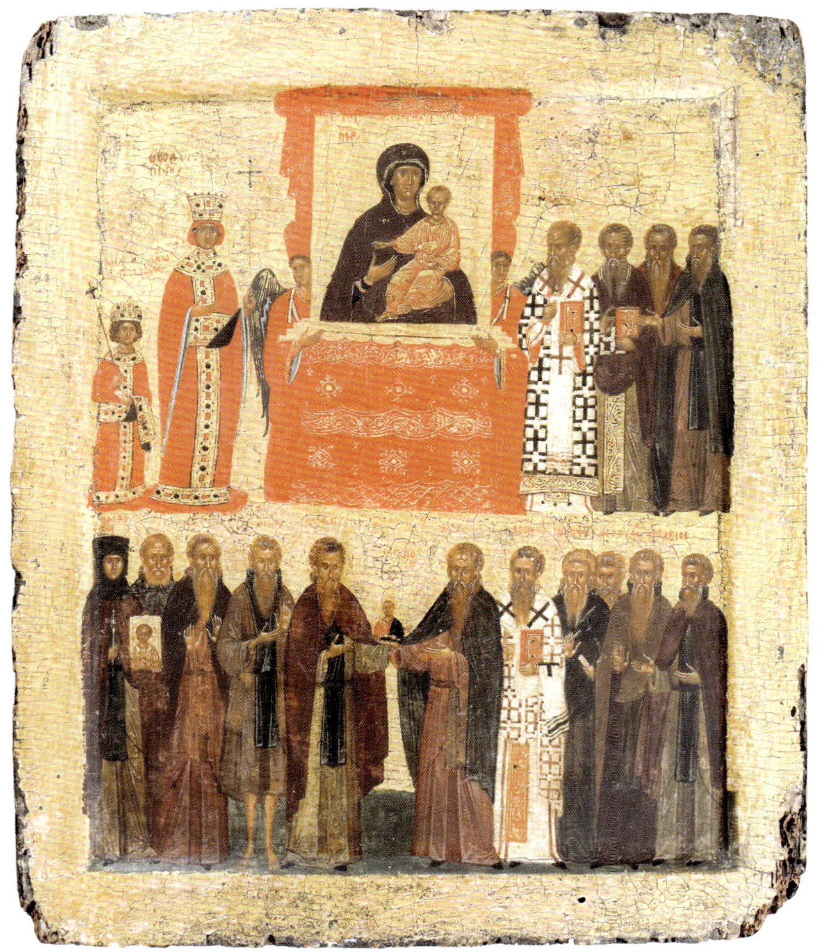

12 The so-called 'Icon of the Triumph of Orthodoxy', late 14th century. Illustrating the importance of images in the Orthodox church, it shows their veneration by those who fought for Orthodoxy during the Iconoclastic period (730–842). Flanking the celebrated Hodegetria icon are the empress Theodora and her son, Michael III, on the left, and the patriarch Methodios on the right.

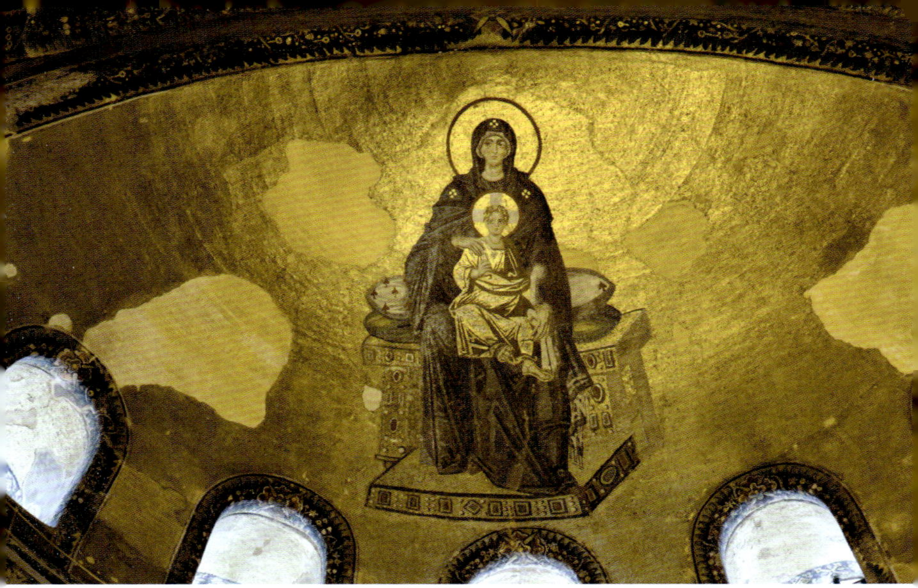

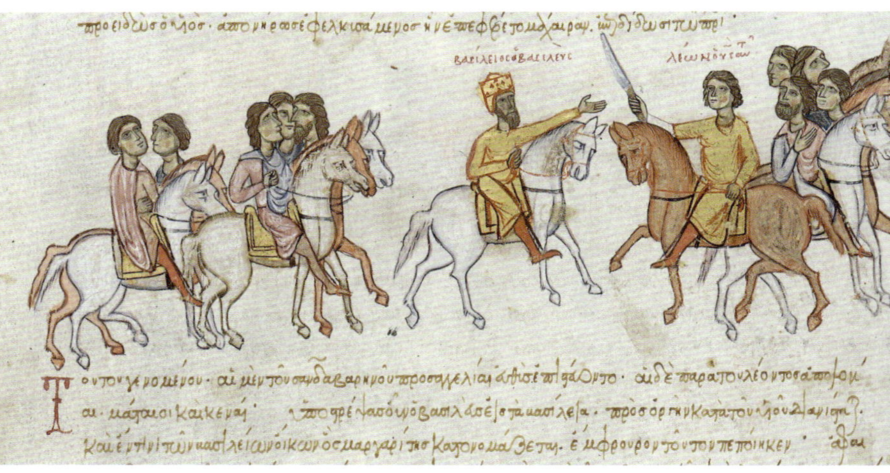

13 Mosaic of the Virgin and Child in the apse of Hagia Sophia, Istanbul, installed during the joint reign of Basil I and Michael III to celebrate the end of Iconoclasm. Patriarch Photios marked the occasion with a homily given on Holy Saturday 867.

14 Miniature from the 12th-century Madrid Skylitzes, showing Leo handing his father Basil I a sword – an act that led to his arrest on charges of attempting to attack the emperor.

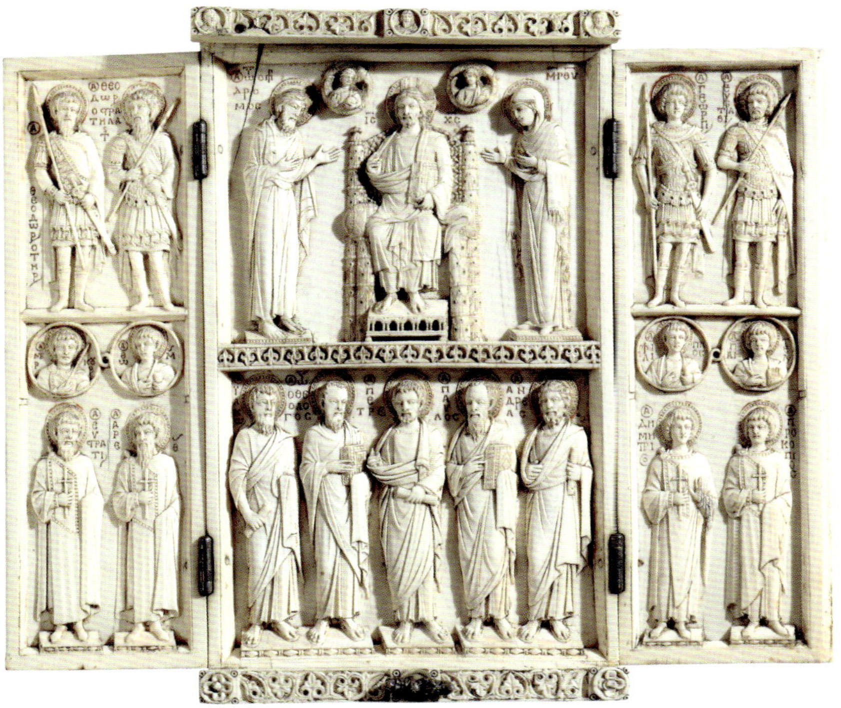

15 The 10th-century Harbaville Triptych, perhaps the finest of all the Macedonian ivory carvings. Despite the formality of the setting, each figure is meticulously carved.

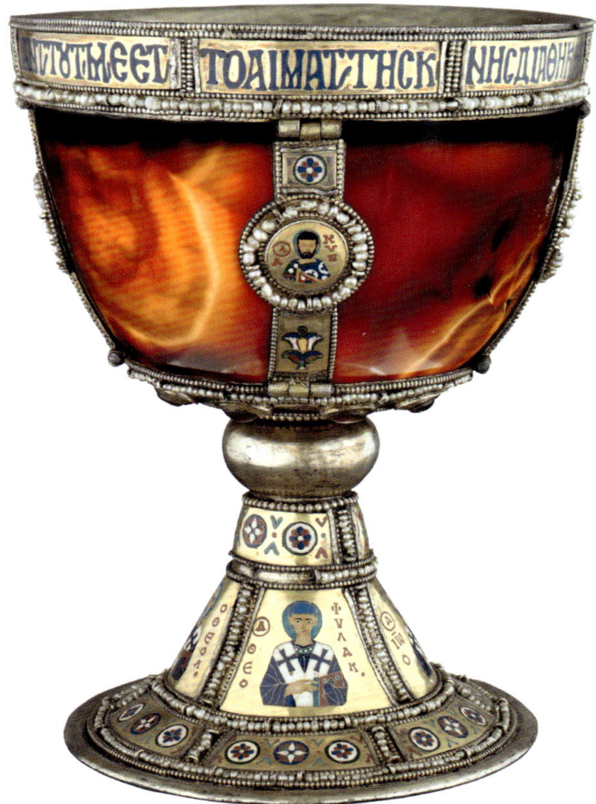

16 The images in enamel around the rim give this vessel its name, the Chalice of the Patriarchs. Dating to *c.* 1000, it is a superb example of court art of the period. The size and splendour of this object, carved from a block of red sardonyx with white flecks, typify the luxury of Constantinople at this time.

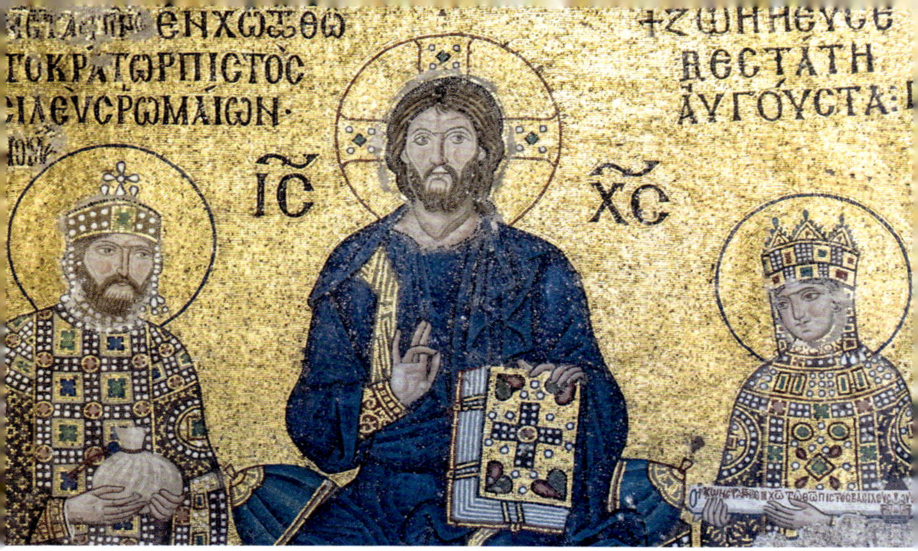

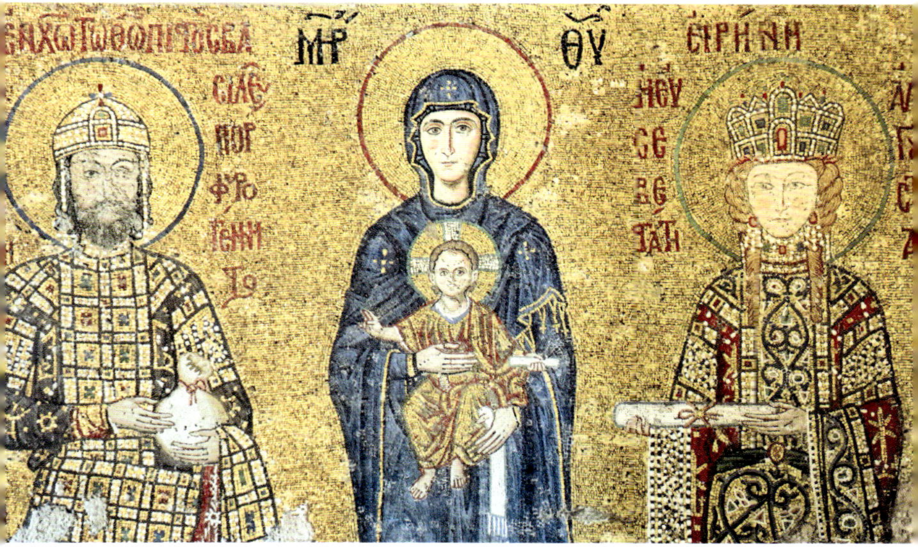

17 The head of Constantine IX (*left*), the third husband of Zoe, on the wall of Hagia Sophia replaced an earlier portrait of Zoe's first husband, Romanos III Argyros — underscoring the fact that their legitimacy as emperor came only through her bloodline, *c.* 1028–34 and 1042–55.

18 Mosaic on the east wall of the south gallery, Hagia Sophia, after 1118. John II and his wife, Irene, flank the Virgin and Child. John is wearing a jewel-studded *loros* cloth and holds a bag of money, symbolizing his beneficence to the church.

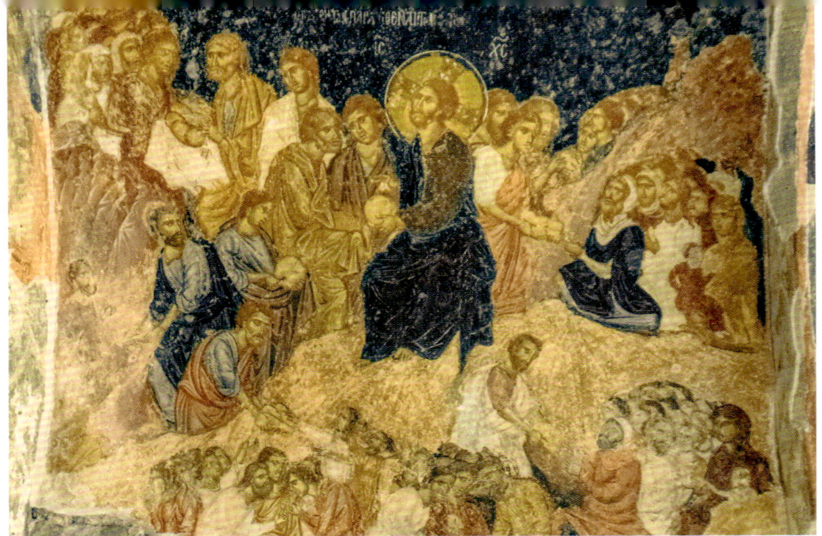

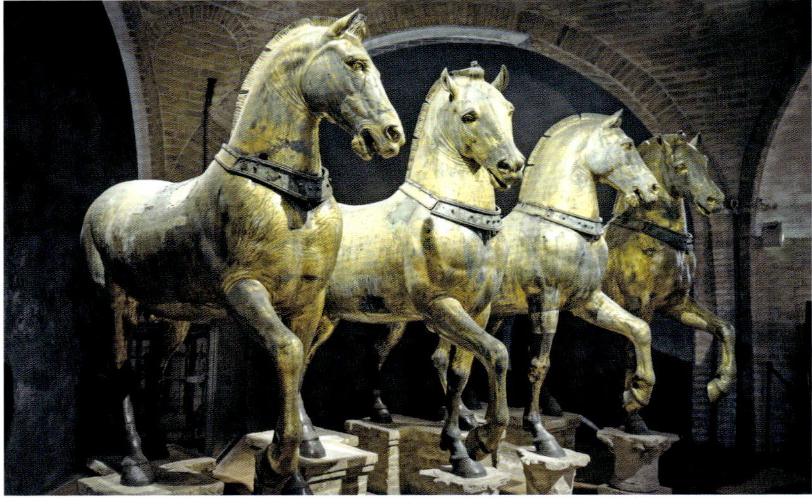

19 Wall painting of the Feeding of the Five Thousand in the church of Hagia Sophia, Trebizond, *c.* 13th century. This shows the beginnings of the late revival of Byzantine art, in the more sophisticated designs, the varied and more vibrant colours, and the increased realism of the figures.

20 The four bronze Horses of San Marco, formerly displayed above the main porch of San Marco in Venice. They were originally part of a quadriga that for centuries stood in the Hippodrome of Constantinople before being looted by the Venetians during the Fourth Crusade. They are probably late Roman or early Byzantine, although some historians believe them to be classically Greek in origin.

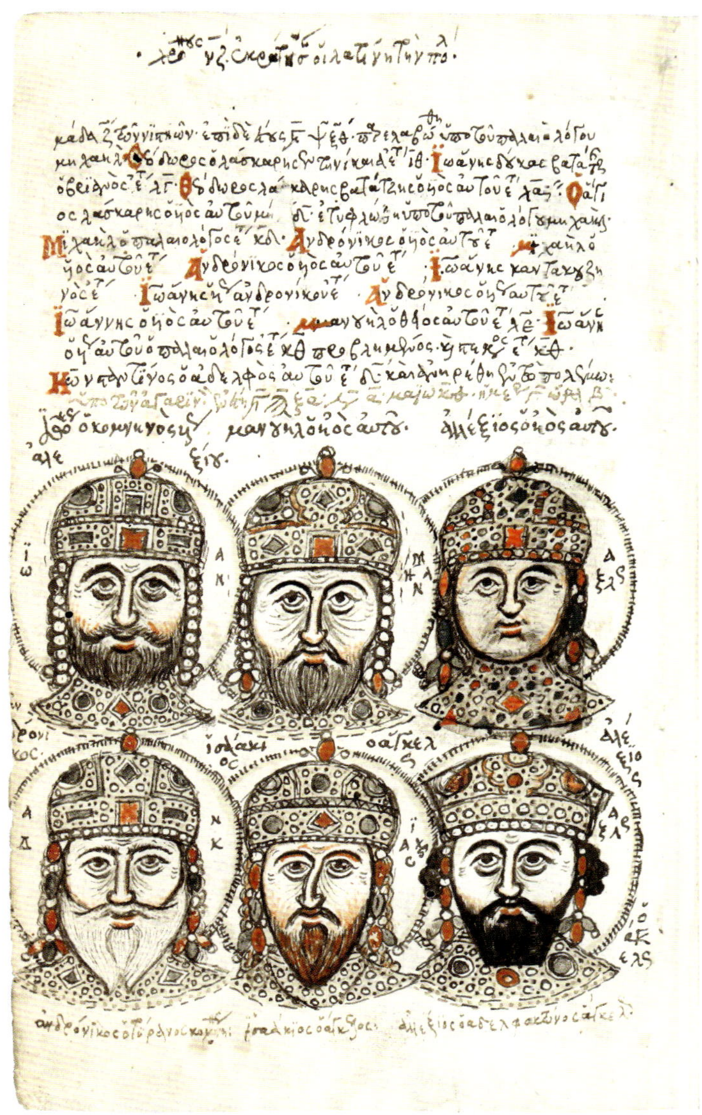

21 The Palaiologoi were the great ruling dynasty of the later years of the Byzantine Empire. Here, from a 15th-century copy of the *History* of John Zonaras, now in the Biblioteca Estense in Modena, are portraits of many of the noble family, drawn in pen, ink and wash. Michael VIII is at bottom left.

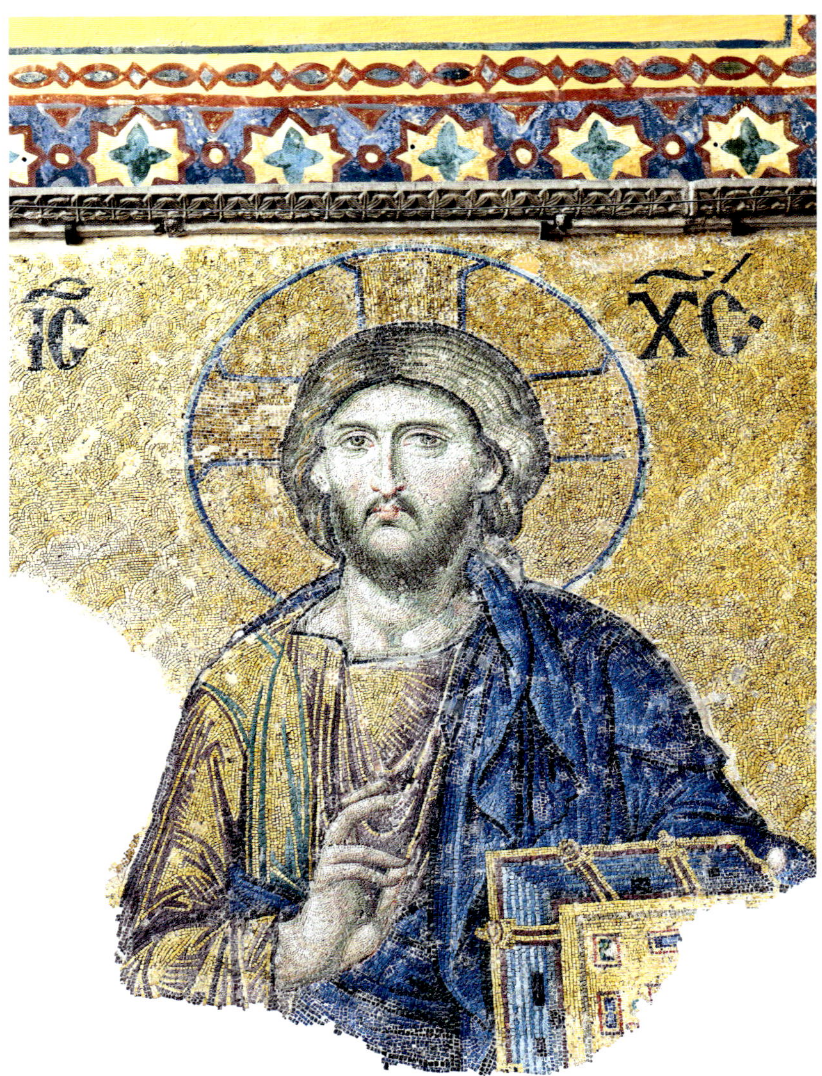

22 There is little evidence of grand mosaic work in the East in the 13th century, although works in manuscript form and icons were produced. So, the unveiling of this famous image of Christ in Hagia Sophia, *c.* 1261 – one of the great masterpieces of Byzantine art – would have been a major event.

was related to the Argyros clan through his mother's marriage to the brother of the emperor Romanos III.

Conscious of the threats that were massing at the empire's borders, Constantine's widow Eudokia realized that she would be unable to manage affairs on her own: she needed a husband and someone who would protect her children. She alighted upon Romanos Diogenes – a choice that was not without its problems, since Romanos had already been imprisoned for attempting to usurp the throne.

Eudokia, far from sentencing Romanos to death for an apparent rebellion against her husband, had listened to the people who held the dashing general in great affection. She came face to face with him, was charmed, and hatched an ingenious plan. Fearing that her sons might be murdered by any opportunistic nobleman ready to take the throne by force, she needed a strong husband to act alongside her as regent to the boys – but at the same time she could not remarry until she had been absolved from her vow of perpetual widowhood. To achieve this end, some claim, she pretended to the patriarch that she wished to marry his brother, whereupon John Xiphilinos, delighted at the idea of being the brother-in-law to the emperor, returned the written oath to her immediately. Eudokia then went straight to Romanos and proposed marriage, which he duly accepted. The couple went on to have two children together, Leo Diogenes and his younger brother, Nikephoros, both of them made co-emperors.

The civil aristocracy, the scheming politician Michael Psellos and the patriarch John Xiphilinos were all outmanoeuvred by this most 'Byzantine' of ploys, and Romanos was duly crowned emperor on 1 January 1068. But they would have their revenge, and everybody would suffer accordingly. The Doukas family was not happy either, seeing Romanos as an upstart who had charmed his way into the affections of Eudokia and denied the rightful heir to the throne – Michael Doukas, son of Constantine X Doukas – his true destiny.

Romanos IV was an experienced and successful soldier who had fought bravely against the Patziniks in the Balkans. Eager to prove himself, he immediately marched east to confront the ever-growing and powerful armies of the Seljuk Turks. Unfortunately, he had overestimated the state of his own forces. It was the best he could assemble in such a short time, but there was no hiding the fact that his army consisted essentially of a rag-tag group of mercenaries from every corner of the empire: Normans, Franks, Bulgarians, Patziniks and Uzes. There was also a homegrown contingent under the command of his stepson, Andronikos Doukas (a traitor in his midst). At first, Romanos's battles were largely successful but inconclusive in their outcomes. He would hear of Seljuk raids in Aleppo and charge off to confront them. The sack of Amorium diverted him again, but he returned to Constantinople without the resounding victories that he so craved and the empire so badly needed.

In 1069 bands of Frankish troops continued to roam Byzantine territories, disrupting the Armeniakon theme and delaying Romanos from his primary concern of facing the serious threat posed by the Seljuk sultan, Alp Arslan, in the east. When the Turkish raided his home province of Cappadocia, the emperor decided to act in a most brutal manner, executing every single captured prisoner, including a Seljuk chieftain. Romanos was getting desperate, and, as well as an impetuous nature with which everyone was familiar, now also revealed that he possessed a streak of cruelty.

In the capital Romanos had to deal with the hostile and unhelpful civil guard, the Doukas family, Michael Doukas's private tutor and eminent politician Michael Psellos, and a population that was getting tired of taxes to pay for an army that had yet to meet expectations by returning to Constantinople with booty. Romanos had also cut back on expensive building projects and flamboyant games in the Hippodrome. To make matters worse, the Norman Guiscard brothers, Robert and Roger, had been besieging Bari, Byzantium's last stronghold in Italy, for almost two years, and the inhabitants were desperate for help. Romanos, arguably two

　　　　　　　　　　　　　　DOUKID DYNASTY

years too late, sent a fleet of ships with soldiers and supplies to relieve them, but they were intercepted and captured by Roger Guiscard. The city's inhabitants, hearing that their last chance of help had vanished, could take no more and finally surrendered. On 15 April 1071 the Byzantine Empire lost Italy for ever.

Convinced that the Byzantines were at a weak point, Alp Arslan prepared himself and his troops for a major assault. The Seljuks headed for the area around Lake Van and eventually found the situation and conditions they had been anticipating. Romanos made some tactical errors, dividing his army, misjudging the size of various Turkish divisions – losing some of his mercenaries (the Uzes) to the enemy, and rejecting some quite favourable terms for peace from Alp Arslan – before deciding to go into full battle. The decisive element in his miserable defeat, one that he probably could not have prevented, was the treachery of Andronikos Doukas, who pretended that the emperor had fallen and took his thousands of troops out of the arena and headed home, leaving Romanos completely exposed. All accounts claim that Romanos fought with courage and skill, but when his horse was wounded and his hand injured he was captured and taken prisoner. It was said that Alp Arslan, needing to be convinced that this bedraggled and dusty man in front of him was really the emperor, sought confirmation from eyewitnesses. As soon as he accepted the truth, he placed his foot on the neck of Romanos as a symbol of victory and proceeded to treat him with great scorn. They were able to strike a deal whereby Romanos would pay an annual tribute to the Seljuks and a handsome sum to ransom himself, and offer military assistance in the fight against a bigger prize for Alp Arslan: the Fatimids in Egypt. These terms were agreed, and Romanos was set free and headed back to Constantinople.

News of the defeat had of course reached the imperial palace, most probably via the traitor Andronikos Doukas. In a coup engineered by Michael Psellos, *caesar* John and Michael Doukas, the emperor Romanos IV Diogenes was formally deposed in his absence and the young Michael VII Doukas crowned emperor by the patriarch. His mother, presumably because she was still considered loyal to Romanos, was tonsured and sent to a monastery.

When Romanos returned, he was treated as an enemy, and those who remained true to him started a civil war. Following defeat in battle, he fled to a fortress near Adana and, with Andronikos Doukas close by, gathered all the money he could muster and sent it to Alp Arslan with the note: 'As emperor, I promised you a ransom of a million and a half. Dethroned, I send you all I possess as proof of my gratitude.'

Romanos had had enough and surrendered himself to the new emperor Michael VII on the condition that his personal safety would be guaranteed. The terms were agreed, signed and then knowingly ignored. He never even managed to reach Constantinople to see his wife and children: he was captured, brutally blinded with red-hot pokers and exiled to the Princes' Islands in the Sea of Marmara, where his wounds turned septic and he died an excruciating death. Eudokia was allowed to give him a funeral, and the hypocrisy of Psellos and others was on full show as they lamented the death of a decent man who tried only to save the empire from its enemies.

Romanos's defeat at Manzikert had been substantial, but the terms he had negotiated were nevertheless bearable for the empire. If adhered to, they would have allowed the administration to get itself in a better state. However, Psellos, John and the now teenage emperor Michael VII refused the terms agreed by Romanos and Alp Arslan, and instead concentrated their energies on politicking in the capital. This infuriated the Seljuks. They turned to Anatolia, which now lay open to them in its entirety, meeting almost no resistance. Following their victory, they promptly set up a sultanate in Iconium, the so-called 'Sultanate of Rum' (i.e. of the Romans) – the first foreign state to occupy an area so close to the empire's capital.

Romanos IV Diogenes had come to power at the wrong time. As a military commander there was a limit to what he could do with such depleted forces, and he had to contend with a civil service that despised him and plotted against him from the beginning. He is remembered as a noble man who tried his best but failed, and allowed the empire's decline to accelerate during his reign.

Michael VII Doukas
October 1071 – March 1078

Michael is a prodigy of our generation and a most adored character. He is inclined to blush.
MICHAEL PSELLOS, MID-1070S

Michael was so naive, ignorant and inexperienced, he was deemed fit only to be a bishop.
MICHAEL ATTALEIATES, *c.* 1080

Michael VII Doukas was crowned on 24 October 1071, as the empire was spiralling out of control. Just 21 years old, he had been manipulated into deposing his stepfather.

Michael's life up to this point had been one of study and court ritual, overseen by the influential Michael Psellos, and he was particularly at ease with religious ceremonies and debate. When his father, Constantine X Doukas, had died in 1067, Michael was young, about 17 years old, but still eligible to rule alone. The combination of a powerful and protective mother and a domineering and ambitious uncle, in the form of *caesar* John Doukas, prevented him from assuming the role, leaving Michael in the background until the disaster at Manzikert.

Once he became the senior emperor, Michael was in thrall to a young eunuch named Nikephoritzes, who began to take control of the day-to-day running of the administration to the point that he seemed to have a vice-like grip on all expenditure. Michael VII, oblivious and probably powerless, did nothing to halt the gradual colonization of the Anatolian heartlands by the Seljuk Turks as they set up their Sultanate of Rum in Iconium. There was no real attempt to take back lands in Italy after the fall of Bari in 1071, and a new rebellion was brewing in the Balkans, where the Bulgarians were looking to re-establish their kingdom on the northern door-step of the empire. Fortunately, the general Nikephoros Bryennios managed to subdue the Bulgar armies and a semblance of order was maintained.

After more uprisings, including one led by John Doukas and his band of mercenaries, the Byzantines were forced to formally acknowledge the Seljuk Turks and all their territories, since they so desperately needed their help in subduing John Doukas. It was at this point that the great Alexios Komnenos emerged as commander of the Byzantine forces, fighting alongside the Seljuk troops led by Malik-Shah I, Alp Arslan having died the previous year, and together they defeated and captured John Doukas.

Back in the capital, matters were going from bad to worse. The eunuch Nikephoritzes was losing control of the state finances, and his policies were failing in front of his eyes. Vast payments to hos-tile neighbours, endless warfare, mercenaries having to be paid in gold – the treasury was spending at a rate it could not sustain, and yet still Michael VII did nothing to stop the decline. He made a disastrous fiscal decision in devaluing the currency by a substantial amount, which gave him the nickname 'Parapinakes', or Michael 'minus a quarter'. He tried to inflate the price of grain – always a recipe for disaster with the crowds in Constantinople – and yet continued to spend money on court ceremonies and vanity building projects, all the while residing in the palace writing poetry. In 1078 there were bread riots in the city, and government build-ings were set alight. Nikephoritzes fled the capital but was captured by the Norman Roussel de Bailleul and tortured to death.

Michael enjoyed one piece of good fortune in the form of his mar-riage to Maria of Alania. Daughter of the Georgian king Bagrat IV, Maria would have a lasting influence in the palace, owing to her intelligence and patronage of artists and writers. Anna Komnene, the daughter of the future Alexios I and one of the most eminent literary figures of the Middle Ages, described her beauty as 'surpassing all description and all art … a joy to all true lovers of the beautiful'. Maria bore Michael VII one son, Constantine.

In 1077 two generals, Nikephoros Bryennios – the commander who subdued the Bulgars – and Nikephoros Botaneiates from the eastern themes, revolted at the same time. Owing to the poor discipline of Bryennios's troops, who delayed their march into the city because they were busy plundering the outskirts, Botaneiates was victorious.

Michael VII, accused of cowardice and shamed by his people, instantly abdicated and fled to the Stoudios monastery, where he seems to have found his place in life. He lived on for another twelve years, eventually becoming bishop of Ephesos. In renouncing the beautiful Maria, Michael VII allowed her to become an empress for a second time when she married his successor, Nikephoros Botaneiates. The abiding memory of the disastrous Michael VII Doukas is one of continual catastrophe, bewildering ineptitude and almost criminal neglect of his duties to the Byzantine Empire.

Nikephoros III Botaneiates
March 1078 – April 1081

His entire body was covered in scars.
CONSTANTINE MANASSES, MID-12TH CENTURY

Nikephoros III Botaneiates came to the throne aged 77. Tired, irritable and stuck in an outmoded way of behaviour, he was unsuitable to lead an empire at any time, let alone through such a difficult period. Coming from a noble and distinguished family, Nikephoros claimed kinship with a previous emperor, Nikephoros Phokas, and had spent his life as a commander in the Byzantine army, clocking up a mixed record of victories and failures on the field. At the death of Constantine X in 1067 he had been considered as a candidate to take over the throne by marrying the dying emperor's widow, Eudokia Makrembolitissa, but she rejected him in favour of Michael VII Doukas – a slight he was not going to forget.

Towards the end of the reign of Michael VII, Nikephoros was one of a number of generals who had grown tired of the emperor's impetuosity and high-handed ways, as well as the excessive power wielded by the eunuch chancellor Nikephoritzes. He decided to gather his army, march on the capital and depose the emperor. To this end he engaged troops from the newly installed leader of the Seljuk Turks, Suleiman ibn Qutulmish, and marched into Nicaea, proclaiming himself emperor. Although Nikephoros Botaneiates was backed by the church and many of the ruling families, Nikephoros Bryennios also had designs on the throne and challenged Botaneiates for the leadership. With the support of the great Alexios Komnenos and his forces, Bryennios was defeated. Botaneiates entered Constantinople on 24 March 1078 and was crowned emperor by the new patriarch, Kosmas I. One of his first orders was to have Bryennios arrested and blinded, and then, snubbing Eudokia's hand in marriage as she had done to him a few years before, he chose Maria of Alania as his wife. Maria accepted because she was desperate to make her son, Constantine, a junior emperor, and pleaded with Botaneiates to crown him accordingly. But he refused, not even allowing Constantine to wear the red shoes of a Byzantine prince. Botaneiates was quoted by Anna Komnene as describing Maria as a perfect wife because, coming from far-away Georgia, she had no troublesome in-laws who might bother him.

Despite his brief reign of just three years, there is a richly described portrait of Nikephoros III Botaneiates in a contemporaneous manuscript of a book of sermons by St John Chrysostom. It reveals in great detail some of the elaborate costumes an emperor would wear in this period and depicts Nikephoros with a full beard, thick black hair and handsome black eyes.

As he grew older and approached his 80th year, Nikephoros realized that he could not cope with the duties and responsibilities of this most difficult of vocations and relied increasingly on the council and military skill of his trusted general Alexios Komnenos, who had suppressed a number of rebellions against him. When Robert Guiscard, the Norman conqueror of Bari, claimed that he was obligated to invade the Byzantine capital, Alexios was placed in charge of repelling him.

It became clear that Alexios was the only figure capable of holding the entire Byzantine world together. With the help of the *caesar* John Doukas and his whole clan, Alexios was persuaded to take arms against the emperor and assume the crown for himself. Botaneiates considered resisting him but could muster no support from any faction and abdicated. He retired to a monastery, as had so many deposed emperors before him, and spent the last year of his life at the Peribleptos monastery, before dying peacefully and almost forgotten. When asked what he missed about being emperor, he is reported to have said: 'Abstinence from meat is the only thing that bothers me.'

Botaneiates had been the last in a long line of ineffectual and incompetent emperors. The empire was financially broken, and besieged on all sides by powerful expansionist enemies.

KOMNENIAN DYNASTY

(II: 1081–1185)

Alexios I Komnenos

April 1081 – August 1118

When he sat on the imperial throne, the fierce splendour of his eyes was like a flash of lightning, and an irresistible radiance shone from his face, nay, from his whole person.

ANNA KOMNENE, *c.* 1150

Byzantium was fortunate that, in its most troubled period for nearly 500 years, a man would take control who had the military skill, the political know-how and the personal support of the ruling families to drag the empire back from the brink of ruin.

Barely 30 years old when he marched into Constantinople as the new Emperor of the Byzantines and was crowned, Alexios I Komnenos was already a seasoned military campaigner, having fought victoriously under the patronage of three successive emperors.

Before he decided to usurp his erstwhile emperor Nikephoros III Botaneiates – a decision he did not take lightly, having being a loyal servant to many emperors before him – Alexios consulted two formidable women who influenced his life significantly: his mother, Anna Dalassene, and his adopted 'mother' (and most probably his lover) Maria of Alania. These women would both offer him counsel for many years. Later, when Alexios was away from the capital on his many campaigns against invaders and rebels alike, Anna effectively ran the government alongside his loyal and redoubtable wife, Irene Doukaina. Uniquely, Alexios made both his mother and his wife *augusta*, something that would cause tension between the two women for years.

Alexios's father was the holder of a senior military office known as *domestikos ton scholon* and was the brother of the emperor Isaac I Komnenos, and his mother came from a noble family. Alexios was thus brought up in close proximity to the palace, mixing with the elite from an early age, where he would have understood immediately that the empire was fundamentally in the hands of a number of powerful landowning and military families.

Before he took the throne and immediately after he had secured it, Alexios rallied the great families around him. According to Anna Komnene, there was a rumour that he wished to marry Maria of Alania, who was a renowned beauty, but his mother insisted that he marry into the Doukas family, without whom the whole enterprise might falter. The 12-year-old Irene Doukaina was selected. Although Alexios may have been indifferent to her at the start, they seemed to grow ever more reliant on each other over the years, and the marriage was long-lasting and stable. They had nine children together, including the next emperor, the future John II.

Once crowned, on 4 April 1081, Alexios reinstated Constantine, the son of Maria of Alania, to the position of co-emperor, and even had his beloved first-born daughter, Anna, engaged to Constantine at an early age. However, when the young Constantine died, the engagement was quickly dissolved and Anna was made to live with her mother and grandmother in the main palace. The lovely Maria, princess of Georgia, wife to two emperors, mother to a co-emperor and adopted mother to the great emperor himself, was eventually dispatched to live in a monastery near her homeland.

Irene Doukaina was a divisive figure within the court. She often clashed with her controlling mother-in-law, Anna Dalassene, and acquired the reputation of a schemer. This was most likely based on her open adoration of her intellectually brilliant daughter Anna and Anna's husband, Nikephoros Bryennios the Younger, whom Irene always wanted to inherit the throne. Alexios took the expedient political route and stuck to his belief that his son John would take over, ensuring more stability for the family and the empire. The great chronicler of the age Niketas Choniates was not an admirer of Irene and described her thus: 'She threw her full influence on the side of her daughter Anna and lost no opportunity to calumniate their son John before her husband Alexios, mocking him as rash, pleasure-loving and weak in character.' Whatever the truth about Irene, she was a pillar of support to Alexios in his later years, accompanying him on campaigns and acting as a nursemaid as Alexios's gout continued to plague him.

Alexios intuitively understood the power of diplomacy and alliances. Throughout his thirty-seven-year reign, he constantly engaged in warfare. Rebellions from within the empire and attacks from outside its borders were a never-ending feature of the period. The constant threat posed by the Seljuks in the heartland of Anatolia was never fully resolved and became caught up in the complexities of the First Crusade. The incursions of the Normans meant that allegiances were sought from far afield, including the German king Henry IV, who was paid 360,000 pieces of gold to attack them from the north and thus to distract them from Constantinople. In Thrace, the Bogomils and the Paulicians joined forces with the Pechenegs to overrun the northern borders, but through a skilful and costly alliance with the Cumans (a Turkic nomadic people inhabiting much of today's Hungary) Alexios managed to defeat them at the Battle of Levounion on 29 April 1091. Alexios was succeeding in defending and expanding the empire but it came at a great cost, both financially and militarily. He had to devalue the currency, and even confiscated church treasuries to melt down the gold and sell the precious stones. By 1092, in order to alleviate some of this financial strain, Alexios had stopped producing the now debased *solidus* coin, replacing it with the *hyperpyron* of 21 carats, which was effective in stabilizing the monetary system.

Always aware that the Seljuks were the most significant long-term problem that the empire faced, Alexios had contacted both

Pope Urban II at the Council of Piacenza and Count Robert of Flanders, asking for help in repelling the Muslim Turks. The concept of a religious crusade was new to the Byzantines. Alexios was essentially requesting the help of Western mercenaries, something the Byzantines had been doing for centuries, but what emerged was a federation fixated on retrieving the Holy Lands, and principally Jerusalem, from the infidel Turks. Jerusalem had not been in Byzantine hands for a very long time and meant little to Alexios, so he was understandably perplexed by this.

Before the true First Crusade even arrived, there was a mass movement, controlled by unscrupulous leaders such as Peter the Hermit, a French priest, that led many thousands of pilgrims through Hungary and the Balkans, looting and plundering on the way. When these troublesome miscreants arrived outside the gates of the capital, Alexios shipped them over the Bosphorus to Asia Minor, where they were promptly slaughtered by the Turkish forces. Later, in 1097, the true leaders of the First Crusade appeared in Constantinople, the Norman adventurer Bohemond, son of Robert Guiscard, Raymond of Toulouse and Godfrey of Bouillon among them. Taking the advice of Alexios, these Western armies sought an alliance with the large Armenian forces and set off towards the Holy Land. They met with some success against the Seljuk Turks, and got as far as the important city of Antioch, where they were temporarily halted. Alexios sent word that he was coming to their aid, but after setting out he decided to turn back. The Crusaders, however, had managed to capture the city in the summer of 1098. Since they felt betrayed by Alexios, they decided to occupy it themselves and not share it with their Byzantine hosts. Alexios was furious and sent a force to confront Bohemond. It was at this time that the Crusaders gave a young boy called John Axouch, almost certainly a Seljuk Turk slave, to Alexios I as a gift. He made the boy a companion to his son, John, and the two grew up together and became life-long friends.

Meanwhile, Raymond of Toulouse had marched on through Syria and took Jerusalem on 15 July 1099. The occupation of the

Holy Land by Western Crusaders had begun, and was to continue for many years.

Bohemond and Alexios continued their feud. With Bohemond still refusing to share Antioch with his Eastern hosts, he left it in the care of his nephew Tancred and set off to raise an army that would attack Albania, thus diverting Alexios's attention from Antioch. Bohemond had spread the word, in the first instance to the Pope Paschal II, whose support he secured, that the Byzantines were as much of an enemy as the Muslims. They were, he claimed, a population of lying, lazy, effete Greeks, led by an emperor who was in religious conflict with the strict Christian beliefs of the pope. This foul slur took hold in the West, and the concept of the disingenuous Byzantines, scheming and tricking their way to power and hindering the progress of the Crusades, took root, coming so soon after the split of the church in 1054. When Alexios was forced to make an alliance with the Seljuk sultan in Baghdad to prevent Tancred from taking more territory in Syria, it served only to fuel the belief that the Byzantines were favouring infidels over their supposed Christian brothers. Treatises were eventually signed to the effect that the two factions could co-exist, saving face but not realistically resolving the problem. Alexios cleverly followed in the wake of the Crusaders' battles and secured towns and areas for the Byzantines. Most of the coastline of Anatolia came back into his hands, as did many important cities in Syria.

All of this activity cost Alexios I a lot of money, and he needed to solicit help. He had already made concessions to the Venetians, in 1082 granting them exclusive and tax-free trading rights to the capital in return for the support of their powerful navy against the Normans. They set up a vast trading post on the Asian shore, and the enormous wealth that Venice later accrued was derived from the trade they managed through Constantinople. Later, in 1111, Alexios made a similar deal with Pisa. Although criticized for doing so, Alexios saw it as a very necessary manoeuvre, since the Italians had controlled trade for some years now.

 KOMNENIAN DYNASTY

Within this world of subterfuge, intrigue and warfare on all fronts, Alexios had surrounded himself with the people he believed he could trust: his extended family. Many of the age-old mechanisms of state bureaucracy were dismantled, and trusted members of his family were given important positions. There can be little doubt that the government now resembled a family-run business rather than the administration of an independent state.

The last years of Alexios's life were spent fighting wars, handling the Crusaders, and coping with his painful and debilitating gout. Both his wife, Irene, and his daughter, Anna, lovingly nursed him until his death on 15 August 1118. They also put pressure on Alexios to change his mind as to who should succeed him, but to no avail. It was always going to be John.

Alexios had rescued the empire from virtual bankruptcy and built alliances with his neighbours when his own armies were in the most terrible state, having been neglected by his predecessors. Every emperor that followed Alexios until the end of the empire was related to him in some way. A truly great man and one of the finest of all the Byzantine emperors, Alexios would be remembered as the subject of one of the great works of the Middle Ages, the *Alexiad*, written by the West's first female historian, his most beloved and talented daughter, Anna.

John II Komnenos
August 1118 – April 1143

As a child he had a swarthy complexion, a broad forehead, hollow cheeks, a nose neither snub nor aquiline but something between the two, [and] very black eyes.
ANNA KOMNENE, *c.* 1150

Having a father who was widely accepted as the saviour of the empire, an older sister who was brilliant, attractive and ambitious, and a mother who openly preferred his sister and wanted her and her husband, Nikephoros Bryennios the Younger, to inherit the throne cannot have made John's early life easy.

As his father, Alexios I, lay dying, John decided to act. With the help of his brother Isaac, he forced his way into the Mangana monastery, took the imperial signet ring off the hand of his father, raced back to the Great Palace and immediately had himself crowned emperor. The next day his father died, and Irene and Anna could do nothing to reverse his actions. John II was so concerned about their intentions that he did not attend his father's funeral, fearing that it might be used for some sort of uprising against him. He remained in power through these nervous few days, and it was not until the following year that he had proof of a plot against him, whereupon he banished his mother to a monastery and placed his sister under house arrest. Despite their behaviour, he eventually forgave them and established relatively good relations with them for the rest of their lives, allowing them to live in comfort. Anna's husband, Nikephoros Bryennios the Younger, distanced himself from the plots and was always loyal to his brother-in-law.

Described by a Latin historian from Jerusalem, William of Tyre, as insignificant in appearance, of medium height, with black hair and swarthy skin – for which reason he is still called 'the Moor' – John rose above all of the sneers and insults to become known as 'Kaloioannes', which means both 'John the Handsome' and 'John the Good'. He was a moral, decent man at a time when cruelty, genocide and general indifference to life were common.

The reign of John II was long and largely successful. Despite constant fighting on the borders and endless shifting alliances with various neighbours, there was a general stabilizing of internal struggles within the empire. Throughout his life he had a constant, capable and loyal companion in John Axouch, a Turkish slave who had been given by the Crusaders to Alexios I and who had grown up with John in the palace. As soon as John became emperor, he made Axouch his *megas domestikos*, or commander-in-chief of the armies, and later his second in command for all matters of state.

John was loyal to the people he trusted. Clearly, one did not have to be a member of the emperor's family in order to flourish in government, and this served to curtail the assumptions of relatives that they had some sort of divine right to high positions. It also sent a signal to those outside the elite that achieving high office was possible, even if they were not connected to one of the ruling families. This was a departure from the practice of his father, Alexios I, who deliberately sought to concentrate power among his extended family.

Other than the constant threat of the Seljuk Turks in the east of Anatolia, the first big military confrontation John II had to manage was with the Pechenegs in the Balkans in 1122. He completely destroyed their army at the Battle of Beroia and, despite getting wounded in the leg, John and his famous Varangian Guard (apparently with a substantial contingent of Englishmen among them) secured a famous victory. There followed a wholesale moving of Pecheneg prisoners into Asia Minor, and an entire people who had so troubled Byzantium for centuries were never to be a threat again.

Less successful was John's attempt to put the Venetians back in their lagoon. He resented their attitude towards the empire and decided to take away their privileged trading rights in the capital. With its strong fleet, Venice took immediate action against the Byzantines, raided the coastline of Asia Minor and its many islands, and captured Cephalonia. John had to admit that he could not match the naval power of Venice and sued for peace, reinstalling their rights to trade exclusively with the largest city in the world and other cities throughout the empire.

With the Balkans subdued, the Hungarians and Serbians now contained and paying homage to the empire, and the Venetians content with their position, John II was able to concentrate his forces against the Seljuk Sultanate of Rum, centred at Iconium, and the more recently established Muslim Emirate of Danishmends, who were based at Amasya and Sivas. Battles were fought with some success, but they had no real, lasting effect. The Byzantine capture

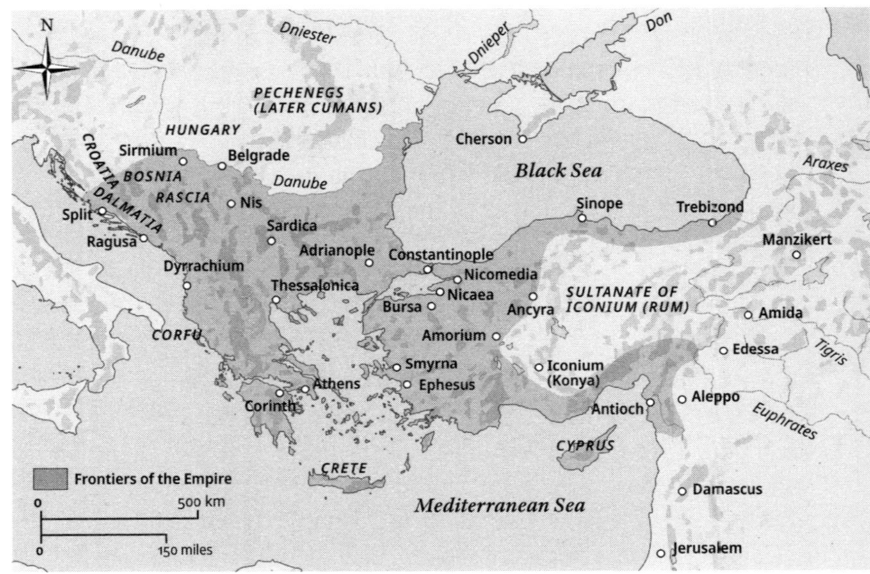

of Kastamonu from the Turks warranted a celebration, but little did John know that, by the time he was back in Constantinople, the Danishmends had recaptured the town.

John II now turned his attention to the Crusader states and in particular to Antioch, which had always been a fortress that the Byzantines wanted for strategic reasons. First, he conquered Tarsus, then Adana, and finally Cilicia, where the ruler, Prince Levon I of Armenia, was brought back to Constantinople as a captive. However, Antioch was under the rule of Raymond of Poitiers, who proved to be a lot more stubborn. Eventually, in 1137, Raymond agreed to become a vassal of the emperor, as long as he remained its prince – a compromise neither party could really claim as a victory.

During the 1130s the Normans had taken the island of Sicily and most of southern Italy, and were once again eyeing the prize of Byzantium under their charismatic leader Roger II. In order to neutralize Roger II's ambitions, John sought an alliance with the Holy Roman Empire in Germany, which was to threaten the Normans in Italy. As part of this agreement John had his son Manuel betrothed to Bertha of Sulzbach, the sister-in-law of King Conrad III. This policy worked to a certain extent, since Roger II was distracted and never tried to invade Byzantium.

In 1142, on what would be his final campaign, John II set out once again to conquer Antioch, but the season was closing in on him and he chose to winter in the Taurus mountains, where he could indulge in one of his few pastimes, hunting wild boar. It was here that he accidentally cut himself with a poisoned arrow. The wound turned septic, and the emperor died in the spring of 1143, away from his capital. Before his death he chose his younger son Manuel to succeed him rather than his elder son Isaac, believing Isaac too erratic and unreliable to rule effectively.

John's personal life appears faultless. An arranged marriage in 1104 to Princess Piroska, the 15-year-old daughter of King Ladislas of Hungary, resulted in eight children, including a set of twins and his successor, Manuel I Komnenos, and he lived a life of religious observance and strict moral discipline. When Piroska, renamed Irene upon her Byzantine coronation, died in 1134, John lived the remaining nine years of his life abstemiously true to the memory of his beloved empress.

John II Komnenos left the empire in a very healthy state – certainly much stronger than when he had inherited it from his father. His building works and charitable donations in the capital were extensive and generous, and along with his wife, Irene, he left behind one of the city's great monuments: the monastery of Christ Pantocrator (now the Zeyrek Mosque), which still stands today. It is perhaps the manner in which he conducted himself that was most impressive. Tolerant, just, pious, faithful to his wife and to his empire, John was one of the best emperors that Byzantium was to have, and in selecting his younger son as his heir he ensured a smooth transition of power.

Manuel I Komnenos
April 1143 – September 1180

A wise and trustworthy prince of great magnificence, worthy of praise in every respect. A great-souled man of incomparable energy.
WILLIAM OF TYRE, *c.* 1180

The youngest son and fourth child of the emperor John II Komnenos and Princess Piroska of Hungary, nephew of the great Anna Komnena, grandson of St Ladislas, king of Hungary, and the grandson of the emperor Alexios I Komnenos – the pedigree of Manuel I was unrivalled. The 12th century belonged to the three Komnenoi, an unbroken line of father-to-son emperors for ninety-nine years, offering hope, stability and success to the entire territory. Manuel I was the last of the great Komnenoi to rule over the Byzantine Empire.

Manuel succeeded his father at the age of 25, selected over his elder brother Isaac for reasons with which nobody seemed to disagree. The transition was not without a brief scare: Manuel was fighting in Cilicia in the south-east of Anatolia at the moment of his father's death and suspected that Isaac might try to take control of the empire in his absence. Manuel therefore sent his trusted general John Axouch to return to Constantinople as quickly as possible and secure the throne for him. This the loyal and capable Axouch did. He had been a great friend and servant to Manuel's father, John II, and was now demonstrating his loyalty to the son. Upon his arrival in Constantinople, Axouch had Isaac arrested and detained in the palace, so that by the time Manuel returned a few days later he could enter as the triumphant, uncontested and rightful heir. He was crowned by the new patriarch, Michael Kourkouas, and just two days later released his brother, promising an annual tribute of 200 silver pieces to the church.

Manuel was everybody's favourite. The great chronicler Niketas Choniates describes him thus: 'Tall of stature, but ever so slightly stooped. In colour, he was not as white and pale as one who is brought up in the shade, nor as dusky as those who are scorched by the sun, but somewhere between black and white and tending more to swarthiness; nevertheless he was very handsome.' His charm was acknowledged by all who met him, friend, foe or Crusader, and in many ways the success that he enjoyed throughout most of his reign was born out of his personal charisma and undeniable force of personality. He was not only clever, educated, curious and forward-thinking, but also a brave warrior who repeatedly led his troops into battle. Particularly intrigued by all matters medical, he would personally tend to the sick whenever he could. He was extravagant to the point of irresponsibility, throwing lavish parties for visitors and friends alike, sparing no expense on gifts for people he wanted to impress, and yet – commendably – he spent very little on himself. This was almost certainly a reaction to the formal, austere and heavily religious court of his father, and the moderation he introduced into matters of court etiquette was welcomed by many.

Manuel was drawn to the West and its culture in many ways. He introduced jousting tournaments to Constantinople, having observed the Crusaders jousting, and even took part in them himself – an activity that some Byzantines found shocking. He would mix with his subjects and his soldiers on a personal level that was unheard of with previous emperors. He employed Western architects to build new buildings, and this openness to Westerners in general encouraged opportunistic Franks and Germans to come to his court seeking their fame and fortune. Both Manuel's wives were Western princesses. The first, Bertha-Irene of Sulzbach, was from an arranged marriage to German royalty when he was very young; they had two daughters. His second wife was the French-speaking Maria of Antioch, with whom he had his son and heir, Alexios II.

Manuel's dream was to try to restore and revive the old Roman Empire, with one church and one supreme authority manifested in himself. However, this romantic notion of recreating the empire as it was in the time of Constantine the Great was never realistic. The world he faced when he took the reins of power was completely different from that of the 4th century. By 1143, much of the empire's former territories had been engulfed by the various armies of Islam, which had invaded and permanently occupied the rich lands of Egypt, Palestine, much of Syria and the whole of North Africa. Not only did Manuel I have to contend with this long-established foe, but there were now new forces pitted against him: the Normans of Sicily, for instance, who had seized all of southern Italy from the empire and threatened further expansion. In the Levant, another new force, the Crusader states, were aggressively establishing themselves as rivals in the east. More worrying still were the powerful Seljuk Turks who were overrunning central Anatolia, the very heartland of the empire. The Balkans, as ever, were largely under control but never straightforward, as rival dynasties, ethnic groups and invading foreigners were always just around the corner, ready to try to wrest control from the Byzantine occupiers.

One of the first real challenges for Manuel was the arrival of the Second Crusade. Both Manuel's brother-in-law, Conrad III of Germany, and Louis VII of France had been convinced that leading a crusade to recapture the Holy Lands from the infidel was imperative, and they each duly raised an army and set forth. Manuel was well aware of the problems these Crusaders would bring: just as his grandfather had adeptly dealt with the First Crusade, Manuel was quick to offer the Crusaders every assistance, but even quicker to have them pass through Byzantine lands as speedily as possible. Their armies were a fearsome liability as they marched through towns and the countryside, taking what they wanted from a supine populace, indiscriminately raping and murdering as they went. Despite being policed by a Byzantine army, there would always be skirmishes, and sometimes quite serious battles, between the Greeks and the Franks. Manuel tried to warn the German army under Conrad III that the Seljuk Turks would be a formidable foe

　　KOMNENIAN DYNASTY

as they passed out of Byzantine lands in southern Anatolia, but the Germans would not listen and marched on towards Jerusalem.

In their first encounter with the Seljuks, the Germans were soundly beaten and slaughtered in their thousands. Conrad escaped with his life and came apologetically back to Constantinople to fall on the mercy of Manuel, who was true to his charming self and became a lasting friend. As Louis VII and his army arrived, they too were defeated with ease by the forces of the sultan of Iconium, forcing Louis and his barons to flee back to Syria. The Second Crusade had been a disaster for everybody except the Turks and Roger II of Sicily, who had used the event to attack Byzantine lands in the Aegean. Manuel I had skilfully avoided any major catastrophe with Conrad III or Louis VII, but the feeling that the Greeks had not assisted their Christian brethren in attacking the infidel Muslims was reinforced by the embarrassed returning forces of Louis, looking for an excuse to hide their incompetence.

In almost all confrontations, Manuel would gain the upper hand either through skilled diplomacy or by using his still considerably well-funded army. The Crusader state of Antioch, under Raymond of Poitiers and, later, Raynald of Châtillon, was eventually ceded to Manuel. Raynald's attack on Cyprus – a Christian assault on fellow Christians – was a low point and particularly brutal: Raynald sent mutilated prisoners back to Constantinople to show Manuel who was in charge. Manuel had his revenge when Raynald came to him begging for help in 1159; he was allowed to live only on the condition that he surrender Antioch to Manuel. Baldwin III of Jerusalem also capitulated to Manuel's forces, and both he and Raynald were made to trail behind the mounted emperor through the streets of Antioch.

With the death of Roger II of Sicily in 1154, Manuel invaded southern Italy and met with great success, taking the towns of Bari, Taranto and Brindisi as the new Norman king, William I of Sicily, struggled to assert his authority. When Manuel himself was leading these expeditions, more often than not they were successful but, as soon as he had accomplished his goal and had to travel to another part of the empire, the area in question inevitably fell back into the enemy's hands.

The one mistake Manuel did make – which would cost the empire dear and, indeed, from which it never fully recovered – was during a battle with his old adversary the Seljuk Turks. Manuel had rightly decided that he must secure his eastern provinces and in 1176 undertook what he believed would be a final defeat of the Seljuks and their sultan, Kilij Arslan II. He arrived to engage with the enemy and capture Iconium, but his army was slow and cumbersome, and at a narrow pass at Myriokephalon it was out-manoeuvred and destroyed by the agile Seljuk forces. This defeat was a humiliation for both the Byzantine Empire and for Manuel personally. He was now seen merely as the king of the Greeks, not the emperor of the Romans as he had so long desired. Much of this perception was not borne out of fact, since the Byzantine army defeated the Turks at a number of battles, notably Hyelion and Leimocheir, but the damage had been done. The Byzantines under Manuel I were unable to defeat their old enemy, just as they had failed at Manzikert a hundred years earlier.

Returning to his capital, Manuel was never quite the same. His energy was sapped, his reputation diminished, and he remained a broken man. Increasingly obsessed with the time and manner of his death, he consulted astrologers. He was told to prepare for a hurricane and started to have underground shelters built beneath the palace before coming to his senses and dismissing all around him. On 24 September 1180 he finally succumbed to a fatal illness and died in his bed.

The empire was not to see the likes of the three Komnenoi on the throne for some considerable time. Manuel had been extremely active in his long and productive reign, defending the empire on all its borders, expanding its territories and influence in all direc-tions, and initiating grand building works throughout, but at an enormous cost. The treasury was almost empty; the army, though still strong, was essentially led by mercenaries and therefore vulnerable to collapse at any moment; his alliances with foreign powers were based more on his character than on solid ground and, with his death, many of them fell away. Lands that had been won in numerous hard battles were quick to fall back into enemy hands. After ninety-nine years of stability and power, the empire was ill prepared for what was to come.

Alexios II Komnenos
September 1180 – September 1183

Thus did Emperor Alexios disappear from the world, not yet 15 years of age. He had reigned for three of these years, but not alone and unaided, for as he was but a child his mother at first governed the realm, and then the affairs of the empire were administered by two tyrants. It was as though the sun were hidden behind the clouds, and it seemed as though Alexios was subject instead of ruler, commanding and doing whatever the rebels proposed until his life was choked out.
NIKETAS CHONIATES, *c.* 1208

The brief and tragic reign of Alexios II Komnenos was in stark contrast to that of his father. When he was crowned emperor as a child aged only 11, his French mother, Maria of Antioch, became his regent. Immediately after her husband's death she had become a nun and acquired the name Xene, meaning 'foreigner', but she did not behave like one, and soon had many suitors. The most persistent among them, and the one who she mistakenly thought would best provide her with protection and power, was another Alexios Komnenos, a nephew of Manuel I who had already acquired the honorific rank of *protosebastos*. It was not the first time Maria had been involved in government: when, at the age of about 16, she had married the 43-year-old emperor, she had been used as an interpreter and unofficial court spy and was experienced in court intrigue and politics.

As his mother and her chosen paramour Alexios were trying to consolidate their power, the young emperor Alexios II was living the life he had always led in the privileged palace environment. He was more interested in games and hunting than anything else. As a boy of 12 years old, he was not eager to get involved in the politics of the Balkans, but his mother kept him away from the world of power in any case, keen to keep it all for herself. He married young: the parents of the young princess Agnes of France had sent her to live with the family of her future husband when she was only 8 years old. She had arrived in Constantinople with great pomp, met by some seventy women from the palace, and married the young Alexios on 2 March 1180. At the marriage her name was changed to Anna.

The elder stepsister of Alexios II, Maria Porphyrogennete, who had married Renier of Montferrat that same year, now decided to make an advance on the throne under the guise of protecting her stepbrother. In 1181 she and her supporters started a riot in the streets, as the people were now impatient with Anna, the foreign girl who seemed to be achieving little except favouring the Westerners in the capital, particularly the Venetian and Genoese merchants. The riot came to nothing, but it opened the door for one of Byzantium's more extraordinary characters to enter the fray: Andronikos Komnenos. He was the grandson of Alexios I Komnenos, a cousin of Manuel I and the present emperor's uncle. He had lived the life of an adventurer and soldier, and through his family connections was the governor of various provinces. He had been in and out of favour with his uncle Manuel I but had always managed to charm his way out of trouble and into the inner circle of Manuel's court. With the death of Manuel, he decided it was time to return to the capital and attempt to usurp the throne for himself. Encouraged by Maria to join her in Constantinople, he played on the people's resentment of Westerners and prepared to come to the aid of his cousin the emperor. At the age of around 16, but fit, ambitious and full of vigour, he marched into the capital

KOMNENIAN DYNASTY

with an army and triggered one of Byzantium's most notorious events: the Massacre of the Latins. This pogrom-like attack on the Roman Catholics of Constantinople was to live long in the memory of the Latins, and was the most violent manifestation of the animosity between the Orthodox Christians and their largely Italian neighbours that had been growing throughout the reign of Manuel I and now, with the French Maria as regent, was almost flagrant. The trading communities of Pisa, Genoa and Venice suffered the most. Men, women and children were all slaughtered by the marauding mob, and Andronikos did nothing to help. Some managed to escape to boats and sail away, but nearly 4,000 of those who survived were sold to the Seljuks as slaves. It was a low point in East–West relations and undoubtedly paved the way for the reciprocal action of the Latins in the Fourth Crusade.

Alexios II would have played no part in this, but Andronikos had anyone that befriended the young emperor removed from the palace and murdered. First, his stepsister Maria and her husband, Renier of Montferrat, were poisoned. Andronikos then had himself proclaimed co-emperor, arguing that Alexios needed help, being so young. To help him achieve this end, he had Alexios's mother, Maria, and her partner, Alexios Komnenos, brought before the court on charges of treason and found guilty: the poor Alexios II was forced to sign the death warrant of his own mother. During this period the defence of the empire was of no concern to Andronikos, and there were invasions from the Hungarians in the Balkans, the Venetians took the Dalmatian coast, and Kilij Arslan II overran parts of western Anatolia. The empire was crumbling.

According to Niketas Choniates, it was not long before Andronikos quoted to his advisors a Greek proverb, 'Better the aged eagle than the fledgling lark', implying that the empire would be better served by one emperor than two. The young Alexios II Komnenos met his terrible end strangled by a bowstring in his rooms in September 1183. His body was brought to Andronikos, who had it dismembered and thrown in the sea – a terrible, ignoble end for a young boy who never had the opportunity to rule as his destiny should have allowed. Byzantium was now on an unstoppable course towards catastrophe, and at its head was a tyrant.

Andronikos I Komnenos
September 1183 – September 1185

He kept his body in excellent shape, was erect, of heroic stature, and even in his old age had a youthful face.
NIKETAS CHONIATES, *c.* 1208

He was by nature so full of contradictions that he could be given the highest praise or the most severe blame, according to which side of his character was being observed.
EUSTATHIOS OF THESSALONICA, *c.* 1190

Andronikos I Komnenos was many things – charming, charismatic, sadistic, manipulative, a competent administrator, a brave soldier – but above all he was a despot.

Born between 1118 and 1120, Andronikos lived a life of privilege and comfort, and little is known of him except that he was imprisoned for an attempt on the life of the emperor Manuel I. He spent nine years in captivity and on one occasion dug a tunnel from his cell through a sewer pipe to escape but was recaptured. Eventually freed, he returned quickly to the ways of his old life. In 1143, while out hunting, he was captured by a band of Seljuk Turkish soldiers who had him imprisoned and ransomed. He remained their prisoner for a whole year before his ever-forgiving cousin Manuel I paid his ransom. Andronikos returned to Constantinople, where his charms worked on the emperor yet again, and he was allowed to live in the palace. His roving eye alighted upon the princess Eudokia Komnenos, the niece of Manuel who resided in the palace, but as soon as he started an affair with her Manuel once more had Andronikos sent away. This time he was given a military command in Cilicia from which he deserted, travelling to the court of Antioch where the reigning prince, Raymond, had a beautiful younger sister, Philippa, just 20 years old. Andronikos seduced her, immediately prompting Manuel to recall him to Constantinople for punishment. To avoid capture Andronikos fled to the kingdom of Jerusalem, where he lent his military skills to King Amalric.

Here Andronikos met his next conquest, the 21-year-old queen Theodora Komnene, another niece of Manuel I and widow of the former king Baldwin III. It seems to have been a genuine love affair; when they were chased out of Jerusalem the pair took off first to Beirut, then lived some years among the Muslims in the east of Anatolia. They had two sons and were relatively settled in Koloneia when the commander of Trebizond managed to capture Theodora and her two sons and take them back to Constantinople. Andronikos immediately travelled to the capital and flung himself on the mercy of Manuel I. Yet again he brought Manuel around enough for himself and his family to be released and sent to a residence in a distant province on the shores of the Black Sea.

Upon Manuel I's death in 1180, Andronikos saw his moment to take the crown that he undoubtedly felt was his by right. Playing on the xenophobic mood of the populace, he marched back to Constantinople, where he played a significant part in the infamous Massacre of the Latins. Three years later he had himself crowned co-emperor, and within a few weeks he had the 14-year-old Emperor Alexios II strangled with a bowstring, promptly marrying his 12-year-old widow. This 65-year-old adventurer, his young bride at his side, now had the empire completely under his command.

At this point Andronikos seems to have fallen into a pattern of paranoia-fuelled revenge. His brief reign saw him torture and murder people at an astonishing rate. Anyone he felt threatened by or who slighted him in any way, he would almost instantly have either blinded or murdered. On one occasion he had every prisoner taken from his cell and killed, so convinced was he of some sort of conspiracy against him. Events unfolding abroad were no less violent: perhaps in retaliation for the Massacre of the Latins some years before, William of Sicily invaded with a large army, killing thousands and sacking Byzantium's second city, Thessalonica. Andronikos was unable to stop them.

If Andronikos could claim one rational policy, it was the stamping out of corrupt systems that had become endemic under his predecessors. He hated the landed aristocracy and curtailed their power at every turn; he is famously quoted as saying, 'Either cease from ill doing, or you will cease from living.' People tended to obey him. His extreme behaviour could not go unchecked for long, however, and as his atrocities multiplied so did his enemies. One of them, Isaac Komnenos, another cousin of Manuel I, fled in open defiance and established a kingdom in Cyprus. Isaac managed to maintain this position for seven years before he was forced to hand the kingdom over to Richard the Lionheart, who conquered the island during the Third Crusade.

A henchman loyal to Andronikos named Stephen Hagiochristophorites, who was rumoured to have strangled the child emperor Alexios II, was sent to arrest Isaac Angelos, a man from a noble family whom Andronikos suspected of treachery. During the confrontation Isaac defended himself to the point of running his sword through Hagiochristophorites, fleeing to Hagia Sophia for safety. Soon a mob appeared and, hearing of the attack, turned on Andronikos, the man they had heralded as their saviour just a few years before. Isaac Angelos was proclaimed emperor, and Andronikos had to flee for his life. He took his young bride with him, along with a mistress, and sailed up the Bosphorus to escape, but winds off the Black Sea prevented him from getting away. He was captured and sent back to Isaac.

Isaac Angelos released Andronikos Komnenos to the mob, who subjected him to the most unspeakably painful and brutal death. Tied to a post, he was beaten senseless, one of his hands was cut off, his hair and teeth were pulled out, and boiling water poured over his head. Finally, he was taken to the Hippodrome and hung

  KOMNENIAN DYNASTY

upside down as two soldiers cut him to pieces. Thus ended the reign of the noble house of Komnenos. Nineteen years later the city would fall to the marauding troops of the Fourth Crusade, and there can be little doubt that the reign of Andronikos was partly responsible.

ANGELID DYNASTY

(1185–1204)

The Angelid dynasty, which stemmed from the female line of the Komnenoi, was unable to prevent the invasion of Anatolian lands by the Seljuks of Rum, and could not curb either the Bulgarian uprising in the north or the Hungarian expansion into Dalmatia. Their most significant disaster, however, was the surrender of Constantinople to the soldiers of the Fourth Crusade in 1204, which ended the unassailability it had enjoyed since Constantine I and marked the beginning of the subsequent diaspora of the noble families.

Isaac II Angelos

September 1185 – April 1195

He sold off government posts like they were vegetables in a market. He had a ruddy complexion and red hair, was of average height and had a stocky body.
NIKETAS CHONIATES, *c.* 1208

Andronikos Doukas Angelos and Euphrosyne Kastamonitissa, the parents of Isaac II Angelos, can arguably be held responsible for Byzantium's worst catastrophe until the city's final demise: their two sons, Isaac II and Alexios III, and one grandson, Alexios IV, ruled the empire for nineteen disastrous years, culminating in the sacking of the great city by the soldiers of the Fourth Crusade. The Angeloi family were brought into the orbit of the Komnenoi when the youngest daughter of the great Alexios I married Isaac's grand-father Constantine Angelos. As a result the Komnenoi continually bestowed important roles upon them, so that these unexceptional aristocrats from Philadelphia in western Turkey had become part of the ruling establishment.

Isaac was at the centre of a popular rebellion against Andronikos, doubtless more on account of the general hatred of Andronikos than through any merit of his own, and entered the palace with a crowd behind him. He was proclaimed emperor and had Andronikos thrown to the mob. At first there was a glimmer of hope for his reign. He defeated the Norman king of Sicily, William II, at the Battle of Demetritzes on 7 November 1185. This was a significant achievement. William had assumed that the chaos in Constantinople would distract the attention of the Byzantine army away from his force of tens of thousands of men, but he was wrong, and suffered a humiliating defeat. Isaac tried to repeat this victory by sending a large fleet of ships to rescue his brother Alexios, held captive in Acre, but the Normans destroyed the fleet in an act of revenge. Isaac's most lasting mistake was to try to win back the island of Cyprus from the usurper Isaac Komnenos, but once again he failed and was mistakenly accused of collaborating with the Muslims under Saladin – an allegation that helped fuel the increasing European mistrust of the Byzantines.

Isaac took steps to establish diplomatic ties with his neighbours by marrying off his niece, Eudokia Angelina, to Stefan Nemanja of Serbia, and his sister, Theodora, to Conrad of Montferrat. He also married for a second time (little is known of the fate of his first wife, Irene Palaiologos, mother of the future emperor Alexios IV). His new wife was Margaret, daughter of the king of Hungary, Bela III, and their son, John Angelos, became a prince.

After this initial flurry of responsibility, and some success in defending the empire, Isaac appears to have turned his attention to nothing but his own pleasure. He had raised a special tax to help pay for his extremely lavish wedding to Margaret, taking money from his people that they could ill afford. From here he seemed to turn his back on running the empire and handed most of the administrative responsibility to his uncle Theodore Kastamonites, and after his death, in 1193, to an official named Constantine Mesopotamites, neither of whom could stand up to the emperor's demands for money to spend on private entertainments, extravagant new buildings and settlements with unruly neighbours. The army was diminishing from lack of funds and motivation and the government was in chaos as Isaac, other than occasionally leading his troops in battle against the Bulgarians, was either oblivious to the decline or powerless to halt it.

Gradually, various parts of the empire fell into the hands of his enemies, and in 1187 the great leader of the Muslim forces, Saladin, took Jerusalem. He had defeated the Latin forces all through Palestine, most notably at the Battle of Hattin. On hearing of the loss of Jerusalem, Pope Urban III reportedly fell down dead of shock, and his successor, Gregory VIII, immediately called for a Third Crusade, to be led by the German emperor Frederick I Barbarossa, Phillip II of France, and the king of England, Richard the Lionheart. Isaac II roused himself from his indulgencies just long enough to realize that it would be very dangerous to have the forces of Frederick I Barbarossa travelling through his lands. Not only would they take what they wanted from the surrounding countryside, as the Crusaders had always done, but Isaac feared that they would make an assault on Constantinople itself. To quell this fear, he pleaded for aid from none other than Saladin, offering to refuse any help to the Crusaders. This incensed the Crusaders, and Frederick threatened to take Constantinople and march against the Byzantines in open war. At this point Isaac capitulated and agreed to help the Latins, offering promises of transport ships and provisions. He also handed over hostages to ensure that he kept his word. The Crusaders marched on but to no avail: Saladin was too strong for them. The Third Crusade collapsed. Aside from Richard the Lionheart's conquest of Cyprus, the Crusaders were removed from Isaac's sphere. This fortunate occurrence meant that he could once again engage in warfare with the new kingdom of Bulgaria.

While Isaac was away from the capital on a hunting expedition, his elder brother, Alexios Angelos, whipped up the beleaguered people of Constantinople and what elements of powerful government remained, and declared himself emperor in 1195. Isaac, who had caught wind of his brother's plans, escaped to Stagira in Macedonia, where he was captured and immediately blinded on his brother's orders. (According to ancient custom, anyone who was disfigured was prevented from ruling.) He was brought to Constantinople and thrown into the palace dungeons, where he would remain in terrible conditions, alongside his young son Alexios, for eight years.

Alexios III Angelos
April 1195 – July 1203

If Isaac II Angelos was universally acknowledged as one of the most inept emperors ever to have ruled Byzantium, his elder brother, Alexios III, was far worse. Alexios presided over the empire at its most notorious moment in all Byzantine history, the only exception being its eventual fall in 1453.

It is surprising that Alexios coveted the throne enough to mount a coup when his brother was out hunting – a brother who had gone out of his way to help him, organizing a rescue operation to free him from Acre, and who had given him the grand title of *sebastokrator*, showering him with luxuries when he was safely back within the walls of Constantinople. That he should then have had his younger brother blinded and hurled into the dungeons of the city is even more revealing of his character.

During his years in charge, Alexios III Angelos Komnenos – he added 'Komnenos' to his name to give it a ring of dignity and to place himself at one remove from his brother's 'Angelos' – had squandered any money he could find in the treasury to keep army commanders and important government officials loyal to his rule. The Holy Roman Emperor Henry VI threatened to attack the city unless he was given 5,000 pounds of gold in tribute, so Alexios paid as much as he could muster by raiding the tombs of his ancestors in the church of the Holy Apostles. The only neighbour with whom

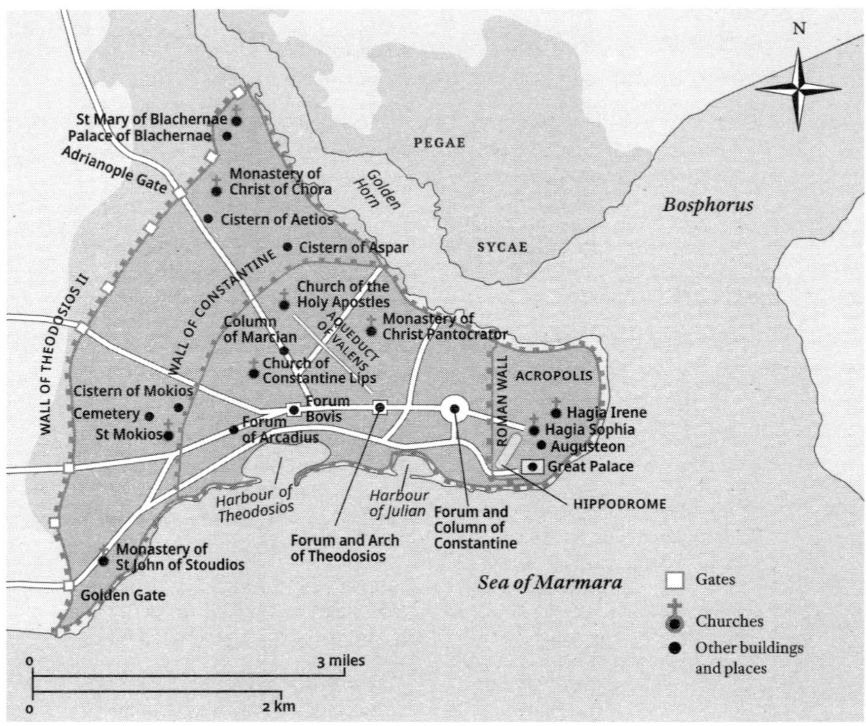

he enjoyed good relations was Serbia, owing to his brother's skill in arranging a marriage between his daughter, Eudokia Angelina, and the king's son, Stefan Nemanja. This union came to an end in 1200, and she was sent back to Constantinople. Alexios III's forceful and somewhat unruly wife, Euphrosyne Doukaina Kamatera, openly had affairs in the palace; and even though Alexios once banished her for a short period, she returned with vigour and continued to exercise much influence over her incompetent husband.

The Fourth Crusade can be seen as a coming together of powerful forces: the various nationalist and imperial ambitions of the Venetians, the Franks and the Genoese; the influential personalities

ANGELID DYNASTY

of figures such as Pope Innocent III and Doge Dandolo, who shaped events; the naivety of Isaac II and his son, the future Alexios IV; and the woeful dereliction of duties of Alexios III.

The Crusade arrived on the emperor's doorstep in June 1203 in the form of thousands of Crusaders camping outside the city walls, one of them being his nephew Alexios IV. He had escaped captivity in the dungeons of Constantinople by bribing some merchants and sailing to Italy to seek the favour of Pope Innocent III or, failing that, from his brother-in-law Philip of Swabia. His plan was to join forces with the Fourth Crusade, remove his wicked uncle Alexios III from the throne, and restore his father, Isaac II, to power in the capital. Waiting outside the walls of the city where he had been held captive for almost half his life, the 20-year-old Alexios IV was completely ignored by the emperor Alexios III. The Venetians lost patience and decided to launch an assault on the city, led by the aged and blind Doge Enrico Dandolo. They scaled the walls and set fire to large parts of the capital before Alexios and a division of soldiers marched in and attacked the invaders. Typically, at the prospect of real fighting Alexios retreated and hid in his palace. Now it was the turn of his courtiers to demand action, and Alexios duly promised to attack the Venetians the following morning. Once more he lied to anyone who would listen, and that same night, 17 July, he grabbed what was left of the treasury – some thousand pounds of gold and precious objects – abandoned his wife and children, except for his favourite daughter, Irene – and escaped to Thrace.

Alexios was never to return to Constantinople, the city he had betrayed and allowed to fall into enemy hands. His life continued in the same vein: in exile he later befriended Alexios V and agreed to give him his daughter Eudokia Angelina in marriage, before turning on his son-in-law and having him blinded. He then escaped to Epiros, where once again he lied and cheated his way into and then out of power, until finally, after picking the wrong side in a battle between Theodore Laskaris and the sultan of Rum in 1211, he was thrown into a monastery in Nicaea and died later that year.

Alexios III Angelos Komnenos created nothing but pain and calamity for those close to him, and caused nothing but catastrophe to the empire.

Alexios IV Angelos & Isaac II Angelos
August 1203 – February 1204

Though they (the accursed Latins) may dissemble friendship, submitting to the needs of the time, they yet despise us as their bitterest enemies; and though their speech is affable and smoother than oil flowing noiselessly, yet are their words darts, and thus sharper than a double-edged sword.
NIKETAS CHONIATES, *c.* 1208

At the young age of 12 or 13, Alexios Angelos was arrested and thrown into prison by his uncle, Alexios III, along with his blinded father. His mother, Irene, appears not to have been present at all in his life, and all we know of her is that she was perhaps in a nunnery long before this time, possibly as early as 1185 when Alexios was an infant.

Having bribed his way out of captivity, Alexios Angelos negotiated with a certain Pisan captain to be taken to his sister, Irene Angelina, who had been married off to Philip of Swabia, the king of Germany. They seemed to welcome the young man, introducing him to influential people at the court, including many Crusaders. He shared his dream with them of returning to Constantinople to free his father and take back the empire from his uncle.

It was here that Alexios's naivety played a significant part in both his trajectory and that of the empire. Enrico Dandolo, the doge of Venice, must have thought that this young prince asking for his help to enter the Byzantine capital was a form of divine intervention. He was not alone. Boniface of Montferrat, one of the Crusade's leaders whose family had close ties to the East, had long coveted the richest city in the world. Encamped with his army, having already sacked the Catholic city of Zara on the Dalmatian Coast and been cut off by Pope Innocent III as a consequence, he discerned a way out of his predicament. What these politically astute characters saw and heard from young Alexios was an opportunity presenting itself.

Alexios must have thought that matters had finally turned in his favour as these skilled adventurers offered their assistance to take him back to his capital ahead of the collective forces of the Fourth Crusade. Heady with misplaced power and benevolence, he made promises to the Crusaders: 10,000 soldiers to help fight the Saracens, 500 knights in the Holy Land maintained at his expense, ships to transport soldiers to their eventual destination, Egypt – and, to cap it all, he was happy to pay off the Crusaders' debts to Venice at the cost of 200,000 silver marks. His next undertaking was more damning than he could have understood. He promised to make the Greek Orthodox church submit to the authority of the pope.

These conditions were, of course, accepted by the Venetians and many others, but not all. Pope Innocent III had seen through the charade of princely protection and did not want the Crusaders engaging in warfare with the Byzantines. Soldiers felt the same way: they had come to fight the Saracens and retake the holy sites, not to engage in battle with fellow Christians, even if their doctrines were skewed.

On 24 June 1203, the fleet arrived at Constantinople and Alexios was paraded outside the city walls as a returning monarch. But the reigning Alexios III and the majority of the populace simply ignored him. They had an emperor already, and they certainly did not want heavily armed Latins coming into their city. And so, after some deliberation, the so-called 'Queen of all Cities' was attacked. By land and by sea, the Crusaders defeated the largely feeble opposition and on about 17 July 1203, as Alexios III fled his capital, the city was captured – the first time it had been taken by force since its founding by Constantine the Great some 900 years before.

For a brief period the people of Constantinople took the initiative and reinstalled their blinded ex-emperor on the throne. Isaac II

Angelos was back in charge and, doubtless at the suggestion of the leaders of the Crusade, had their puppet, Alexios IV, crowned as co-emperor. Very quickly the invaders demanded the payments Alexios had promised; although he tried his best, he simply did not have the money. The city was broke, the people had been taxed to the limit, and Alexios had nothing to keep them at bay. Furthermore, he had angered his own people by inviting Latin mercenaries into the capital in the first place. There was a riot.

In January 1204 riot turned into rebellion, and a hitherto minor player in the government of Byzantium, Alexios Doukas Mourtzouphlos, visited the emperors and induced them to hide, claiming that they were surrounded by the populace who wanted to tear them apart for siding with the Latins. Alexios IV was thrown into prison and murdered, and at about the same time Isaac II was poisoned, strangled or simply died of shock.

Father and son had tried their best to save the empire but were not capable of affronting the challenge. They were spared the ultimate indignity of being in charge as the city actually fell.

Alexios V Doukas Mourtzouphlos
February 1204 – April 1204

He was extremely clever by nature and arrogant in his manner, and he believed deception to be the mark of shrewdness.
NIKETAS CHONIATES, *c.* 1208

Alexios V Doukas was known as 'Mourtzouphlos' on account of his eyebrows, which were black, met in the middle and overhung his eyes. The word might also indicate that he was 'melancholy and sullen'. At the court of Alexios IV and Isaac II he occupied the position of *protovestiarios*, which gave him unrestricted access to all areas of the royal apartments.

On the night of 28 January 1204 Alexios Doukas hurried into the sleeping quarters of Alexios IV, convinced him that he must escape immediately, and led him to the dungeons, where the young man was poisoned and strangled. Crowned Alexios V, he would not rule for very long.

In the years before 1204, Alexios V had fallen in love with Eudokia Angelina, the daughter of Alexios III and the spurned wife of Stefan Nemanja of Serbia. He carried on an open affair with her, despite having been married twice before, and later agreed to marry her. Despite his appalling route to power, Mourtzouphlos proved himself an able and energetic leader. He immediately set about strengthening the city defences and tirelessly tried to rouse the populace to come together and defend their homes, their city and their lives. But there was nothing he could do to protect the beleaguered capital from the far superior forces of Doge Dandolo and Boniface of Montferrat. As they stormed through the city, raping, pillaging, looting and setting fire to whole areas, Mourtzouphlos assembled his beloved Eudokia, her mother, Euphrosyne, and others close to him, and set out in a fishing boat for Mosynopolis in Thrace, where Alexios III Angelos was hiding. Once he had arrived, he married Eudokia and began to plot with his father-in-law on how to regain the capital from the Latins. However, something went very wrong, and the ever-treacherous Alexios III had his son-in-law captured and blinded, probably so that he would not challenge Alexios for the throne. Now abandoned to his fate, Alexios V was captured by the Latins and brought back to Constantinople to stand trial for treason. The charge laid against him was the murder of the young emperor Alexios IV, no doubt designed to make the Latin usurpers appear more noble, but Alexios V claimed that it was his predecessor who had really committed treason by inviting the Latin Crusaders into the city. Alexios V was, of course, found guilty and condemned to death. He was taken to the top of the Column of Theodosios and hurled to the ground.

Alexios V Doukas Mourtzouphlos was the last to reign in Constantinople before the Latin Empire was established.

LATIN CONSTANTINOPLE AND THE EMPIRE IN EXILE

The original purpose of the Fourth Crusade, as with the previous three, was to conquer Egypt and the Holy Land, and liberate Jerusalem from the hand of the Muslim invaders. Power, opportunity and greed intervened, however, and diverted these soldiers of fortune, who instead sacked Constantinople and set up the Latin kingdoms. It was a merciless and relentless attack by Christians upon Christians, and it was a catastrophe for the Byzantines, who fled their capital to form a number of new Byzantine states in Epiros, Trebizond and, most importantly, Nicaea. It was from the last that a virtual 'government in exile' launched its recovery of the capital nearly sixty years later.

The Latin Occupation of Constantinople
(1204–1261)

These were the outrageous crimes committed by the Western armies against the inheritance of Christ. Without showing any semblance of humanity, they stole from everyone all their money and chattels, homes and clothing, leaving them with nothing at all.

NIKETAS CHONIATES, *c.* 1208

The 'Latin' rulers who reigned as emperors from Constantinople between the years 1204 and 1261 contributed very little to the lives of the Byzantines whom they had so brutally conquered. Essentially opportunistic brigands, they found themselves unsuitable and unable to rule a large empire, and once settled in the capital they spent more time plundering whatever they could from their conquered foe than trying to create anything new and lasting.

The shock of their occupation forced the Byzantine ruling class to flee and set up rival states in different parts of the empire, principally in Nicaea, but also in Trebizond on the Black Sea coast and Epiros in western Greece. It made them re-examine their systems and, indeed, their purpose. Who were they now that they had been defeated and banished from their own capital?

The Byzantine Empire had essentially ceased to exist at the point that the Latin rulers, led by Baldwin of Flanders, sat on the throne of Constantinople and were crowned in Hagia Sophia by a new patriarch, the Venetian Tommaso Morosini. On the surface, the new rulers took on a system of government similar to that of the Byzantines, but in practice the territory was divided up into smaller fiefdoms and ruled virtually independently by despots. The rot was to set in immediately, as some former knights were unhappy with their allocation. Chief among them was Boniface of Montferrat, who had been given lands in Asia Minor but wanted more on the European side; after failing to be elected as emperor, he invaded Macedonia and Thrace, establishing himself as the new king in Thessalonica. His actions would have serious consequences, allowing the Empire of Nicaea to flourish when Byzantium was at its most vulnerable. Unsurprisingly, the local people – mainly Greek-speaking Orthodox Christians – did not welcome these new masters. Only in the Morea, today's Peloponnese, did the populace manage an uneasy truce and remained largely independent from the ensuing fight for control.

It was the Venetians who were most focused on what they wanted from the defeated Byzantine state: a strengthened ability to dominate trade throughout the Eastern Mediterranean. They controlled not only the port of Constantinople, but the ports all along the Adriatic coast, many of the islands in the Aegean, and the strategically vital island of Crete.

The Latins' fall from power, led by a resurgent Byzantine government in exile based in Nicaea, was sixty years in the coming, but these usurpers and sons of usurpers were always going to fail

in an alien land, and ultimately were seen as a destructive interlude in the story of Byzantium. They fought among themselves,
misjudged the strength of their neighbours (notably the Bulgars
and the Serbs), underestimated the power of the Seljuk Turks,
ignored the will of the people who longed for the return of the true
Byzantine way of life and, perhaps most importantly of all, they
ignored the populace's unshakeable Orthodox faith and its hatred
of the Catholics and its popes.

It is worth noting the effect of the looting, destruction and plunder of great works of art that occurred under these rulers. When
the Latins took over, Byzantium was a city that was still the envy
of the world. Rich in all forms of art and learning, it had treasuries filled with works from its own culture and many others – the
most recognizable and symbolic being the four bronze horses that
once surveyed the Hippodrome and are now housed inside San
Marco in Venice (those on the basilica's roof are modern replicas).
However, in the wake of the Fourth Crusade the city was stripped
of these and many other treasures. Niketas Choniates writes of the
wanton destruction of churches, tombs and royal apartments by
Crusaders who, he claimed, 'were in want of money, for the barbarians are unable to sate their love of riches'.

The Despotate of Epiros

(1204–1337)

For a while, the Despotate of Epiros seemed the place most likely to
provide a successor to the Latin emperors in Constantinople. The
despotate would last for 140 years but was ultimately not militarily or politically strong enough to prevent the emperors of Nicaea
from claiming the imperial throne. It was Michael Angelos, a cousin
of Isaac II and Alexios III, who took control of this part of western Greece and formed a capital, Epiros, at Arta. Under his vigorous leadership, the Epirotes fought all who stood in their way: the

　　　　　　　　　　　　　　LATIN CONSTANTINOPLE

Venetians, the Frankish kingdom of Thessalonica and even their former colleagues in Nicaea. Michael Angelos was succeeded by his half-brother Theodore, who had rather grandly assumed the name Theodore Angelos Komnenos Doukas in order to claim as much legitimacy as possible. He too fought bravely and successfully, even capturing the Latin emperor Peter of Courtenay and subsequently taking Thessalonica. At this point he had himself crowned emperor of Byzantium, setting himself up as the only rival to the emperor of Nicaea and the one true heir to the throne of Byzantium.

However, Theodore overstretched himself. When battling with the resurgent Bulgaria under the strong leadership of John Asen II, he was defeated at the Battle of Klokotnica in 1230 and was captured and blinded. Retreating to their small base at Epiros, his forces remained subservient to the more powerful emperor of Nicaea, John III Doukas Vatatzes, and his successors for the rest of the despotate's duration. The royal palace has long since disappeared, but the main church in their capital, Arta, remains, the church of the Parigoritissa. Built in the late 1280s, it is a rather clumsy provincial affair.

The Empire of Trebizond
(1204–1461)

Shortly before the Fall of Constantinople in 1204, two brothers, Alexios and David Komnenos, grandsons of the tyrant Andronikos I Komnenos, set up an empire of their own in Trebizond, on the Black Sea coast. The two ruled jointly, and at their zenith they controlled much of Paphlagonia and established dominance over the strategic ports of Cherson and Kerch in the Crimea. However, events conspired against them. They met their match in the cunning and dynamic Theodore Laskaris of the Empire of Nicaea, who eventually became the true emperor of Byzantium in exile. They fought and lost some significant battles against the Seljuk Turks, and when David died, sometime around 1212, their drive for expansion had dissipated. Their empire remained intact for another 250 years, centred in Trebizond, but the state was subservient to the Byzantine emperors in Constantinople and never again attempted to challenge them for leadership or territory. Ironically, they outlived their more illustrious masters in the capital, finally falling to the Ottomans in 1461.

Artists in Trebizond produced work of high quality and in a distinctive style. No mosaics exist from this time, but there are some wonderful examples of wall painting in the church of Hagia Sophia in Trebizond itself. Murals were undoubtedly cheaper to produce: there was no need for vast glass factories making countless small tesserae. It also gave the people a way to exhibit their own individual style. A subtler use of colour – indeed, a whole new style altogether – began to emerge. Horses were painted a deep red, houses bright yellow, and oxen were green, in what can be seen as a deliberate reaction against realism. The influence of their Persian neighbours may well have played a part here, since realism was never taken at face value in the courts of Persia or by the Ottomans, whose use of colour was always dynamic and imaginative. The intellectuals and artists of Trebizond were often forced to travel to other areas for work, and not just Constantinople. In Russia and the Balkans their influence is apparent. The monastery at Gračanica on the Serbian–Kosovo border is a fine example: the king of a largely independent Serbia, Stefan Milutin, built the monastery in 1321, and beside a fresco of him donating the church is an inscription that reads: 'I have seen the ruins and the decay of the Holy Virgin's temple of Gračanica, so I have built it from the ground and painted and decorated it both from inside and outside.' The frescoes are fine examples of Serbian Trebizond-influenced painting of the early 14th century.

     LATIN CONSTANTINOPLE

THE EMPIRE OF NICAEA

(1208–1261)

The Laskarids were the largest and ultimately the most success-ful group of aristocrats who had fled Constantinople following the Latin invasion of 1204. They ruled in exile from Nicaea, just 100 km (60 miles) from Constantinople.

Theodore I Laskaris
Emperor of Nicaea 1208–1222

He was small in stature but not excessively so, quite dark, with a flowing beard forked at the end, and with eyes differing slightly in colour.

GEORGE AKROPOLITES, AFTER 1260

Theodore Laskaris was the son-in-law of the emperor Alexios III, having married the emperor's daughter Anna Angelina in 1199, and in the chaos that followed the loss of the capital in 1204 had as good a claim to the throne as anyone else. He came from a noble but not particularly distinguished family and had fought bravely in defending Constantinople from the first onslaught of the Latin soldiers of the Fourth Crusade. His brother, Constantine Laskaris, was briefly and unofficially named emperor in Constantinople in the confusion of the Latin occupation. However, Theodore quickly established himself as leader of the Byzantines in exile and was joined by his brother shortly afterwards.

At first Theodore's task must have seemed daunting. Nicaea (the modern Turkish town of Iznik) is less than 100 km (60 miles) from Constantinople, and the victorious Latins under their various military overlords would have looked very capable of crossing the Bosphorus and marching through the countryside towards them. There was confusion among the diaspora of Byzantine aristocracy, as the rump states established in Epiros and Trebizond also claimed to be the true government in exile. The Seljuk Turks were close by, settled in Asia Minor with a capital in Iconium. To a lesser man this may have been enough to cause him to simply surrender to one of the other contenders, but Theodore was steely, clever and patient. He did not have himself crowned emperor immediately, possibly in deference to his father-in-law and his brother, who were both theoretically emperors in their own right. Nicaea was besieged on all sides, and an early encounter saw his brother Constantine die, presumably at the hands of Henry of Flanders, at the Battle of Adramyttion in 1205. This hastened Theodore's need to be seen as the undisputed leader of Nicaea: after appointing a patriarch, Michael IV Autoreianos, he was duly crowned emperor in 1208.

Theodore entered into an alliance with the powerful Kaloyan of Bulgaria, and together they stalled the Latin advance at Adrianople. A surprising problem arose when Theodore's father-in-law Alexios III found refuge with the old enemy, the Seljuk Turks, and their leader, Sultan Kaykhusraw I of Rum. Under the pretence of helping Alexios III to regain his Byzantine throne, the Seljuks attacked Theodore and the Empire of Nicaea in a pitched battle at Antioch on the Meander river. According to the historian George Akropolites, during the battle – in which both leaders led their troops in combat – Theodore found himself in hand-to-hand fighting with the sultan himself. Kaykhusraw managed to throw Theodore off his horse but was then felled himself by the Byzantine emperor hacking at the legs of his own horse. Once the sultan was on the ground, Theodore I Laskaris killed him himself. This was a highly important moment for Theodore: it won him not only the battle, but also the reputation of a legendary fighter, which allowed him never to have to join in battle personally again. He was now able to capture his untrustworthy father-in-law, whom he imprisoned in a monastery for the rest of his days.

In seeking an alliance with the Latins in Constantinople, Theodore was offered the hand of Marie of Courtenay, the teenage daughter of Peter II of Courtenay and Yolande of Flanders. Peter had been captured by Theodore Angelos Komnenos Doukas of Epiros, so his wife, Yolande, was *de jure* regent for her captured husband. She agreed to the marriage of her daughter, and in about 1219 Marie and Theodore I Laskaris were married in Nicaea. He was 45, and Marie about 14 years of age.

Theodore died peacefully three years later of unknown causes. He had skilfully manoeuvred the Empire of Nicaea from its status as a small group of exiled aristocrats on the verge of annihilation into a legitimate force capable of recapturing the capital and reinstating the Byzantine throne. That was to take another forty years, but Theodore played a vital role in establishing the dynasty that could achieve it. The throne passed to his daughter Irene Laskaris, from his first marriage, and her dynamic and capable husband, John III Doukas Vatatzes.

John III Doukas Vatatzes

Emperor of Nicaea December 1222 – November 1254

He was a gentle man, always inclined to compassion.
GEORGE AKROPOLITES, AFTER 1260

John III Doukas Vatatzes was the greatest of the Nicaean emperors. Throughout his long reign, the government in exile came ever closer to recapturing the capital and ousting the detested Latin rulers. It was only his debilitating epilepsy that prevented him from taking back the capital himself. Having gained the throne through his marriage to Irene Laskaris, he remained faithful to her – by no means a common attitude among the Byzantine nobility. Irene was badly injured in a riding accident shortly after the birth of their son,

Theodore, and could have no more children. She helped her husband in many aspects of the Nicaean court and its government's administration, and is credited with nurturing an environment of cultured learning and charitable enterprise that helped maintain and strengthen the Byzantine values of study and religious contemplation. Something of a polymath, John III established hospitals, schools and libraries, which attracted many intellectuals and artists to his court, laying the foundations for what later became known as the 'Palaiologan renaissance'.

John's real skill was as a political diplomat, and in the long and revered tradition of Byzantine emperors he managed alliances with his neighbours as effectively as any before him. Chief among these was John Asen II of Bulgaria, with whom he remained on good terms, even laying siege to Constantinople alongside him in 1235. The year before, John III had arranged for his son, the future Theodore II, to marry Elena of Bulgaria, John Asen's daughter. Later, some years after his beloved Irene Laskaris had died, he made an alliance for himself with the brilliant and successful Frederick II Hohenstauffen, king of Sicily and Holy Roman Emperor, marrying his daughter, at the very young age of just 10 (John was now about 50 years old).

There were some dissenters at home, however: it seems John expelled Michael Palaiologos (later to become an emperor himself) from the Nicaean capital for allegedly trying to stage a coup. However, they were few in number, and John generally enjoyed the support of all in his empire.

John was preoccupied with restoring the foundations for a strong economy, and through creative taxation he (somewhat controversially) discouraged the buying of foreign – particularly Venetian – products and encouraged the empire to buy goods only from itself. Farms were made more efficient, and their produce was controlled centrally. Famously he had a crown made for Irene that was fitted only with egg-shaped jewels, paid for by taxes raised on the sale of eggs from his own estates. The great Flemish traveller William of Rubruck, who passed through the court of

THE EMPIRE OF NICAEA

John III, remarked that John and his entourage were very well read, noting that John himself had a copy of what purported to be the missing books of Ovid's *Fasti*. It seems clear that the court of John III Doukas Vatatzes in exile was a centre of learning, patronage, sound economic policy and traditional Roman–Byzantine justice that would have rivalled any other court of the time. John died in Nymphaion, on the Crimean peninsula, in 1254 without achieving his great goal of recapturing Constantinople, but he successfully established the systems and diplomatic alliances that would make it inevitable. Canonized some fifty years after his death as 'John the Merciful', he was honoured with a feast day, on 4 November; it is still celebrated, though today he is more popularly referred to as the 'Father of the Greeks'.

Theodore II Laskaris

Emperor of Nicaea November 1254 – August 1258

A kind and gentle soul.

GEORGE AKROPOLITES, AFTER 1260

The short reign of Theodore II Laskaris was dominated by his ill health. A scholarly, suspicious and generally embittered young man, he came to the throne at the age of 33 and was dead four years later. His father, John the Merciful, was not the most loving of parents. He was strict with the young Theodore, never affording him the title of co-emperor that was most common among first-born sons; he seems to have given him the best of educations but little paternal affection, believing that too much flattery at court would corrupt the young emperor-in-waiting. Instead it was left to his invalid mother, Irene, to bring Theodore up among her circle of literary and learned friends in Nicaea. It is telling that Theodore, who inherited his father's epilepsy, took the name Laskaris from his mother rather than his father's name of Vatatzes.

A prolific writer of discourses on all subjects and a poet of some note, Theodore wrote the *Megas parakletikos kanon*, or 'Great Supplicatory Canon to Our Lady', which is still in use in Orthodox church ceremonies, and throughout his life he preferred the company of learned men, often from the middle classes, to that of aristocrats. One of the people he did not see eye to eye with was the future emperor Michael VIII Palaiologos, and their poor relationship was to prove fatal for Theodore's young son, John.

Despite his academic leanings, when the Bulgarians attacked part of the empire in Thrace Theodore personally led his forces into battle and defeated the young king Michael Asen I, acquiring more territory for the empire and getting ever closer to regaining Constantinople. He also acquired the cities of Durrachion and Servia from Epiros by holding Theodora Petraliphaina, wife of Theodore Angelos Komnenos Doukas, and her son to ransom. Theodore seems to have been content with his own wife, Helen Asen, a princess of Bulgaria, who had been brought over to the court as a little girl in preparation for their marriage. They had at least four daughters and one son, who would succeed him as John IV. When Helen died Theodore never remarried, and his health deteriorated quite rapidly. Knowing he had little time left, he decided to install his oldest friend, George Mouzalon, as regent to his 7-year-old son. This was not a popular move with the aristocratic families: Mouzalon was not from a noble family and had been disliked by the powerful at court for many years.

Despite his ill health and obvious vulnerabilities, Theodore II Laskaris upheld the high levels of scholarship instigated by his parents and maintained the Nicaean Empire's position as the inevitable successor to the Latin rulers of Byzantium.

John IV Laskaris
Emperor of Nicaea August 1258 – December 1261

Upon the death of his father, the 8-year-old John IV Laskaris became an orphan. His mother, Helen Asen, had died some years earlier, and his father's last instructions were that his lifelong friend George Mouzalon was to be the boy's regent until John came of age. Alas, George Mouzalon had many enemies and had always been resented by the aristocratic families of the government in exile in Nicaea – so much so that, as he attended Theodore II's funeral just nine days after his death, he was assassinated. It was a brutal slaying, in which his two brothers were also killed by mercenaries most probably carrying out the orders of the ambitious and ruthless Michael Palaiologos. The young John IV was present at the killings but was spared; Michael Palaiologos wanted to be positively associated with the young emperor and became his guardian immediately after the murders. The patriarch Arsenios, who had been appointed by John's father, Theodore II, was powerless to intervene and eventually crowned Michael VIII Palaiologos as co-emperor to the young John IV on 1 January 1259, four months after the death of Theodore II.

For the remainder of his life, the child John was kept within the palace and brought out to meet people only when it suited the usurper Michael VIII. Documents were signed in their joint names, but when Michael's generals had taken Constantinople the boy was not present during the celebrations and was never mentioned again. A few months after the victory, John was taken to the dungeons and blinded on the orders of Michael VIII, now sole emperor. The empire had finally regained its capital, but its treatment of the rightful heir was shrouded in secrecy and cruelty. John IV is revered as a saint in the Russian Orthodox church.

PALAIOLOGAN DYNASTY

(1261–1453)

The last and longest-serving dynasty of the Byzantine era oversaw a cultural revival, with significant developments in literature, art and philosophy. However, despite several attempts to unite the Eastern Orthodox church with the Catholic church of Rome, the many Palaiologan emperors failed to find a way of securing religious union with, and military help from, the West. The ruling family were racked with internal divisions, most notably during the fifty-year reign of John V, who was made a vassal to the Ottoman sultan, was usurped by his own son Andronikos IV, and then restored to power, before being once again usurped, this time by his grandson John VI. The eventual end of the Byzantine Empire under the last emperor, Constantine XI, was both inevitable and tragic. Constantine XI died on the walls of the great city, vainly fighting the vast Ottoman army of Mehmed II, known as 'the Conqueror'.

Michael VIII Palaiologos
December 1261 – December 1282
(Emperor of Nicaea 1259–1261)

The final and longest-lasting dynasty in Byzantium's history, the house of Palaiologos was founded by Michael VIII in 1261. His effective and at times brilliant reign began with a ruthless and brutal act. His despicable treatment of John IV – having him blinded and murdered while still a child – caused the usurper great difficulties with the people of Constantinople and members of the ruling class. The patriarch, Arsenios, had Michael VIII excommunicated for his acts of cruelty against the former emperor, before he himself was removed and a puppet put in his place. Michael survived, and it could be argued that the Byzantine Empire was fortunate to have such a diplomatically astute, cunning and ruthless leader at this most delicate of times in its history.

Michael Palaiologos was born of a noble family, and through his mother claimed descent from the emperor Alexios III. He was ambitious as a young man, and despite his youth resented the fact that the 'low-born' emperor John III Doukas Vatatzes was in a superior position to himself. He was summoned by the emperor, accused of plotting against him and ordered to suffer 'trial by ordeal'. This involved holding a red-hot poker to prove one's innocence. If you were unharmed, you were cleared of all charges, but if your hands were burnt you were considered guilty. According to George Akropolites's account, the confident Michael replied to the challenge by saying that if Phokas, the adviser to the emperor, would take the iron with his own hands and pass it to him he would happily receive it in the belief that truth would be restored. Phokas declined and Michael was set free.

John III must have felt some fondness towards the arrogant Michael as he allowed him to marry his grandniece Theodora. Michael was always mistrusted, however; after the death of John III, fearing the wrath of the new emperor, Theodore II Laskaris, Michael and some friends escaped the Byzantine territories and signed up as mercenaries for the Seljuk sultan Kaykaus II of Rum, in whose service he fought against the Byzantines for several years. As soon as Theodore II died, Michael returned to Nicaea and positioned himself as the guardian of the 8-year-old child emperor John IV Laskaris, before being proclaimed co-emperor in Nymphaion on 1 January 1259.

Already ruling as if he were sole emperor, having locked John away in the palace, Michael gathered his forces and won an important victory against an alliance of Latins and Theodore Angelos

Komnenos Doukas, the despot of Epiros, at the Battle of Pelagonia in 1259. His triumph not only subdued his enemies but also lent Michael legitimacy as a successful leader and commander-in-chief.

The big prize was to recapture Constantinople from the detested Latin emperor Baldwin II. After an unsuccessful attempt in 1260, Michael signed the Treaty of Nymphaeum with the Genoese to help him defeat the powerful Venetian navy that blocked his seaward entry into the city. However, this move suddenly proved redundant. One of his generals, Alexios Strategopoulos, was outside the city walls on a reconnaissance mission when some loyal Greek insiders informed him that most of the Latin forces were away fighting a battle against other enemies. The gates were opened, allowing Alexios inside the city. Constantinople was recaptured on 25 July 1261 with virtually no resistance at all, and Michael VIII was just several days' march away in Meterion. According to Akropolites, Michael was told the news by his sister, who apparently woke him early in the morning by telling him, 'Christ has conferred Constantinople upon you.'

Entering the city through the Golden Gate on 15 August 1261, Michael VIII Palaiologos celebrated with great ceremonies and the pageantry so beloved by the Byzantine people. He even had the holiest of icons, the Virgin Hodegetria – 'She Who Points the Way', reputedly painted by St Luke himself – paraded in front of him as he walked through the streets, cheered on by the adoring crowds and heralded as their saviour from the Latins.

The Constantinople that Michael saw around him was a far cry from the great city it had once been. The buildings were collapsing and its past riches had been looted: even the lead from church roofs had been stripped for making coinage. The great imperial palace at Blachernae was a virtual ruin, and the city was altogether a desolate and under-populated place. The measures Michael took were to reinvigorate the capital with new building projects and a policy of rapid repopulation. But the act of blinding the young co-emperor John IV and his subsequent incarceration severely

   PALAIOLOGAN DYNASTY

tempered Michael's popularity: despite his great achievements over the next twenty years, he was never beloved by the people.

Michael's life as emperor was spent manoeuvring the reborn Byzantine state into a position of power and influence once more. The task was Herculean: there was little money in the treasury, the army was a shadow of its former self, and the navy non-existent. Threats of invasion were all around: the Seljuks in the south and east; in the west the Despotate of Epiros and the remaining Latin principalities; and to the north the resurgent Bulgarians whose king had married the young John IV Laskaris's sister. Michael used his family to help make alliances, marrying off one illegitimate daughter to the Mongol leader, Abaqa Khan, and another to the Tartar prince, Nogai. He received the Hungarian princess Anna as a bride for his eldest son, Andronikos, which undoubtedly managed to keep this enemy at bay for many years.

Perhaps the greatest threat of all, however, was the powerful kingdom of Sicily, under the ambitious and ruthless Frenchman Charles of Anjou. Charles had a large army in Sicily waiting for a papal blessing to launch a Crusade against the schismatic Christians and the 'usurper' Palaiologos in Constantinople. Michael cleverly approached Pope Gregory X directly and made overtures to the effect that he would like to heal the rift between the two churches and submit the Orthodox congregation to the will of the papacy. This move effectively prevented Charles of Anjou from launching his desired Crusade, since the pope would not give Charles his blessing as long as he could see a bigger prize: unification of the church under his own authority. And so it was that, in 1274, at the Council of Lyon, through Michael's envoy, the historian George Akropolites, the schism between the two branches of Christendom was healed. The Orthodox branch had finally submitted to papal supremacy.

This monumental capitulation worked with the West but not with Michael's own people. Their long-held hatred of the Latins and their heretical Catholic ways could not be erased by the signing of a treaty in Lyon, and Michael could not convince them otherwise.

When a new pope, Martin IV, was elected in 1281 – a Frenchman and a sympathizer of the king of Sicily – the Byzantine emperor was immediately excommunicated, and Charles of Sicily and Anjou prepared his far superior military forces for the long-awaited Crusade. Michael now needed a miracle.

It is said that, in March 1282, as a crowd of worshippers stood outside the cathedral of Palermo, a French soldier tried to rape a local Sicilian girl. The crowd intervened to protect the girl, and news of the incident spread like wildfire. The mob turned on the soldiers, and for the next few days the whole island erupted in dissent against its French masters in the rebellion known as the 'Sicilian Vespers'. Peter III of Aragon invaded and took control of Sicily. Whether Michael was behind the revolt is unclear, but the empire's safety had been secured, and no Byzantine blood had been shed in the process.

This great triumph was the last Michael saw. A few months later, while crossing the Sea of Marmara in bad wintery conditions, he caught a chill and died. Such was his unpopularity with the people that he was not granted the traditional funeral honours of an emperor. Instead, he was placed in a modest grave before being exhumed some years later by his emperor son Andronikos II. His surprisingly intact remains were sent to a monastery in Selymbria. It is recorded that his body was 'too wicked to return to earth'.

Never loved, never given a proper burial, and quickly forgotten by his people, Michael VIII Palaiologos – the founder of the longest dynasty in Byzantine history – is a curious figure in the long story of Byzantium. Brilliant, ruthless, charming as a young man but disliked by all as emperor, he undoubtedly kept the empire alive at a time when it could so easily have been destroyed by its legion of more powerful enemies. His descendants would rule Byzantium until the end of its existence, but he himself was denied the credit and affection that he perhaps deserved. His people never forgave him for his two unforgivable acts: blinding a child emperor, and agreeing to submit the Orthodox church to the will of the papacy.

     PALAIOLOGAN DYNASTY

Andronikos II

December 1282 – May 1328

He was tall of stature and handsome of face,
but above all venerable, as if born to rule.
NIKEPHOROS GREGORAS, 1330S–50S

Andronikos II Palaiologos was the eldest son of Michael VIII and was at his father's side when he died of a fever in 1282. In many ways he was the opposite of his father: where Michael was astute and cunning, Andronikos was naive and trusting; where Michael was ruthless and showed no interest in religious matters, Andronikos was weak-willed and a devout Orthodox Christian. Devoid of his father's judgment and leadership qualities, Andronikos oversaw the empire's irreversible decline, presiding over territorial loss, financial ruin and military disasters. Yet because he was an educated, kind, intellectual and religious man, there was a flourishing of arts and culture at the court. He presided over the so-called 'Palaiologan renaissance', a gathering of great scholars including the statesman and philosopher Theodore Metochites and the astronomer Nikephoros Gregoras.

According to extant illustrations, Andronikos's beard was a magnificent spectacle. It was thick and brown and cut straight across the bottom contrary to the presiding fashion of the day, and this, together with his kindly face and tall elegant demeanour, doubtless helped him look the part of emperor, even if he failed miserably at the task itself. Finding himself devoid of state funds, Andronikos tried to raise taxes but could not persuade the wealthy landowners and aristocratic families to pay their dues. Instead, disastrously, he decided to save money by cutting back on military spending. He abolished the navy and reduced the army to less than a few thousand troops, most of whom were mercenaries. This was a catastrophic mistake, as it allowed the Turks to occupy the whole of Asia Minor and left the newly dominant tribe of Osmanli – known to us as the Ottomans – totally unopposed. Meanwhile, in the Balkans, the Serbs and the Bulgarians had seized almost full control, to the extent that nearly all Byzantine rule and influence in the area was lost. Both the Venetians and the Genoese continued to command the trade that passed through Constantinople, accruing the wealth that had belonged to their once all-powerful landlords.

The next disastrous decision by the unlucky and hapless Andronikos was to attempt to rectify the situation caused by his military cutbacks by inviting a group of mercenaries from Spain into his capital. They were known as the Catalan Grand Company, and were run by a ruthless Sicilian tyrant of German descent known as Roger de Flor. It had seemed like a positive and decisive action, since the ferocious and well-armed fighters were seen in the capital as powerful defenders. Roger de Flor was even offered the hand of the emperor's teenage niece, Maria, in marriage. However, on their wedding night, the Catalan Company's celebrations spiralled out of control and turned into a riot, aimed mainly at the Genoese; the rape, plunder and murder lasted for days. Several thousand Genoese were killed before Roger took action and ordered his men to stop. It was a taste of what was to come, in that the Catalans chose to maraud their way through the Byzantine cities rather than fight the Ottoman Turks. They took no notice of the pleas to stop of their emperor and employer, and simply did as they pleased. It was only when they visited the young co-emperor and son of Andronikos, Michael IX Palaiologos, in his base at Adrianople that events took a turn. According to the historian George Pachymeres, Roger de Flor and a few close friends were dining as guests of Michael, when they were set upon by mercenaries he had hired and murdered where they sat. The leaders of the loathsome Catalan Grand Company were thus removed, but it was some time before the troops left Byzantine lands completely. They headed for Athens, which at this time was part of the Frankish Crusaders' domain, where they took over the duchy and caused trouble for the empire for a further seventy years.

Throughout this period Andronikos also had personal tragedies to contend with. His first wife, Anna of Hungary, had died at the age of 22, having given birth to the future Michael IX and another boy, Constantine. Two years later Andronikos married, sight unseen, Yolanda, the daughter of William of Montferrat, in what he hoped would be an astute diplomatic manoeuvre. Yolanda came to Constantinople in 1284 as a girl of 11, married the Byzantine emperor and converted to the Orthodox faith. They lived together in relative harmony for many years and had several children together, including a daughter, Simonis, born in 1294. The Serbian king Milutin – a vicious despot who had already married three times – now, at the age of 45, wanted a real Byzantine princess as his next wife. If he did not get one, he threatened Andronikos, he would simply take Thessalonica from the empire by force. Trapped, Andronikos reluctantly sent his infant daughter, then just 5 years old, to be married to the Serbian king, who promptly abused her and kept her for many years within his palace. She would occasionally be allowed home to see her father, and on these visits would beg to be allowed to stay in her parents' home. They could not risk the wrath of the Serbian king, however, and she was sent back time after time. Only when Milutin died in 1321 did the wretched and abused young woman return to Constantinople to live out the rest of her life.

According to Nikephoros Gregoras, Andronikos's wife Yolanda began to resent her stepson Michael, who was destined to inherit the throne at the expense of her own children. She began to agitate against Michael and pleaded with her husband to split the empire equally between all his children. But Andronikos, choosing to adhere to tradition, would never agree, so Yolanda eventually left him and went to live in Thessalonica until she died, in 1317.

Michael IX, co-emperor and devoted son to Andronikos II, fathered two sons, Andronikos and Manuel. The young Andronikos grew up to be a happy-go-lucky prince who kept several mistresses. One particular mistress he seemed to love more than his wife, and he would spend most evenings with her. Increasingly jealous, he began to suspect her of seeing other men, and had his bodyguards hide in the darkened alleys around her apartments with instructions to kill any suitors who might visit her. One dark night in 1320, Andronikos's younger brother came to find him at his mistress's house; not recognizing him, the bodyguards beat him to death. When the news reached Michael IX that one of his sons had been the cause of his other son's murder, he suffered a heart attack and died. Upon hearing of these events, Andronikos II turned against his grandson, the heir to the throne, refusing to speak to him and openly treating him with contempt. But the young Andronikos was a proud man and had many friends in the palace. He challenged his grandfather to either crown him as co-emperor or disown him. Eventually Andronikos II acquiesced, and in 1325 had his grandson crowned as Andronikos III Palaiologos.

The years 1321 and 1322 saw civil war break out between the two, during which many were killed on both sides. After several more years of tension, Andronikos the grandson decided it was time to take over. He had a new wife now, Anna of Savoy, who had given him children – a fact that gave him the motivation to strike. The fighting continued until 1328, when Andronikos II, now aged 70 and with his sight failing, heard that Andronikos had entered the capital and abdicated. He lived for two years in the palace, looked after by his daughter Simonis, before giving up his worldly life and retiring to a monastery, where he lived for two more years as Brother Anthony. He died peacefully in 1332.

During the reign of Andronikos II Palaiologos the empire diminished in every way. It was a disastrous time in which, paradoxically, culture and artistic endeavours reached new heights. The emperor had tried his best but had failed at every turn. The fate of the empire that had lasted for a thousand years now rested in the hands of his fratricidal grandson.

Andronikos III
May 1328 – June 1341

Andronikos III styled himself 'Doukas Angelos Komnenos Palaiologos', keen that everyone should appreciate his descent from all the great families of Byzantium. As a young man he was completely indulged by his father, Michael IX. He was the playboy prince whom everybody liked, and was also a favourite of his grandfather, the emperor Andronikos II. The ruling class were often very young when they came to power, and it happens that Andronikos's grandfather was only 38 years old when his grandson was born. It was Andronikos's role in the accidental death of his younger brother, Manuel, that set his life on a different course. With his father dead of a heart attack at the age of 43 and his grandfather forced to abdicate, the way was now clear for Andronikos III to rule alone.

Throughout his entire life, Andronikos had a best friend in John Kantakouzenos, a brilliant and capable man who also enjoyed the backing of a rich and ambitious mother behind him. John was his *megas domestikos* (commander-in-chief) and the effective chief administrator of the empire. Thanks to this popular and principled man, who allowed his beloved friend Andronikos to play the emperor more than he truly embodied the role, everything appeared to be on an even keel after the terrible civil wars under Andronikos II. John helped introduce legal reforms intended to address state corruption, which were largely effective, and in effect instituted the first supreme court, named the 'Universal Judges of the Romans'. It is said that Andronikos III often asked John to be co-emperor alongside him, but Kantakouzenos always nobly refused.

The vigorous new emperor soon found a suitable wife in Anna of Savoy, but after their wedding in 1326 problems began to arise between Kantakouzenos and the new empress consort. Anna, just 20 years old herself, had to contend with the attitude of her playboy husband and his inseparable friend John, the power behind the throne. There were, it could be said, three of them in the marriage.

In the wider sphere of the empire, the deterioration that had set in under Andronikos II continued. The Ottoman Turks grew stronger and occupied almost all the territory in Asia Minor. Andronikos III, always prepared to go to battle, faced up to the Ottoman sultan Orhan at the Battle of Pelekanon in 1329 but was roundly defeated. In the north, the Serbians defeated the Bulgarians in the famous Battle of Velbuzd, which made them all-powerful in the Balkans.

Tragedy struck in 1341, when Andronikos III contracted malaria and died quite suddenly. His young son John, probably named after his best friend Kantakouzenos, was only 9 years old, so the issue of who would act as regent was of utmost importance. Obviously, Anna of Savoy, the empress consort and mother of the new child emperor, assumed she would be governing on her son's behalf, but John Kantakouzenos had other ideas. What followed was a chaotic civil war that raged for six years and ripped the heart out of the empire.

John V

1341–1347 (*first reign*)

John V Palaiologos ruled over the empire for five decades, from 1341 to 1391, but his reign was interrupted on no fewer than three occasions. He would have been the longest-serving emperor in Byzantium's history were it not for these intervals; however, from the sources available to us it appears that he was also a fickle, petty and stupid man who caused irreparable damage to the realm.

John V cannot be held responsible for the early years of his reign, which saw a battle between his ambitious and rather talentless mother, Anna of Savoy, and the effective prime minister John Kantakouzenos. Just 9 years old at the time of his succession, John V was to take little part in government proceedings until he was of age. The period up to 1347, when John VI Kantakouzenos became senior co-emperor, was marked by civil war on a scale

 PALAIOLOGAN DYNASTY

that practically ruined the empire. Anna formed a council of regency that included the patriarch John XIV Kalekas and the newly installed *mega doux*, or commander of the fleet, Alexios Apokaukos. She then began her persecution of her late husband's most loyal and brilliant friend, plundering his house and placing his noble and aged mother under house arrest. Kantakouzenos fled to Didymoteichon in Thrace, gathered his forces around him and declared himself emperor in 1341. From this moment until he successfully took the capital six years later, the two sides fought. He and Anna both spent money that they could ill afford on mercenaries to fight their battles for them. It was a ruinous period for the whole of Byzantium. Anna sold her crown to the Venetians for 30,000 ducats, and John sent one of his daughters to be held as hostage at the Ottoman sultan's court.

Eventually, Kantakouzenos was victorious and entered the capital. Pronounced emperor John VI Kantakouzenos, senior co-emperor, he immediately tried to heal the wounds between himself and the young emperor John V. At his coronation, his imperial diadem was made of painted leather and cut glass rather than the magnificent gold and jewels of the past. He offered his 14-year-old daughter Helena's hand in marriage to John V as a sign of reconciliation.

John VI Kantakouzenos

May 1347 – 1354

The Byzantine Empire's long-serving loyal subject John VI Kantakouzenos was a man who endlessly tried to assist the empire in every way he could, first as *megas domestikos*, then as virtual prime minister under his friend and emperor Andronikos III Palaiologos, and then as co-emperor alongside the boy named after him by his father. Now, reigning as senior emperor after six punishing years of civil war against the young emperor's mother, Anna, and

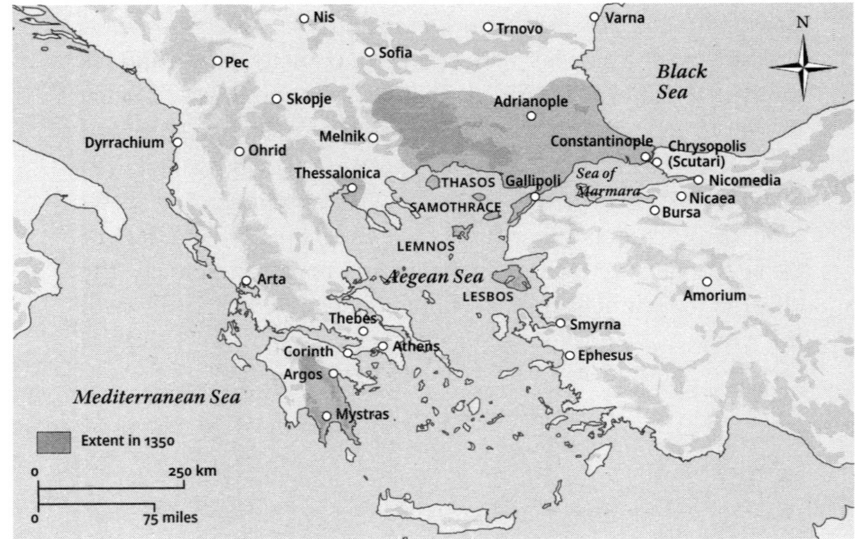

her advisers, he was faced with an empire in a terrible state. There was no military strength to speak of, the treasury was bankrupt, and the population had been ravaged by conflict for many years. Both the Genoese and the Venetians had a stranglehold on the valuable trading rights of the city, depriving the treasury of much-needed income. Yet all of this was as nothing compared to what was about to land on their shores: the Black Death.

Bubonic plague killed almost half the population of Constantinople. It ravaged the empire and most of Europe and Asia, claiming well over 100 million lives over a five-year period. Constantinople did not suffer more than many other cities at the time, but productivity, tax revenues and general manpower all went into serious decline.

PALAIOLOGAN DYNASTY

Highly indebted to the Turks who had funded many of his wars, John VI annexed Kallipolis to the Ottomans, which gave them their first foothold in Europe.

Always an honest man, John VI had promised John V and his mother that he would rule for only ten years, until John V came of age as the rightful emperor. John VI Kantakouzenos retired to a monastery in 1354, changing his name, as was the custom, to Joasaph Christodoulos. For many years he remained on good terms with his emperor, acting as a representative of the Eastern Orthodox church at various councils and trying to reconcile the differences between the two churches. He died peacefully with his sons by his side at Mystras in the Peloponnese, at the age of around 90, having served the empire for many years.

John V
1354–1376 (*second reign*)

The second reign of John V continued in much the same vein as the first: utterly ineffectually. For the next twenty years John ruled over an empire that had little influence, no money and negligible military power. He believed that the only way to protect it from the seemingly unstoppable Ottomans was to get help from the West. In 1366 he visited Hungary in an attempt to garner support from Louis I. It is rumoured that they met with great pomp in the royal city of Buda, when John made the mistake of not dismounting from his horse, leaving the king standing. Taking great umbrage, the Hungarians sent John away, refusing to offer support unless he agreed to surrender the Orthodox church to the will of the pope. John declined and moved on to Italy, where he met with Pope Urban V in Rome. Again, Urban asked him to end the schism between the churches by submitting to his, and this time John agreed. He converted to Catholicism in St Peter's Basilica. However, without the involvement of his own patriarch, his change of heart was not given much credence. Humiliated and rejected, John made his way back to Constantinople. He stopped off in Venice on his return and was ignominiously held captive until his debts could be paid off by his son Manuel, despot of Thessalonica.

When he arrived back in his impoverished capital, John was obliged to let Byzantium become a vassal state of the Ottoman sultan Murad I and to pay tribute to the Ottomans so they did not take more of his ever-diminishing territories. While he had been in Europe, attempting to raise help, he had left his ambitious and venal son Andronikos in charge. This was a move he would come to regret.

Andronikos IV

1376–1379

Born in 1348 as the first son of John V and his wife, Helena Kantakouzenos, Andronikos was made co-emperor in 1352 by his father. He was always destined to inherit the throne but, since John V was only 15 years old at the time of his birth, it was likely to be a long wait. Andronikos never really got on with his father and appears to have been a rather surly adolescent, all too eager to gain power for himself. He had little time for his younger brother, Manuel, a more agreeable and studious man.

It was when Andronikos's father departed Constantinople to seek help from the Europeans in 1366 and left him in charge of running the empire that his true character emerged. Wilful and domineering, he acted as if his father was never coming back and, as the reigning emperor in the capital, expected his word to be final. When John V was held captive in Venice until his debts were paid, Andronikos ignored his father's pleas and deliberately found reasons not to help him raise money. When told by his father to sell off some church treasures, Andronikos claimed it would be impious. Only the actions of his younger brother, Manuel, who travelled to Venice and pleaded for his father's release, enabled John V to return.

It was the submission of his father to the Ottoman sultan Murad I in 1373, when John paid an annual tribute to his enemy and accepted the position of an Ottoman vassal, that spurred Andronikos to act openly and take the throne from him. He had found a shared understanding in the person of the sultan's son, Savci Beg, who was in exactly the same position as the impatient, ambitious Andronikos; together they hatched a plot to overthrow their old and domineering fathers and take the thrones for themselves. Both rebellions failed miserably, and Sultan Murad had his son blinded so savagely that he allegedly died of his wounds. Murad insisted that his vassal John V do the same to his son, and indeed Andronikos's 2-year-old son. Although John V would have been furious with Andronikos, he had not contemplated blinding both him and his own grandson; however, if he did not obey his overlord, the entire city could be razed to the ground. Reluctantly, he complied. After the blinding he locked Andronikos and his family in the windowless Tower of Anemas, adjacent to the crumbling Blachernae palace. Miraculously, after just a few weeks it was declared that Andronikos could see once more in one eye and that little John, with the help of his mother's magic salve, had totally regained his sight. This must have appeared to some as God's work, to others as deliberate.

Andronikos IV was removed from the line of succession and his younger, altogether more honest brother Manuel designated as the new co-emperor. Andronikos was not one to give up on his aspirations, however, and, with the help of the Genoese and secret communications with the Ottomans, he managed to escape and fled to Pera, the Genoese stronghold just across the water. Although it appeared odd for the sultan to support Andronikos against his father, the crafty Ottoman chief merely wanted to sow discord among his enemies. With the backing of both the sultan and the Genoese navy, Andronikos laid siege to his father and his brother for over a month before finally taking the city and declaring himself the new emperor, taking the name Andronikos IV Palaiologos. He immediately imprisoned his family in the very tower where he himself had been held captive, the Tower of Anemas, where they languished for three long years.

Once he was in power, there is little evidence that Andronikos achieved anything. When John V and Manuel finally escaped from the Tower of Anemas in 1379, they did so with the help of the Venetians, who were constantly looking to outwit their Genoese rivals and take control of Constantinople's trading privileges. They gambled on John V being their ally once he was reinstalled on the throne. Andronikos IV did not disappear, however. True to his character, he kidnapped his own mother, Helena Kantakouzenos, and her two elderly sisters, as well as their father, the monk Kantakouzenos, who was now well into his eighties. He threw them in a prison that had recently housed victims of the plague. The weak and pathetic John V gave in to his demands and, when the family hostages were released, was granted his freedom and reinstated as co-emperor and successor to his own son. Only Manuel, the decent, long-serving brother, lost out, as he was stripped of his title and stood to inherit nothing.

Andronikos IV moved away from Constantinople and became governor of the nearby city of Selymbria. Finally, in 1385, while preparing yet again to attack his father's forces, he suddenly fell ill and died. Relief spread through the empire as this destructive human being was laid to rest in the great monastery of Pantocrator, within the walls of the city he had damaged so critically.

John V
1379–1390 (*third reign*)

Once back in power, John V Palaiologos reverted to his previous ways of governing by doing very little. The city was now clear of the bubonic plague, but it had had a devastating effect on the empire, slowing down economic growth severely. The Venetians were in the ascendency thanks to their control of trade coming through the capital and, most worrying of all, the Ottoman Turks were now in power in Asia Minor and were circling around the capital as they started to conquer areas in the Balkans.

John's trusted and capable son Manuel had moved out of the capital and was running Thessalonica as his own fiefdom, almost totally independently of his father. Although he never openly declared his intentions, Manuel attracted a circle of nobles and military men to his city as hope in John V's efficacy faded. He had some early successes against the forces of the Ottomans, but by 1383 the Turks had surrounded the second city of Byzantium and settled in for a long siege. Manuel was reluctant to leave, but as the years passed the situation grew ever more hopeless. In 1387 the starving and beleaguered inhabitants asked their leader to make his escape and surrender the city to the Turks. In a surprising move Manuel did not return directly to Constantinople but instead went to the island of Lesbos and sought refuge with his cousins, the ruling Gattilusio family. He spent some months on the island, planning his return to the capital, before going to Bursa and subjecting himself to the sultan Murad. Upon the death of his elder brother, Andronikos IV, Manuel returned to serve his father as co-emperor. It was at this moment that Andronikos's son, John VII, returned from Genoa, where he had been living, and laid claim to his grandfather's throne. John V fled to the fortress at the Golden Gate while the young John VII was crowned emperor. Deposed by a member of his family yet again, John V languished for a short period while John VII Palaiologos ruled as *basileus*, but all the while was really dancing to the tune of the Ottoman sultan.

John VII
April 1390 – September 1390

Spending his early years in prison was not the easiest of beginnings for the scheming John VII. He was supposed to have been blinded at the age of 3 on the orders of the Ottoman sultan Murad but managed to avoid this fate. He was then sent to live with relatives in Genoa until he returned to Constantinople and led a successful coup against his grandfather John V in 1390.

The 20-year-old emperor was not capable of ruling his empire while those around him were more loyal to his grandfather, who was at that time hiding in the tower at the Golden Gate. The government of John VII and his makeshift ministers collapsed after just five months in power. He escaped to Europe, where he sought help to regain his throne but found none. He even tried, unsuccessfully, to sell his title to a French lord in return for a castle in France.

Years later, following the death of John V, he was made co-emperor at the unexpected behest of his uncle Manuel II. In this capacity he behaved surprisingly well, even acting as regent when Manuel II took a long trip to Europe in the desperate hope of finding support from his Christian brothers. Upon Manuel's return, John VII was allowed to keep his title of co-emperor and moved to Thessalonica, where he was made imperial governor. In 1408, at the age of 38, he fell fatally ill. As was often the custom, he became a monk, changing his name to Brother Joasaph, and died that same year. His tenure as emperor had been a farce, and yet another element in the whole Palaiologan demise.

John V
September 1390 – February 1391 (*final reign*)

The final year of John V's long reign was as disastrous as the previous forty-nine. Restored to power after his grandson John VII's usurpation, he made his younger son, Manuel, co-emperor and heir to the throne. However, his condition for doing so was that the son who had always been loyal to his father, and who had once again worked to restore him to power, had to be sent as a hostage to Sultan Bayezid of the Ottomans.

Thus ended the long and catastrophic reign of John V Palaiologos. He witnessed the ruination of his lands, as the Ottoman Turks were poised to conquer all before them. Weak-willed and indecisive, he

 PALAIOLOGAN DYNASTY

was unable to control his own family, let alone the empire. He was not a malicious or evil man, just inept and weak. At the age of 58, having spent fifty years as emperor, he died peacefully in his bed.

Manuel II
March 1391 – 1425

The ability to write is clearly better than being rich, is sweeter than all sweet things and, indeed, brings the greater glory.
MANUEL II PALAIOLOGOS, *c*. 1383

Manuel II had played a significant role in the government of the empire for many years before he became sole emperor in 1391. He had helped his father, John V, on numerous occasions, and had even offered himself as hostage to the Ottoman sultan Bayezid in Bursa where he was forced to fight alongside the Turkish forces, capturing cities that had once been part of the Byzantine Empire. He was still in the service of the sultan when news of his father's death reached him, and he fled Bursa to take control of the ailing empire, particularly concerned with the role his untrustworthy and scheming nephew John VII might play.

Manuel was in his early forties when he became sole ruler. He was an imposing and distinguished man. He favoured wearing white robes, the Byzantine colour of mourning, as an acknowledgment of the state of the empire. With his long white beard and flowing white hair, he was positively remarked upon wherever he went. He had chosen not to marry until he was emperor, but soon after his coronation, on 10 February 1392, he married a Serbian woman, Helena Dragas. She went on to have at least six children, including the last two emperors of Byzantium, John VIII and Constantine XI. She outlived her husband and became a nun upon his death. Her skull, a holy relic, can be found in the monastery of St Patapios in Loutraki in the Peloponnese, and her saint's day is commemorated on 29 May, the day Constantinople fell to the Ottomans.

Manuel tried his best to maintain standards within what was left of the empire; he restarted building works in the capital, and there was a renewed interest in all matters scholastic. During his earlier imprisonment alongside his father in the infamous, windowless Tower of Anemas, he spent many hours studying and reading, composing long treatises on matters both religious and political. Manuel II was a prolific writer of all types of literary works: poetry, theological treatises, even an 'Oration on the Death of his Brother Theodore'. He fostered an environment in which fairness and consideration were held in high esteem, and it was in this context that his nephew John VII was reinstated as co-emperor.

From 1394, Constantinople was besieged by Sultan Bayezid I – a situation that lasted for seven long years. Five years in, confident in the power of the city's defences, Manuel II entrusted the defence of the empire to John VII and, together with a group of forty trusted friends, decided to make a journey to the great courts of Europe. His object was to seek help to defend Constantinople and Christendom against the Muslim Turks – a policy that cemented his reputation as a noble and worthy emperor, unlucky to be born at a time when the end seemed unavoidable. He first made his way to the court of Charles VI in France, then the most powerful kingdom within Christendom, where he was greeted with enormous interest. The French court was mesmerized by the stature, dignity and scholarship of this athletic 50-year-old man. However, Manuel was to discover that the king of France was highly unpredictable. Charles VI would have bouts of complete lucidity and then would be unable to function at all. Manuel eventually left France having won many admirers, but with no guarantees of help to stem the Ottoman invasion.

In 1400 Manuel came to the court of Henry IV of England and stayed over the Christmas period at Eltham Palace. The first Byzantine monarch to visit England since Constantine the Great over a thousand years before, he similarly made a great impression on all he met. Henry IV laid on a special jousting tournament,

PALAIOLOGAN DYNASTY

banquets were given, and even a masquerade was staged for him. However, Henry IV had troubles of his own and could afford no real help to the Byzantine emperor. Manuel went on to meet with the Holy Roman Emperor, Sigismund, Martin of Aragon and Margaret I of Denmark. Many had already contributed soldiers to the mini-Crusade against the Muslims in 1396, during which, at the Battle of Nikopolis, their combined forces had been roundly beaten by the superior Ottoman army. It was too soon for them to commit again. It appeared that all was lost for Manuel II and his mission to garner help from the West.

Fortune struck in an unlikely fashion. In 1402, news reached Manuel that the Turkoman warlord Amir Timur, known as Tamerlane in the West, had just defeated the Ottoman forces in a monumental battle at Ankara. His empire would rule Central Asia for a century and destabilize the region that the Ottomans had seemingly so safely secured. The Ottomans were thrown into disarray and withdrew from their siege of Constantinople. Manuel II hurried back to his capital and made the most out of the breathing space Timur had given him. He rewarded his nephew John VII for holding out against the Turks during his trip to Europe by making him *basileus* of Thessaly for the rest of his life.

The survival of Byzantium continued to depend on diplomacy, however. During the struggle over the Ottoman succession, Manuel II skilfully backed the right son of Sultan Bayezid to take over the throne. The new all-powerful sultan, Mehmet I, knew that Manuel II Palaiologos had played a large role in helping him secure power, and throughout the rest of Manuel's reign there was an easy truce between the two. For twenty years it looked as though the tiny Byzantine state, which now consisted of just the city and its environs and parts of the Morea, could co-exist with the enormous, dominant Ottoman Empire entirely surrounding it.

This relationship also meant that Manuel could strengthen that part of the empire that was not at odds with the Ottomans' expansionist desires. In the Morea, Manuel's young son, Theodore II, replaced his brother Theodore, who had ruled as despot for many years but had recently died. Determined to protect this last precious piece of empire, in 1415 Manuel and his son started to repair and rebuild the Hexamilion, a wall 6 miles (9.7 km) long, originally built in the 5th century and restored by Justinian I, that stretched across the Isthmus of Corinth and would protect the Morea from invasion.

When Manuel II was ill and exhausted at the age of 72, he gave the task of governing to his son John VIII. In the tradition of many of the Palaiologoi, Manuel II decided to become a monk, changing his name to Brother Matthew and retiring to a monastery, where he died after a few months of retirement, at the age of 75.

Few emperors of Byzantium were as universally admired and respected as Manuel. To his people, his family and even his enemies in the Ottoman camp, he was a trusted and esteemed ruler. If he had been in charge of the empire when it had power and money and a military force of note, he would have been supreme. As it was, he miraculously extended the life of the realm he loved so much and served so well.

John VIII
1425 – October 1448

My son, the basileus, is a worthy basileus, yet not so for today's world. He sees and thinks on a grand scale, which in past times resulted in the prosperity of our forefathers. But today, when our troubles are heaped upon us, our state wants not a basileus but a custodian. And I fear that his schemes and endeavours may lead to ruin for this house.
MANUEL II PALAIOLOGOS, JOHN VIII'S FATHER, AS QUOTED BY GEORGE SPHRANTZES, 1470S

A black beard on a pale face, hair and eyebrows the same. The eyes between grey and green, and the stooped shoulders of a small person.
PISANELLO, *c.* 1439

     PALAIOLOGAN DYNASTY

When he was crowned co-emperor in 1421, John VIII disagreed with his ageing father about how to deal with the successor to the recently demised Sultan Mehmed, Murad II. Manuel recommended an alliance with Murad, but John made an error of judgment, deciding to back a rival for the sultanate. Murad II was furious and immediately attacked Constantinople. Thanks only to the skilled diplomacy of the old emperor could the Ottoman leader be persuaded to withdraw, but at great cost. The Byzantines were now a tribute-paying vassal of the sultan.

When his father died, John VIII was alone, facing an array of problems that would have tested anyone. His most immediate issue was a hostile Sultan Murad, who had agreed to leave Constantinople alone but instead turned his attention to Byzantium's second city, Thessalonica. It had been ceded to the Venetians in 1423, but they were only ever interested in how it could improve their trading capacity and, as soon as the city was under real threat and needed investment in its defences and necessary expenditure on mercenaries to defend it, the Venetians boarded their ships and fled.

In 1430 the frustrated Ottoman forces subjected Thessalonica to a terrible sacking. Thousands were killed or enslaved, and the great church of the Acheiropoietos was converted into a mosque. The Ottoman army broke through the Hexamilion, and all that Manuel had so painstakingly won over the previous twenty years was undone. Only the Despotate of the Morea survived these years intact.

John VIII, like his father and grandfather before him, believed that the only way to keep the Turks at bay was to get help from the West. He therefore set off for Italy with a fantastic entourage of 700 people and arrived in Ferrara at the invitation of Pope Eugenius IV. Yet again the emperor and his party were a spectacle of great fascination for the Italians. Their sumptuous costumes, their strict adherence to a rigidly defined code of manners and behaviour, and their high standard of learning and scholarship all engendered admiration and envy. John VIII had calculated that, in order to initiate a new Crusade against the Muslims funded and staffed by the Western powers, he would have to make a significant concession to please his Catholic hosts. The only leverage he had left was the age-old dispute over the two churches, and it was his intention to reunify them by submitting to the pope's will. The negotiations went on for months, taking so long that the cost of hosting this vast contingent of Byzantines – as well as an outbreak of the plague at Ferrara – forced them to be moved to Florence, where only the wealthy Medici family could afford to accommodate them.

The debate was heated and stuck on the same, unresolvable issue of the *filioque* and the supremacy of the pope. Alongside John was the cream of early 15th-century Byzantine intellectuals: the patriarch Joseph II, the first to attend a meeting in the West; Demetrios, the brother of the emperor and great philosopher of his age; George Gemistos, known as Pletho; Georgios Scholarios, the theologian; and George Amiroutzes representing the Platonist view while George of Trebizond argued from the Aristotelian tradition. Supporting them were eminent clerics including Bessarion, bishop of Nicaea, who would eventually become a cardinal. The Renaissance had now firmly taken hold in the minds of many Italians, and these highly learned, native Greek-speaking intellectuals were a source of knowledge and insight that could not be found anywhere else in Christendom.

On 6 July 1439 a statement known as the 'Union of Florence' was signed, to the effect that the pope would send an army of Crusaders to help defend Constantinople from the Muslim Turks. John had thus achieved a certain success that had eluded his predecessors: the West had finally agreed to send an army to help their Christian brothers. Alas, it was too little too late: despite the pope's promise of tangible support, the people of Constantinople, stubborn to the end, did not agree with their emperor over the union of the churches, and most definitely did not accept the superiority of the pope over the patriarch.

Throughout this period John had a problematic personal life. He had been married three times, and all three wives had died. He returned to his palace and his capital having failed in his attempt to unify the churches, without the joy of marriage, and having witnessed no sustainable victories of the Western armies against the Ottomans. At the age of 55 he was childless and alone. On 31 October 1448, ill and exhausted, he named his younger brother Constantine as his successor and died. Owing to his policy of appeasement without submission to the Latin church, the Orthodox clergy would not afford him the religious rites normally given to an emperor. He was buried alongside his third wife, Maria, in a simple grave in the monastery of the Pantocrator.

The fusion of the cultures of the old Latin kingdoms and the Eastern-facing Byzantines made for a vibrant and dynamic combination, and artistic and intellectual activity flourished. John VIII is remembered over and above some of his predecessors simply because great Italian artists such as Pisanello and Benozzo Gozzoli represented him in frescoes, drawings and, in Pisanello's case, in bronze, adorning the first ever Renaissance medal. This portrait in bronze was drawn from life and showed John VIII wearing a magnificent Greek hat and viewed in profile – something no Byzantine would have accepted previously, since it was considered bad luck not to see the whole face of a subject.

John VIII was the last Byzantine emperor to have had a wife as empress consort, the last to die peacefully at home, and the last to believe that there might be hope for the continuation of the empire that had lasted for over eleven hundred years. John VIII Palaiologos had tried his best to save Byzantium but had bequeathed to his brother Constantine XI an empire on the brink of extinction.

Constantine XI Dragases
October 1448 – May 1453

There was a long-held prophecy that the last emperor of Byzantium would have the same name as the first. The Palaiologoi had paid attention to this prediction for nearly two centuries, and Manuel II probably thought that it was safe to name his eighth child and fourth son Constantine, since the likelihood of him becoming emperor was slim. The future Constantine XI Dragases Palaiologos could not have thought that he would ever be emperor, having spent much more of his adult life in the Morea than in the city that bore the same name as his own.

Having inherited the empire from his brother, Constantine faced a monumental task. He decided not to be crowned by Gregory III in Constantinople, since the patriarch was still loyal to the terms of the Union of Florence, and Constantine wanted no association with that heresy. Instead, he chose to be crowned in Mystras, and as soon as he entered Constantinople he sought and was granted permission to ascend the throne from his overlord and sultan, Murad II. This would be one of the last formal acts of Murad II, who died in 1451; he was succeeded by his son Mehmed, just 19 years old and full of ambition and vigour. Constantine underestimated Mehmed, attempting to agitate against him – a fact that allowed Mehmed to claim that the terms of their long-standing peace treaty had been broken. The new Ottoman sultan was now able to declare war on the Byzantines and attack their capital. In 1452 Mehmed began his assault by building a fortress on the European shore of the Bosphorus, which still stands today as Rumeli Hisar. He thus effectively cut the city off from all access. The Muslims surrounded Constantinople on all sides.

Constantine XI, like his forebears, appealed once again to the West, and a cardinal, Isidore, arrived in the capital with 200 archers to help defend the city. What the cardinal really wanted was a ratification of the terms of the Union of Florence, which, with characteristic expediency, the Latins succeeded in obtaining by having it read aloud in Hagia Sophia. The majority of clerics and the people of the city ignored it, but to the cardinal and the pope back in Rome it was the final sanction they had longed for since the treacherous Fourth Crusade.

Mehmed was now preparing for a massive assault. A Hungarian engineer named Urban had come to Constantine to build a cannon bigger than anyone had ever seen, of a kind that would revolutionize warfare from this point on, but of course Constantine had neither the funds nor the material to give him. Urban then crossed the Bosphorus and made the same offer to Mehmed, who instantly agreed and paid the Hungarian four times what he was asking. Urban built an artillery of seventy cannon, which sank a Venetian ship that had sailed into the Bosphorus to help the Byzantines. A previous ship had also been destroyed by the cannon at Rumeli Hisar, and on that occasion, with the all too familiar brutality of the time, every crew member had been decapitated, and their captain impaled and left on the roadside for all to see.

It was Easter Monday, 2 April 1453, when the sultan's troops first appeared outside the walls of Constantinople. By 22 April the Ottoman navy was also in place. The cannon then started to batter the walls, keeping up a continuous bombardment for weeks until Mehmed felt they were weakened enough for his soldiers to attack. On 28 May Mehmed gave his soldiers a day of rest, and the Byzantines, in both a noble and somehow pitiable act of defiance, gathered in Hagia Sophia and took part in the last Christian liturgy in the Byzantine world.

Constantine and his defenders were heroic. They were heavily outnumbered, with a mere 4,000 Byzantine defenders facing around 100,000 Ottoman troops. Inevitably the walls were breached, and the attackers swarmed through them. Constantine was seen discarding his emperor's robes and fighting to the last. His body was never found – a fact that gave rise to the myth that he had become the 'Marble Emperor', who was not really dead but always waiting to return and restore the Byzantine Empire.

There was widespread looting and killing. Anything of value that was left now belonged to the sultan, and thousands of the city's inhabitants were slaughtered where they stood. Young and old, women and children, were either sold into slavery or simply put to the sword. Some killed themselves rather than surrender. Many had taken refuge in the churches and of course in Hagia Sophia itself. But this gave them no protection, and they died where they prayed. By the end of the third day the sultan called for an end to the killing and the plunder, marched into Hagia Sophia, converted it to a mosque and had an imam recite prayers from the pulpit. The capture of the city was complete. The prisoners, many of them from Byzantine noble families, were at first pardoned, but then Mehmed changed his mind and had every male captive beheaded.

What stands out in the story of the Fall of Constantinople is the bravery of the emperor and his loyal subjects. The legacy of Byzantium continued in many ways – through its learning and its art, and through its influence on the Italian Renaissance – but this extraordinary empire, which had lasted for over 1,100 years, was extinguished the moment that its emperor, Constantine XI Dragases Palaiologos, was killed, valiantly but unsuccessfully defending the great city that he loved. His last words, in response to an offer from Mehmed II to spare his life if he surrendered, were preserved by the contemporary historian Doukas: 'The right to surrender the city to you belongs neither to me nor to anyone who dwells therein. Rather than to have our lives spared, it is our common resolve willingly to die.'

  PALAIOLOGAN DYNASTY

FURTHER READING

General surveys

As *The Emperors of Byzantium* is
designed to be a first encounter with
the world of the Byzantines, listed
below are recommended overviews
that are readily available.

Cameron, Averil, *The Byzantines*,
 Oxford, 2007
Gregory, Timothy E., *A History of
 Byzantium*, Oxford, 2010
Harris, Jonathan, *The Lost World of
 Byzantium*, New Haven and
 London, 2016
Herrin, Judith, *Byzantium:
 The Surprising Life of a Medieval
 Empire*, London, 2007
Mango, Cyril, *The Oxford History of
 Byzantium*, Oxford, 2002
Norwich, John Julius, *Byzantium:
 The Early Centuries*, London, 1988
——, *Byzantium: The Apogee*, London,
 1991
——, *Byzantium: The Decline & Fall*,
 London, 1995
Runciman, Steven, *Byzantine Style and
 Civilization*, new edn, London, 1990
Sarris, Peter, *Byzantium: A Very Short
 History*, Oxford, 2015
Stathakopoulos, Dionysios, *A Short
 History of the Byzantine Empire*,
 London, 2014

The following works treat the subject
in slightly different ways but together
give a more detailed and rounded view
of the whole subject. Although written
years ago and in many ways out of date,
they can still be recommended.

Bury, J. B., *A History of the Eastern Roman
 Empire* [1912], Cambridge, 2015
Gibbon, Edward, *History of the Decline
 and Fall of the Roman Empire* [1776–
 88], 3 vols, London, 1995

Ostrogorsky, George, *History of the
 Byzantine State* [1940], Oxford, 1959

More recent surveys

The Cambridge Ancient History: vol. 13,
 The Late Empire, AD 337–425,
 eds A. Cameron and P. Garnsey,
 Cambridge, 1998; vol. 14, *Late
 Antiquity: Empire and Successors*,
 AD 425–600, eds A. Cameron,
 B. Ward-Perkins and M. Whitby,
 Cambridge, 2000
*The Cambridge History of the Byzantine
 Empire, c. 500–1492*, ed. Jonathan
 Shepard, rev. edn, Cambridge, 2019
The New Cambridge Medieval History,
 ed. C. Allmand, vols 1–7, Cambridge,
 1995–2005
The Oxford Dictionary of Byzantium,
 ed. A. P. Kazhdan, 3 vols, Oxford, 1991

For yet further reading, the
bibliography of Dionysios
Stathakopoulos's *A Short History of the
Byzantine Empire* is comprehensive.

Original sources in translation

Akropolites, George, *The History*, ed. and
 trans. Ruth Macrides, Oxford, 2007
Ammianus, Marcellinus, *The Later
 Roman Empire*, ed. and trans. Walter
 Hamilton, intro. Andrew Wallace-
 Hadrill, Harmondsworth, 1986
Choniates, Nicholas, *O City of
 Byzantium*, trans. Harry J. Magoulias,
 Detroit, 1984
Constantine Porphyrogenitus,
 De Administrando Imperio, ed. Gyula
 Moravcsik, trans R. J. H. Jenkins,
 4th edn, Washington, DC, 2002
Eusebius, *Eusebius' Life of Constantine*,
 trans. Averil Cameron and Stuart G.
 Hall, Oxford, 1999
——, *The History of the Church from
 Christ to Constantine*, trans.

G. A. Williamson, Harmondsworth, 1989
Kinnamos, Johannes, *Deeds of John and Manuel Comnenus*, trans. Charles M. Brand, New York, 1976
Komnene, Anna, *The Alexiad*, trans. E. R. A. Sewter, London, 2009
Leo the Deacon, *The 'History' of Leo the Deacon*, trans. Alice-Mary Talbot and Denis F. Sullivan, Washington, DC, 2005
Liudprand of Cremona, *The Complete Works of Liudprand of Cremona*, trans. Paolo Squatriti, Washington, DC, 2007
Procopius, *On Buildings*, trans. H. B. Dewing, Cambridge, MA, 1954
——, *The Secret History*, trans. G. A. Williamson and Peter Sarris, London, 2007
Psellus, Michael, *Fourteen Byzantine Rulers*, trans. E. R. A. Sewter, Harmondsworth, 1966
Skylitzes, John, *A Synopsis of Byzantine History 811–1057*, trans. John Wortley, Cambridge, 2011
Theophanes Confessor, *The Chronicle of Theophanes Confessor*, trans. Cyril Mango and Roger Scott, Oxford, 1997

Byzantine art and architecture

The following books illustrate and describe most of the existing Byzantine works of art and architecture around the world.

Beckwith, John, *Early Christian and Byzantine Art (Yale University Press Pelican History of Art)*, New Haven and London, 1992
Byzance: L'art byzantin dans les collections publiques françaises, exh. cat., Louvre, Paris, 1992
Byzantine Antiquities, exh. cat., Moscow Kremlin Museums, 2013
Byzantine Art, exh. cat., Royal Scottish Museum, Edinburgh, 1958
Byzantium 330–1453, exh. cat., Royal Academy of Arts, London, 2008
Byzantium and Islam: Age of Transition, exh. cat., Metropolitan Museum of Art, New York, 2012
Byzantium: Treasures of Byzantine Art and Culture, exh. cat., British Museum, London, 1984
Coche de La Ferté, Étienne, *L'Art de Byzance*, Paris, new edn, 2001
Cormack, Robin, *Byzantine Art*, Oxford, 2000
Eastmond, Antony, *The Glory of Byzantium*, London, 2013
From Byzantion to Istanbul: 8000 Years of a Capital, exh. cat., Sakıp Sabancı Museum, Istanbul, 2010
From Byzantium to El Greco: Greek Frescoes and Icons, exh. cat., Byzantine Museum of Athens; Royal Academy of Arts, London, Athens, 1987
The Glory of Byzantium, exh. cat., Metropolitan Museum of Art, New York, 1997
Lowden, John, *Early Christian & Byzantine Art*, London, 1997
Mango, Cyril, *Byzantine Architecture*, London, 1986
Rice, David Talbot, *Art of the Byzantine Era*, London and New York, 1985
The Road to Byzantium: Luxury Arts of Antiquity, exh. cat., Somerset House, London, 2006
The Treasury of San Marco, Venice, exh. cat., British Museum, Milan, 1984
Underwood, Paul A., *The Kariye Djami*, 3 vols, Princeton, 1966
Wessel, Klaus, *Byzantine Enamels from the 5th to the 13th Century*, Greenwich, CT, 1968

History as informed by the study of numismatics

Grierson, Philip, *Byzantine Coins*, London, 1982
Ratto, Radolfo, *Monnaies byzantines*, sale catalogue, Lugano, 1930, reprinted Amsterdam, 1959
Sear, David, *Byzantine Coins*, London, 2010

FURTHER READING

Tekin, Oğuz, *Byzantine Coins: The Yapi Kredi Collection*, Istanbul, 1999
Whitting. P. D., *Byzantine Coins*, London, 1973
Wroth, Warwick, *Catalogue of the Imperial Byzantine Coins in the British Museum*, 2 vols, London, 1908
——, *Catalogue of the Coins of the Vandals, Ostrogoths and Lombards ... in the British Museum*, London, 1911

Other works

Cameron, Averil, *Byzantine Matters*, Princeton, 2014
Garland, Linda, *Byzantine Empresses: Women and Power in Byzantium AD 527–1204*, London, 1999
Harris, Jonathan, *Constantinople: Capital of Byzantium*, London, 2017
Head, Constance, *The Emperor Julian*, Boston, 1976
——, *Imperial Byzantine Portraits*, New Rochelle, NY, 1982
——, *Imperial Twilight*, Chicago, 1977
Hughes, Bettany, *Istanbul*, London, 2017
Kaldellis, Anthony, *A Cabinet of Byzantine Curiosities*, Oxford, 2017
—, *Streams of Gold, Rivers of Blood: The Rise and Fall of Byzantium, 955 AD to the First Crusade*, Oxford, 2017

Lenski, Noel (ed.), *The Cambridge Companion to the Age of Constantine* rev. edn, Cambridge, 2012
Luttwak, Edward, *The Grand Strategy of the Byzantine Empire*, Cambridge, MA, 2011
Nicol, Donald M., *A Biographical Dictionary of the Byzantine Empire*, London, 1991
Potter, David, *Theodora: Actress, Empress, Saint*, Oxford, 2015
Rosen, William, *Justinian's Flea: Plague, Empire and the Birth of Europe*, London, 2007
Runciman, Steven, *The Emperor Romanus Lecapenus and his Reign*, Cambridge, 1988
——, *A History of the Crusades*, 3 vols, London 1990–91
Tougher, Shaun (ed.), *The Emperor in the Byzantine World: Papers from the 47th Spring Symposium of Byzantine Studies*, London, 2019
Treadgold, Warren, *The Middle Byzantine Historians*, Basingstoke, 2013
Walker, Alicia, *The Emperor and the World: Exotic Elements and the Imaging of Middle Byzantine Imperial Power, Ninth to Thirteenth Centuries CE*, Cambridge, 2012

ACKNOWLEDGMENTS

I am indebted to the many people who had a hand in this book. The team at Thames & Hudson for all their support and insight: Mohara Gill, Sam Ruston, Sally Nicholls, Julia MacKenzie. Special thanks must go to Sam Wythe, whose editing was spectacular, and to Roger Thorp, kindly introduced to me by Will Gompertz, who turned the initial discussion of the idea about Byzantine emperors into a reality.

Many thanks go to Bettany Hughes, for her eloquent and insightful introduction, and for connecting me with Professor Dionysios Stathakopoulos, and to Robert Peston for his typically articulate foreword. I'm most grateful to Gang Wu for his astute knowledge and precision, as well as Tom Eden for his numismatic wisdom, and Sam Fogg, medievalist supreme.

The two literary giants of this world, John Julius Norwich and Steven Runciman, need special mention, as their writings and knowledge on all matters Byzantine set me on the path to write my own.

Lastly, the long-suffering Lygo family, my wife Suzy and my beautiful children, Madison and Eliot, who saw me scuttling away into my study on so many occasions when I should have been mucking about with them – thank you. Hope you like it ...

PICTURE CREDITS

Frontispiece: akg-images/Erich Lessing

1   © Artur Bogacki/123RF.com
2   © vicspacewalker/123RF.com
3   State Hermitage Museum, St Petersburg
4   Panther Media GmbH/Alamy Stock Photo
5   DEA/G. Dagli Orti/Getty Images
6   © gonewiththewind/123RF.com
7   © Konstantinos Michail/123RF.com
8   DEA/G. Dagli Orti/Getty Images
9   akg-images/Erich Lessing
10 akg-images
11 Photo Scala, Florence
12 Trustees of the British Museum, London
13 © İhsan Gerçelman/123RF.com
14 Biblioteca Nacional de España, Madrid
15 akg-images/Erich Lessing
16 akg-images/Cameraphoto
17 © ozdereisa/123RF.com
18 ©Andrii Sarymsakov/123RF.com
19 © Sirio Carnevalino/Dreamstime.com
20 © Viacheslav Lopatin/123RF.com
21 akg-images/Album/Oronoz
22 © Zzvet/123RF.com

INDEX

Byzantine emperors are shown in **bold**.
Page numbers in *italics* refer to
illustrations and maps.

Abbasids 9, 111, 112, 122, 127, 129, 132, 151
Adramyttion, Battle of (1205) 240
Adrianople, Battle of (378) 34
Akropolites, George 239, 240, 241, 243,
    247, 249
Aleppo 155, 164, 169
Alexander 2, 141, 145, 146–47
Alexandria 20, 39, 41
Alexios I Komnenos 190, 198, 201,
    202–7, 224
Alexios II Komnenos 213, 217–20, 221,
    222
Alexios III Angelos 224, 225, 226, 231,
    233, 239, 240, 246
Alexios IV Angelos 224, 227–32, 233
Alexios V Doukas Mourtzouphlos 229,
    232–33
Alp Arslan, sultan 191, 195, 196, 198
Ammianus, Marcellinus 21, 30, 32, 33
Amorium 108, 127, 133, 135, 194
Anastasios I Dikoros 48, 55–59, 61–62, 68
Anastasios II Artemios 102–3
Anatolia 37–38, 49, 79, 88, 92–93, 94, 97,
    108, 127, 163, 182, 183, 190, 191, 197, 204,
    206, 214, 215, 221, 224
Andronikos I Komnenos 219–23, 225, 237
Andronikos II Palaiologos 249, 250,
    251–54
Andronikos III Palaiologos 254, 255–56
Andronikos IV Palaiologos 246, 260–62,
    263
Anna of Savoy (wife of Andronikos III)
    254, 255–57
Anthemius (guardian of Theodosios II)
    43, 45
Anthemius (Western Roman emperor)
    50, 54
Antioch 30, 33, 41, 63, 72, 129, 157, 160,
    169, 205, 210, 215
Antioch, Battle of 240
Arcadius 36, 40–42; *plate 4*

Ardzen, Battle of 182
Ariadne (wife of Zeno and Anastasios I)
    48, 49, 50–51, 52, 53, 55, 58; *plate 8*
Arian sect 20, 25, 33, 37–38, 62
Armenia/Armenians 24, 29, 41, 68, 73,
    82, 89, 94, 100, 103, 108, 139, 150, 157,
    159, 164, 181, 189, 192, 205, 210; *see also*
    Leo V the Armenian
Artabasdos 108, 109
Aspar the Alan 44, 45, 47, 48–49
Athos, Mount 157, 160, 165, 274
Attila the Hun 44, 46
augustus/augusta/augusti 14, 15, 16, 22, 42,
    72, 74, 145, 187, 203
Avars 71, 73, 75–76, 79, 80, 82–83, 94
Axouch, John 205, 208–9, 212

Baldwin III of Jerusalem 215, 221
Baldwin of Flanders 235
Balkans 71, 79, 82, 87, 137, 190, 194, 198,
    205, 209, 214, 219, 238, 252, 256, 263
Bardas (uncle of Michael III) 134–36, 137,
    138, 141
Barletta, Italy 47
Basil I 137, 139–43, 147, 150; *plates 13, 14*
Basil II Bulgaroktonos 139, 155, 156, 157,
    159, 161–65, 166, 167, 178, 179, 186
Basil Lekapenos 159, 162, 163
basileus 83, 116, 122, 142, 263, 267
Basiliskos 13, 49, 50, 52–53
Belisarios, general 68
Beroia, Battle of (1122) 209
Bertha of Sulzbach 211, 213
Bohemond 205–6
Boniface of Montferrat 230–31, 233, 235
Britain 16, 22, 33
Bryennios, Nikephoros 183, 198, 199–201
Bryennios, Nikephoros the Younger 203,
    208
Bulgars/Bulgaria 91–92, 94, 97, 99, 101,
    103, 105, 109, 111, 112, 114, 117, 119–20,
    122–23, 124–25, 130, 136, 142, 144, 147,
    148, 150, 151, 160, 174, 192, 198, 224, 225,
    226, 235, 237, 240, 242, 244, 249, 252, 256
Busir, *khagan* of the Khazars 98–99

You may also be interested in:

The Ottomans
A Cultural Legacy
DIANA DARKE

'Seeks to remind us of the glories, triumphs and successes of what was once one of the world's greatest empires'
Peter Frankopan, *Financial Times*

'This gorgeous, wide-ranging and utterly fascinating book is the perfect introduction to the art and architecture, as well as cultural, religious and political history, of one of the most important and surprising empires'
William Dalrymple, author of *The Anarchy: The Relentless Rise of the East India Company*

'Exquisitely written ... this delightful book brings five centuries of Ottoman culture to life'
Eugene Rogan, author of *The Fall of the Ottomans*

24 illustrations · 256pp · ISBN 978 0 500 298183 paperback

Medieval People
From Charlemagne to Piero della Francesca
MICHAEL PRESTWICH

This engrossing and often witty account tells the life stories of nearly 70 individuals who made the Middle Ages. They range from the important, such as El Cid or Frederick Barbarossa, to the little known, such as the dissolute Venetian nun Clara Sanuto. Some were astonishingly successful, others were failures. Full of intriguing historical insights, eminent historian Michael Prestwich shows how medieval people lived in an era that was more one of invention and innovation than of superstition and backwardness.

26 illustrations · 272pp · ISBN 978 0 500 293850 paperback

A History of Ancient Greece in 50 Lives

DAVID STUTTARD

'A few great men operating in isolation – too often this is the way ancient Greece is described to us. Stuttard puts the very greatest into their historical, political and cultural contexts and coaxes some of the lesser known centre stage'
Bettany Hughes, author and historian

'David Stuttard's career represents an admirable commitment to popularizing classical culture and making it accessible to new non-specialist audiences'
Current World Archaeology

29 illustrations · 304pp · ISBN 978 0 500 295519 paperback

Islamic Civilization in Thirty Lives

The First 1000 Years

CHASE F. ROBINSON

'A beautifully written set of brief, vividly drawn portraits'
Times Higher Education

'An elegant digest'
The Economist

'Fascinating ... a unique introduction to Islamic history ... not to be missed'
Timeless Travels

19 illustrations · 288pp · ISBN 978 0 500 293782 paperback